3/65

Edward R. Thornton is Assistant Professor
of Chemistry at the University of Pennsylvania.
He received his Ph.D. from the Massachusetts
Institute of Technology. Dr. Thornton has held
a National Institutes of Health Post-doctoral
Fellowship at both M.I.T. and Harvard
University.

MODERN CONCEPTS IN CHEMISTRY

EDITORS

Bryce Crawford, Jr., University of Minnesota
W. D. McElroy, Johns Hopkins University
Charles C. Price, University of Pennsylvania

BOOKS PUBLISHED

MICHAEL J. S. DEWAR, University of Chicago—*Hyperconjugation*
JACK HINE, Georgia Institute of Technology—*Divalent Carbon*
LARS MELANDER, Nobel Institute of Chemistry, Stockholm—*Isotope Effects on Reaction Rates*
EDWARD R. THORNTON, University of Pennsylvania—*Solvolysis Mechanisms*

BOOKS IN PREPARATION

B. E. CONWAY, University of Ottawa—Theory of Electrode Processes
R. CLINTON FULLER, Dartmouth Medical School—Photosynthesis
PHILIP GEORGE and ROBERT J. RUTMAN, University of Pennsylvania—
Thermodynamic Driving Force in Biosynthetic Reactions
HAROLD HART, Michigan State University—Carbonium Ions in Organic Reactions
HAROLD S. JOHNSTON, University of California, Berkeley—Gas Phase Reaction Rate Theory
MICHAEL KASHA, Florida State University—Molecular Excitation
JOHN L. MARGRAVE, Rice University—High Temperature Chemistry
PATRICK A. McCUSKER, University of Notre Dame—Organo-Boron Compounds
E. E. MUSCHLITZ, JR. and THOMAS L. BAILEY, University of Florida—
The Mass Spectrometer as a Research Instrument
C. G. OVERBERGER, Polytechnic Institute of Brooklyn; JOSEPH G. LOMBARDINO, Charles Pfizer and Co., Inc.; and JEAN-PIERRE ANSELME, Polytechnic Institute of Brooklyn—Chemistry of Organic Compounds with Nitrogen-Nitrogen Bonds
BERNARD PULLMAN and ALBERTE PULLMAN, University of Paris—Chemical Carcinogenesis in Molecular and Quantum Biology
HANS SCHMID and RICHARD BARNER, University of Zürich—Claisen Ether Rearrangement
MICHAEL SZWARC, State University of New York College of Forestry—
Free Radicals: Their Formation and Disappearance
Reactions of Free Radicals: Addition and Atom Abstraction
HOWARD G. TENNENT, Hercules Powder Co.—Organometallic Polymerization
JOHN S. WAUGH, Massachusetts Institute of Technology—Analysis of Nuclear Resonance Spectra
JOHN E. WERTZ, University of Minnesota—Electron Spin Resonance
HAROLD H. ZEISS, Monsanto Research S.A., Zürich—Benzenoid Complexes

SOLVOLYSIS
MECHANISMS

EDWARD R. THORNTON
UNIVERSITY OF PENNSYLVANIA

THE RONALD PRESS COMPANY · NEW YORK

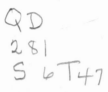
Library of Congress Catalog Card Number: 64–21462

To Jo

Preface

Although solvolysis reactions have always occupied a large part of physical organic chemists' time, the understanding of their detailed mechanisms is quite incomplete. It is possible to discuss many possible mechanisms, however, and many ingenious theoretical and experimental tools, by surveying this broad expanse of chemistry.

In some ways the carbonium ion is the child of all this study of solvolysis reactions. Carbonium ions provide the unifying concept to explain data that cannot be explained by simple, concerted mechanisms. Yet our understanding of carbonium ions is far from complete, because the structure of a carbonium ion in polar solution must be quite different from its structure in the gas or crystalline phase.

This book, a volume in the "Modern Concepts in Chemistry" series, is an attempt to survey the important ideas generated by the study of simple solvolysis mechanisms. The subject matter is largely limited to simple displacements at saturated carbon although, in the broadest sense, every reaction in solution involves some participation by solvent.

Many of the theories presented apply to all areas of chemistry. The book may therefore be useful as an introduction to theoretical organic chemistry.

Each chapter ends with a brief discussion of pertinent references for the reader interested in further study.

My special thanks go to Miss Rose Schwartz, Mr. Guido E. Rubenis, Mr. Louis J. Steffa, Miss Elizabeth D. Kaplan, and my wife for their help with the technical aspects of bringing this book into print. To my former teachers and to the students with whom I have had the good fortune to be associated, I owe a scientific debt which will be apparent to them and cannot be expressed adequately in words.

EDWARD R. THORNTON

Philadelphia, Pennsylvania
April, 1964

Contents

SOLVOLYSIS
MECHANISMS

1

Introduction

If the solvent participates in a reaction by combining with the substrate, the reaction is called a solvolysis reaction. Although many kinds of solvolysis reactions can be visualized, by far the most common involve the displacement of some leaving group by the solvent. Many years' experience has shown that we do not fully understand the simplest solvolyses; this fact may partially excuse the emphasis in this book on the simple reactions.

The literature about solvolysis is enormous. I can only hope to choose for discussion a few topics which I have found especially interesting, a process which probably leads to overemphasis of some areas. Solvolysis is discussed in recent textbooks of physical organic chemistry (1, 2), and there is an excellent book on the subject (3).

MECHANISM

The mechanism of a reaction is a complete description of the motions of all the particles (electrons + nuclei) in question as the reactants are converted into products. Usually the chemist is satisfied to know partially the structure of all *intermediates* and *activated complexes* which occur during the course of the reaction. An intermediate is a molecule (possibly an ion or free radical) which is formed during the course of reaction and is usually less stable (has higher free energy) than either reactants or products. The structure corresponding to a free energy barrier which must necessarily be overcome during the reaction is called an activated complex. It is a metastable arrangement of particles, analogous to an infinitely sharp pencil standing on its point. Intermediates and especially activated complexes are usually elusive, however. It is frequently difficult to establish their existence experimentally, to say nothing of determining their structures. Indirect means are necessary. For example, determining the ultraviolet, infrared, Raman, or n.m.r. spectra of reacting solutions will sometimes establish the existence of an intermediate. Activated complexes are so unstable that no spectral method has yet been capable of detecting them; therefore, even less direct methods must be used to investigate their structures. The rate of a reaction is determined by the energies of the activated complexes which occur, so that rate measurements are the principal means of learning about activated complexes.

Most known solvolysis reactions of organic molecules proceed by mechanisms which involve nucleophilic substitution on carbon. This last phrase means that some molecule or ion X which has a "lone pair" of electrons eventually replaces some molecule or ion Z which was attached to a carbon nucleus in the reactant: $X + RZ \rightarrow XR + Z$. Z ends up with an extra lone pair of electrons. "Nucleophilic" means "nucleus-loving," *i.e.*, a lone pair of electrons on X seeks out a carbon nucleus in the course of the reaction; X is a nucleophilic reagent. Two major nucleophilic substitution (SN) mechanistic types are known. The SN2 type involves simultaneous formation of the XR bond and breaking of the RZ bond, the activated complex containing X, R, and Z. The numeral 2 indicates that the rate of reaction is expected to be dependent on the RZ concentration times the X concentration, a second-order reaction (Fig. 1A). The other, SN1 type, involves rupture of the RZ bond before formation of the XR bond. In this case an intermediate forms, presumably a carbonium ion

R^+, then the carbonium ion reacts rapidly with X to form XR. This mechanism usually requires two activated complexes, one occurring as the RZ bond ruptures, the other as the XR bond forms. The numeral 1 indicates that the rate of reaction is expected to be dependent on the RZ concentration and independent of the X concentration, a first-order reaction (Fig. 1B). The SN2 mechanism is exemplified by the reaction of optically active (about the carbon atom bearing I) 2-octyl iodide with radioactive iodide ions in acetone solution (4)

$$CH_3(CH_2)_5CHICH_3 + *I^- \rightarrow CH_3(CH_2)_5CH*ICH_3 + I^-$$

wherein it was also shown that the second-order rate constant for substitution of radioactive iodide is essentially equal to that for inversion of optical configuration, indicating that iodide ion always attacks the opposite side of the carbon nucleus from the side to which the leaving iodide ion is attached. This backside attack is known as Walden inversion. The SN1 mechanism is exemplified by the reaction of benzhydryl chloride with different nucleophiles in liquid sulfur dioxide solution (5)

$$(C_6H_5)_2CHCl + X \rightarrow (C_6H_5)_2CHX + Cl^-$$

wherein the initial rate of reaction is the same with each of three nucleophilic reagents X and is (except for small ionic strength effects) independent of the concentration of nucleophile. It is necessary to compare initial rates because the situation is complicated by competition of X and Cl^- for the carbonium ion $(C_6H_5)_2CH^+$, producing both $(C_6H_5)_2CHX$ and $(C_6H_5)_2CHCl$, the latter product being able to react again.

There are at least two other cases of interest, which do not fall neatly into SN2 or SN1 prototypes. It is conceivable that a carbonium ion could form in a first-order reaction but react with X with zero activation energy so that the activated complex for combination of X with R^+ has very nearly the same free energy as R^+ itself. In this case the reaction has a

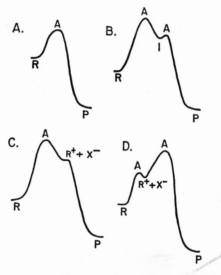

Fig. 1. Free energy diagrams for various mechanisms. Ordinate is free energy and abscissa is reaction coordinate. R = Reactant(s); P = Product(s); A = Activated complex; I = Intermediate.

rate independent of X concentration but the carbonium ion has a very small lifetime, so that the mechanism has some SN1-like properties and some SN2-like properties. It would be very difficult to differentiate experimentally from a "normal" SN1 mechanism wherein the carbonium ion can be truly considered a distinct intermediate (Fig. 1C). The other case is a reaction which proceeds via a fast, equilibrium rupture of the RZ bond to form $R^+ + Z^-$, followed by a slow attack of X upon R^+. In this case a distinct carbonium ion intermediate is formed, yet the rate is second-order, depending on the concentration of X times the concentration of RZ. Again we have SN1-like and SN2-like properties. This mechanism is sometimes distinguishable experimentally from the "normal" SN2 mechanism. In the "normal" SN2 mechanism, adding extra Z^- ions would not affect the rate of the forward reaction, while if the equilibrium $RZ \rightleftarrows R^+ + Z^-$ is set up, adding extra Z^- ions would decrease the equilibrium concentration of R^+ and thereby slow the rate of formation of product, a phenomenon known as the "common ion effect" (Fig. 1D).

The differences between mechanisms are sometimes more easily visualized in terms of a free energy diagram. The ordinate is free energy and the abscissa is some measure of the amount by which the reaction has progressed, usually called the "reaction coordinate." These are plotted in Fig. 1 for the four mechanisms mentioned in this section. (See, however, the footnote on page 182.)

STRUCTURE

Obviously, the SN1 and SN2 mechanisms depend not only on the structures of X and RZ, but also on the solvent molecules surrounding these reactants. These solvent molecules can have profound effects on the free energy of reactants, intermediates, and transition states. In some cases it is possible to observe a changeover in mechanism—a given reaction proceeding by the SN1 path in some solvents and by the SN2 path in other solvents.

The particular mechanism which occurs may therefore depend on changes in the structure of X, R, or Z and the solvent medium. Also, changes in conditions such as temperature and pressure may have minor effects.

One of the most useful methods of investigating mechanisms has been to study the effect of small changes in structure on the products and rates of reactions. In this way one can more or less isolate a certain structural factor in the transition state, hoping to keep all other effects constant. For example, electrical effects can be investigated in the absence of steric (size) effects by inserting a rigid structure between the reacting center and the point where the structure is changed. The rates of a series of *meta-* and *para*-substituted anilines as nucleophiles towards the same reactant RZ might be investigated. Here the planar benzene ring is inserted between the reacting center (nitrogen) and the points of structural change (the *m*- and *p*-substituents). This technique may be applied even to the subtle changes which occur on substituting one isotope for another, *e.g.*, deuterium for protium. Only the weight of a nucleus is changed; the distributions of electrons are essentially identical. It is obvious that the main factor which affects rates and mechanisms is the electron distribution, since it is responsible for the bond strengths and nuclear positions. Nevertheless, isotopic substitution does affect reaction rates, and the magnitude of this isotope effect can be exceedingly useful in finding out about the structures of transition states.

A difficult problem in studying reaction mechanisms is in defining terms. To take a ridiculous exaggeration, the concept of "simultaneous bond-making and bond-breaking" must be subject to a relativistic effect. If the observer were moving fast enough (close to the speed of light) relative to the reaction solution, he could also observe XR bonds being formed before RZ bonds broke and RZ bonds breaking before XR bonds formed, depending on the orientation of the activated complexes with respect to his motion. We should therefore define simultaneous as being relative to an observer stationary with respect to the activated complex. This illustrates the problems encountered as we strive for a more and more detailed understanding of reaction mechanisms, and the increasing difficulty of making experimental observations which will differentiate between closely related mechanisms. The difficulty of such problems is compensated by the interesting results which can be obtained.

REFERENCES

Both Hine's book (1) and Gould's book (2) give a broad picture of the subject of physical organic chemistry, including various solvolysis reactions. Streitwieser's book (3) is a detailed account of solvolysis and related reactions, very complete through 1955 but with only a brief Supplement dealing with work since 1955.

2

Structural Effects

SOLVOLYSIS

When the mechanism of solvolysis is considered in the light of the SN1 and SN2 mechanisms for nucleophilic displacement, the analogy is seemingly complete: instead of the nucleophile X attacking RZ, a solvent molecule plays the role of attacking nucleophile. There should then be SN1 and SN2 solvolysis mechanisms. The most distinctive feature of the ordinary displacement mechanisms is their kinetic order with respect to X. If the activated complex contains X, the rate is dependent on the concentration of X. However, when X is a solvent molecule the dependence of rate on X concentration cannot be determined. The concentration of solvent cannot vary appreciably through the course of a kinetic run, and cannot be varied between one kinetic run and another, without changing the medium itself (*i.e.*, its dielectric and solvating properties) in addition. Many attempts to determine experimentally and theoretically the nature of solvolysis transition states have therefore been made. The problem is still unsolved. Many investigators think that SN1 and SN2 mechanisms are useful distinctions for solvolysis reactions, while many others think that the distinction is incomplete and that there are borderline mechanisms which are neither SN1 nor SN2, but somewhere between.

9

The solvolysis reaction puts restraints on the type of structural changes in reactants which can be investigated. Small changes in the structure of the nucleophile include, by definition, changes in the properties of the solvent, so that it is difficult to determine these effects separately.

STRUCTURE

Since the structures of molecules are so important in determining mechanisms, a brief discussion of current qualitative ideas about structure is necessary at this point.

Structural factors affecting the potential reactivity of a molecule may be divided into four semi-independent contributions—inductive, delocalization, field, and steric effects.

The inductive effect simply involves a polarization of electrons through the effect of a substituent. For example, much of the influence which makes chloroacetic acid a stronger acid than acetic acid is attributed to the relative inductive effects of chlorine and hydrogen. The chlorine substituent withdraws electrons from the O—H bond of the carboxyl group, weakening that bond and increasing the acidity.

A delocalization effect is involved in the stabilization of the "double" bonds of benzene relative to, say, cyclohexene. The electrons in the benzene "double" bonds are actually free to circulate around the ring, and this leads to a stabilization. In general, structures which have conjugated double bonds in a classical structure are capable of electron delocalization which leads to "extra" stability beyond that expected for localized electrons.

A field effect is an electrostatic effect of charges or dipoles interacting across space. The acidity of the rigid carboxylic acids

$$Z-C\underset{CH_2-CH_2}{\overset{CH_2-CH_2}{\underset{\diagdown}{\diagup}}}CH_2-CH_2-C-CO_2H$$

with various substituents Z showed that probably the field

effect *and* the inductive effect together are necessary to explain
the results (6).

Steric effects are caused by the repulsions of non-bonded
substituents which are close together in space. The hindered
rotation about the bond joining the two rings in properly substituted biphenyls is generally considered to be a steric effect.

All these four factors are at work to greater or lesser extents
to determine the mechanism of solvolysis reactions. Of
course, they operate in the substrate, the activated complex,
and the solvent itself.

Steric factors can exert a most profound effect in the
phenomenon of optical activity, where a tetrahedral carbon
atom with four different groups attached can exist in two different configurations—right- and left-handed, or D and L. The
conformation of a molecule is also determined by steric factors,
the classical example being cyclohexane, which is largely in
the chair form rather than a planar or a boat form (7). There

CHAIR   BOAT

are two different types of positions, a (axial) and e (equatorial).
Large substituents tend to occupy equatorial positions, where
they are out of the way of the axial hydrogen atoms.

An example of the effect of structure of reactants is the
fact that primary halides, $e.g.$, CH_3Cl or CH_3CH_2Cl, tend to
undergo mainly SN2-type reactions, while tertiary halides,
$e.g.$, $(CH_3)_3CCl$, tend to undergo mainly SN1-type reactions.
All four effects listed above probably operate to make $(CH_3)_3C^+$
a more stable carbonium ion than CH_3^+. Molecules which
have the possibility of forming relatively stabilized carbonium
ions usually have a tendency to do so.

SOLVENT

The solvent affects reactivity in two ways simultaneously·
First is any specific interaction of solvent with substrate in
the activated complex, such as nucleophilic attack on carbon.
Second is the gross effect called solvation. The reactant may
have completely different solvation properties from the activated complex, so that changing the solvent atmosphere may
affect the reactivity or even the mechanistic type. For a
first guess about such effects, a useful rule is that the creation
or concentration of charges should be accelerated by a solvent
better at solvating ions, while the destruction or spreading out
of charges should be accelerated by a solvent less efficient at
solvating ions (8). This is certainly reasonable because the
interaction energies of charges with polar solvents are well
known to be very large.

A concept which has been controversial, but which no
doubt has many elements of truth to it, is that of the "push-
pull mechanism" (9). This idea is that simultaneous attack
by solvent on both the atom undergoing displacement and the
leaving group is necessary in any solvolysis reaction. The
nucleophilic attack on carbon "pushes" the leaving group
away, while an electrophilic (electron-seeking) attack on the
leaving group "pulls" it away. The controversy centers
around the question of whether the push and pull are very

specific bonding interactions, or merely generalized, nonspecific solvation effects. In any case it seems that the solvent must exert both push and pull in one form or another, if we care to use that terminology.

PRODUCT

Although the product(s) of a reaction is believed to exert no direct influence on the forward rate, it can be of importance to mechanistic studies. The product is the single most important piece of evidence for a reaction mechanism, for in order to speculate about activated complexes and intermediates, it is necessary to know "where the reaction is heading." If an alkyl halide reacts with solvent to produce a rearranged product and not a simple displacement product, the mechanism must obviously take account of this. For example, neopentyl iodide reacts with water in the presence of silver ion as catalyst to give a rearranged alcohol but, as far as is known, no neopentyl alcohol (10):

$$(CH_3)_3C-CH_2-I \xrightarrow[H_2O]{Ag^+} (CH_3)_2C-CH_2CH_3$$
$$| \\ OH$$

The stability (free energy) of the product may have an indirect influence on possible intermediates or activated complexes. The structure of an activated complex for a SN2 reaction, say, should be different if the over-all process is highly favored (ΔF negative) than if it is the reverse. This important idea will be discussed in Chapter 4.

The products of individual steps (intermediates) are also of great importance. If a carbonium ion forms, our speculations about mechanism will be quite different from what they are if no carbonium ion is present. The structures and properties of such intermediates are therefore a very important aspect of solvolysis studies. For example, the properties of carbonium ions can be studied in concentrated sulfuric acid solutions, where many are stable enough to yield ultraviolet, infrared, and n.m.r. spectra (11). In addition, the chemist may attempt to prove the presence of such intermediates by deliberately adding some suitable extraneous reagent to the solvolysis reaction mixture in the hope of "trapping" the intermediates and isolating the product of trapping. There is one pitfall in such studies: the fact that a certain "intermediate" (*e.g.*, a carbonium ion) is present in the solution does not prove it is involved in the pathway between reactants and products. It might be merely a reversibly formed by-product. It is an exceedingly subtle problem to find out whether such a species is part of the reaction path or not.

REFERENCES

Eliel's book (7), *Stereochemistry of Carbon Compounds*, is an excellent source of information on structural effects and stereochemistry. Of course, (1), (2), and (3) contain much information on this subject, too. For physical methods such as ultraviolet, infrared, and n.m.r., one good source is *Determination of Organic Structures by Physical Methods* (Academic Press, New York; Vol. 1, edited by E. A. Braude and F. C. Nachod, 1955; Vol. 2, edited by F. C. Nachod and W. D. Phillips, 1962). For a good treatment of molecular structure on the theoretical level, see J. C. D. Brand and J. C. Speakman, *Molecular Structure* (Edward Arnold (Publishers) Ltd., London, 1960).

3
Theories

REACTION RATES

There are two major approaches to the theory of reaction rates, the collision theory and the transition-state theory. The main idea of these theories is that equilibrium exists between reactants and activated complexes. In the simplest collision approach the number of collisions per second of reactant molecules is multiplied by the probability that the colliding molecules will have sufficient energy, giving the rate. In the transition-state approach the equilibrium concentration of activated complexes (transition states) is calculated and multiplied by the frequency of decomposition of these transition states to products, giving the rate.

The collision theory of reactions in solution is the subject of a book (12) which also contains a nice comparison of the collision and transition-state theories. The transition-state theory is the subject of a book also (13). In addition, a discussion of these subjects is contained in books on chemical kinetics (14).

Rate Constants. Before discussing these theories, we should consider the form of kinetic rate expressions. It is experimentally true, and the assumption of equilibrium between reactants and activated complexes implies, that the rate of a reaction is proportional to the concentrations of reactants. For a simple decomposition of a single reactant A (provided the rate of the reverse reaction is much smaller than that of the forward reaction),

$$\text{rate} = -\frac{d(A)}{dt} = k(A)$$

where (A) is the concentration of A, t is time, and k is the first-order rate constant for the reaction. To find k, this expression can be integrated as follows:

$$-\frac{d(A)}{(A)} = k\, dt = -d \ln (A)$$
$$-\ln (A) = kt + \text{constant}$$

When $t = 0$, the constant is seen to be $-\ln (A)_0$ where $(A)_0$ is the initial concentration of A. Then

$$\ln \left[\frac{(A)_0}{(A)} \right] = kt$$

A plot of $\ln [(A)_0/(A)]$ *vs.* t has a slope of k.

A bimolecular reaction between A and B to give product(s), if the reverse reaction is very slow compared to the forward reaction, has a rate

$$-\frac{d(A)}{dt} = -\frac{d(B)}{dt} = k(A)(B)$$

The equation can be integrated also, giving

$$kt = \frac{1}{(A)_0 - (B)_0} \ln \left[\frac{(B)_0(A)}{(A)_0(B)} \right]$$

This rate expression applies to a typical SN2 process. If a solvolysis reaction had a SN2-type mechanism, A would be the reactant which is destroyed, but B would be a solvent molecule. The concentration of solvent is so large that generally $(B) = (B)_0$, in which case the rate expression is

$$-\frac{d(A)}{dt} = k(B)_0(A) = k_{\text{OBS}}(A)$$

The observed rate is then pseudo-first-order, but the observed first-order rate constant contains the (constant) concentration of solvent.

A SN1 reaction involves an intermediate carbonium ion. The mechanism is

$$RX \underset{k_{-1}}{\overset{k_1}{\rightleftharpoons}} R^+ + X^-$$

$$R^+ + B \xrightarrow{k_2} product(s)$$

Since the carbonium ion is such an unstable intermediate, it may be that the reverse reaction of R^+ with X^- can in some cases compete with the reaction of R^+ with B. The rate of formation of product(s) (P) is

$$\frac{d(P)}{dt} = k_2(R^+)(B)$$

The problem is that the concentration of R^+ is unknown in terms of the initial concentrations and the concentration of P, which are the only quantities that are easily measured. There are conditions under which the rate can be expressed in terms of known concentrations. The rate of formation of R^+ is

$$\frac{d(R^+)}{dt} = k_1(RX) - k_{-1}(R^+)(X^-) - k_2(R^+)(B)$$

We assume that the reversion of products to R^+ and B is very slow compared with the rate of formation of products.* If $\frac{d(R^+)}{dt}$ is very small compared with all the other terms in the above equation,

$$k_1(RX) - k_{-1}(R^+)(X^-) - k_2(R^+)(B) - \frac{d(R^+)}{dt} = 0$$

reduces to

$$k_1(RX) - (R^+)[k_{-1}(X^-) + k_2(B)] = 0$$

* This is true if the reverse of the reaction with rate constant k_2 has a rate constant k_{-2} which is much smaller than any of the other rate constants.

This is known as the steady-state assumption. Solving for (R^+),

$$(R^+) = \frac{k_1(RX)}{k_{-1}(X^-) + k_2(B)}$$

The rate is then

$$\frac{d(P)}{dt} = \frac{k_1 k_2 (RX)(B)}{k_{-1}(X^-) + k_2(B)}$$

This rate expression is fairly complicated. In certain cases, it can be further simplified. If $k_2(B) \gg k_{-1}(X^-)$,

$$\frac{d(P)}{dt} = k_1(RX)$$

a first-order reaction. This means that if the rate of reaction of R^+ with B is very fast, the rate is simply determined by the rate of formation of R^+. If $k_{-1}(X^-) \gg k_2(B)$,

$$\frac{d(P)}{dt} = \frac{k_1 k_2}{k_{-1}} \frac{(RX)(B)}{(X^-)}$$

This would be a second-order reaction if a large amount of X^- were added initially so that (X^-) were essentially constant throughout the course of the reaction. In this case

$$\frac{d(P)}{dt} = \frac{k_1 k_2}{k_{-1}(X^-)_0} (RX)(B) = k_{OBS}(RX)(B)$$

The second-order rate would, however, be slowed by increasing $(X^-)_0$, the common-ion effect mentioned in Chapter 1. In this case kinetic measurements could prove the existence of an intermediate in the mechanism. In a solvolysis reaction B is the solvent, which is constant, and the rate in the presence of excess X^- simplifies to

$$\frac{d(P)}{dt} = \frac{k_1 k_2 (B)}{k_{-1}(X^-)_0} (RX) = k_{OBS}(RX)$$

In a solvolysis where no X^- is initially added,

$$\frac{d(P)}{dt} = k_{OBS} \frac{(RX)}{(X^-)}$$

A more complex situation arises when the concentration of R^+ is not small. When the first step is considered to be essentially irreversible,

$$RX \xrightarrow{k_1} R^+ + X^-$$
$$R^+ \xrightarrow{k_2(B)_0} \text{product}$$

it is possible to integrate the rate expression to give

$$(RX)_0 - (P) = (RX)_0 \left\{ \frac{k_1}{k_1 - k_2(B)_0} e^{-k_2(B)_0 t} - \frac{k_2(B)_0}{k_1 - k_2(B)_0} e^{-k_1 t} \right\}$$

which can be shown to reduce to the proper expressions for cases in which the first or the second step is completely rate-determining. Sometimes more information can be obtained (15) if the rate of change of concentration of R^+ itself can be measured (usually by a characteristic ultraviolet or visible absorption).

If we have a first-order reaction which is reversible,

$$A \underset{k_{-1}}{\overset{k_1}{\rightleftarrows}} B$$

then the rate is

$$\frac{d(B)}{dt} = k_1(A) - k_{-1}(B)$$

or, since $(A)_0 - (A) = (B)$,

$$-\frac{d(A)}{dt} = (k_1 + k_{-1})(A) - k_{-1}(A)_0$$

which can be integrated to give

$$\ln \left[\frac{k_1(A)_0}{(k_1 + k_{-1})(A) - k_{-1}(A)_0} \right] = (k_1 + k_{-1})t$$

At equilibrium $d(B)/dt = 0$, so

$$k_1(A)_e = k_{-1}(B)_e = k_{-1}[(A)_0 - (A)_e]$$

where the subscript e refers to equilibrium concentration.   The rate equation then simplifies to

$$\ln \left[\frac{(A)_0 - (A)_e}{(A) - (A)_e} \right] = (k_1 + k_{-1})t$$

The approach to equilibrium therefore appears to be first-order, but with an effective rate constant equal to the sum of the actual rate constants for forward and reverse reactions.

It is worthwhile mentioning a few common fallacies in kinetic studies.   Failure to determine products can lead to errors.   At least 80 per cent of the products should be isolated and characterized (more if possible).   The homogeneity of a reaction should be tested.   Reactions occurring on the walls of the vessel can be detected by adding enough glass wool to give at least ten times more glass surface and checking the rate to see whether it is increased.   Reactions occurring on the surface of precipitated products can be detected by adding new reactants to a completed run to see whether the rate is increased.   Especially in free radical reactions, one should check for light, metallic ion, or air catalysis.   The medium should be kept constant with respect to solvent, pH, and ionic strength, because the rate may be changed by changes in these factors during the course of the run (*e.g.*, if acid or ions are products of the reaction).   Finally, the rate plot should be carried out to 90 per cent reaction, because plots of two different kinetic orders may both be linear in the range up to 50 per cent reaction.   If possible, a range of initial concentrations should be used also.

At 300°K., a change in activation energy of 1.37 kcal./mole corresponds to a rate ratio of 10.   Near 300°K., a 10° increase in temperature gives approximately a factor of 3 in rate, for "ordinary" reactions (activation energy *ca.* 20 kcal./mole).

Collision Theory.   Perhaps the more intuitive and easier to visualize of the two theories is the collision theory.   Let us consider the case of a bimolecular reaction of two atoms A and B which goes through a single activated complex A---B in which the bond between A and B is partially formed (16). It is known from the kinetic theory of gases that the average velocity of a perfect gas molecule in a single direction is

$$u = \left(\frac{kT}{2\pi m}\right)^{1/2}$$

where k is Boltzmann's constant, T is the absolute temperature, and m is the mass of an individual molecule. Since this velocity depends on mass and temperature, but not on state of aggregation, we may assume that it applies to velocities in solution as well as in the gas phase.* In any case, we will derive the rate constant without explicitly considering the role of the solvent. If there are n molecules of solute per cm.^{3}, the number reaching unit area in the solution in one second is simply

$$Z = n \frac{molecules}{cm.^3} \times u \frac{cm.}{sec.} \times 1 \ cm.^2 \ area$$
$$= nu \ molecules/sec.$$

On an area S cm.^{2} it is nSu molecules/sec. So

$$Z = nS \left(\frac{kT}{2\pi m}\right)^{1/2}$$

Now we wish to calculate the number of collisions $_1Z_B$ of B atoms with a single A atom. This is the number of B atoms reaching the surface of a sphere of radius $r_A + r_B$ where r_A and r_B are considered to be the effective collision radii of atoms A and B. This is true because $r_A + r_B$ is the distance at which A and B collide, and since they are atoms this distance is spherically symmetrical. The area of a sphere is $4\pi r^2$, so

$$_1Z_B = n_B 4\pi (r_A + r_B)^2 \left(\frac{kT}{2\pi \mu}\right)^{1/2}$$

---

* This assumption is not far wrong, and may be nearly exact. Typically, about 10^{12} collisions per second occur in solution between solute molecules at $1M$ concentration; however, these collisions happen in sets of 10–100 collisions between the same two partners before the two molecules can diffuse apart through the solvent "cage."

where μ is the reduced mass of A and B,

$$\frac{1}{\mu} = \frac{1}{m_A} + \frac{1}{m_B} \qquad \text{or} \qquad \mu = \frac{m_A m_B}{m_A + m_B}$$

It is necessary to use the reduced mass instead of merely the mass m_B because we now want the relative velocity of A and B rather than the absolute velocity of B, *i.e.*, A is not fixed but is in motion also.   Now the number of collisions per second of all A atoms with B atoms $_AZ_B$ is just $n_A \, _1Z_B$ or

$$_AZ_B = n_A n_B (r_A + r_B)^2 \left(\frac{8\pi kT}{\mu} \right)^{1/2}$$

The assumption of the collision theory is that the rate of reaction is equal to the number of collisions between reactant molecules multiplied by the fraction of those collisions in which the atoms possess enough energy to cross the energy barrier leading to products.   This latter fraction is proportional to exp $(-E/RT)$ where E is the critical energy increment, *i.e.*, the difference in energy between reactants and activated complex, and **R** is the gas constant.*   In the case of two atoms colliding, the fraction is nearly equal to exp $(-E/RT)$.

$$\text{rate} = \frac{dn}{dt} = {}_AZ_B e^{-E/RT} = n_A n_B (r_A + r_B)^2 \left(\frac{8\pi kT}{\mu} \right)^{1/2} e^{-E/RT}$$

The rate constant in units of liters mole^{-1} sec.$^{-1}$ is easily shown to be

$$k = \frac{dn}{dt} \cdot \frac{1}{n_A n_B} \cdot \frac{N_0}{1000}$$

where N_0 is Avogadro's number (the number of atoms in a gram atomic weight).   Therefore

$$k = \frac{N_0}{1000} (r_A + r_B)^2 \left(\frac{8\pi kT}{\mu_{AB}} \right)^{1/2} e^{-E/RT}$$

* This is the simple Boltzmann law for a system at equilibrium obeying the laws of classical motion.   It can be "derived" by probability arguments but its best justification is probably its success in predicting velocity distributions and other gas properties.

The mathematics becomes much more complex for reactions involving polyatomic molecules as one or both reactants. It has been found that for many reactions the simple collision theory must be modified, as might be expected for reactions of complex molecules. Electrostatic interactions must be taken account of when we deal with molecules which are ionic or dipolar. The problem is usually that the reactions are much slower than would be predicted from the simple calculation of Z. This means that many of the collisions between reactants are ineffective even when the proper energy of activation is available. Such discrepancies are very logical since in many cases reaction could be expected to occur only if the reacting molecules collided while oriented in a precise manner. For example, in a SN2 reaction the backside attack at carbon is by far energetically more favorable than any other mode of attack, so that collisions only with a very small part of the total area of the reactant molecule will be effective. This orientational factor and the possibility that certain solvent molecules must be properly oriented as well (*cf.* the push-pull mechanism, Chapter 2 and Ref. (9)) are capable of explaining the large discrepancies, sometimes as much as 10^{-8}, which are observed. It is usual to add another factor P to the rate expression to allow for this effect:

$$k = PZe^{-E/RT}$$

so that the predicted rate can be correlated with the experimentally observed Arrhenius relationship:

$$k = Ae^{-E/RT}$$

Recent, precise kinetic measurements generally show that the Arrhenius equation is not exact in that A is temperature-dependent:

$$k = BT^{C/R}e^{-E/RT} \tag{3-1}$$

Eq. (3–1) fits experiment better. If we generalize the definition of activation energy as

$$E_A = \mathbf{R}T^2 \frac{d \ln k}{dT}$$

where E_A is the apparent activation energy, we find

$$E_A = E + CT$$

The reasonableness of this result is seen when we recognize
that C plays the role of a heat-capacity term in E_A. The
apparent activation energy is made up of a critical energy
difference E between activated complex and reactants, plus a
term CT, where C is the difference in heat capacities between
activated complex and reactants. C is usually negative;
hence the heat capacity of the activated complex is less than
that of the reactants. Differences in heat capacities will be
discussed in Chapter 5.

It should be mentioned that even this expression for E_A is
approximate. The general classical (non-quantized) form of
the Boltzmann distribution for polyatomic molecules is (17)

$$p = e^{-E/\mathbf{R}T} \left[\frac{(E/\mathbf{R}T)^{s-1}}{(s-1)!} + \frac{(E/\mathbf{R}T)^{s-2}}{(s-2)!} + \cdots + 1 \right] \quad (3\text{–}2)$$

where p is the fraction of molecules possessing energy of at
least E and 2s is the "number of squared terms in the energy
of activation." For translational motion in a single direction
the (classical) energy of a molecule is

$$\epsilon = \tfrac{1}{2}mu^2,$$

a single "squared term." In our former case of two atoms A
and B reacting, the activation energy was made up of the
translational motion of each molecule toward the other, or
two squared terms, so that s = 1. In this case the only term
appearing in brackets in p is unity, so $p = \exp(-E/\mathbf{R}T)$ as

we already assumed. A harmonic oscillator has (classical) energy

$$\epsilon = \tfrac{1}{2}fx^2 + \tfrac{1}{2}\mu v^2$$

where f is the force constant, x the displacement, μ the reduced mass, and v the velocity. This is two squared terms for each degree of vibrational freedom. In case $E \gg RT$,

$$p \approx e^{-E/RT} \frac{(E/RT)^{s-1}}{(s-1)!}$$

which gives a rate constant of the same form as Eq. (3–1), with $s - 1 = -C/R$. When E is not $\gg RT$, other terms than the first will be important in Eq. (3–2), so that Eq. (3–1) is actually a simplification.

Partition Functions. Since the transition-state theory is most easily derived in terms of statistical thermodynamic expressions, and since isotope effects are also usefully discussed in such terms, we will now briefly discuss this topic. The ideas are really very simple; the difficulty of statistical thermo-dynamics is merely the complex mathematics involved in (a) attempting complete rigor or (b) making absolute calculations for complex systems. Fortunately, we need not attempt either (a) or (b).

The fundamental basis of this theory is simply the Boltz-mann distribution law, which says that in any system of molecules at equilibrium, the number possessing an energy ϵ is proportional to exp $(-\epsilon/kT)$, expressing the fundamental logarithmic relationship between energy and probability. For example, a molecule having an energy 2ϵ has a probability proportional to

$$e^{-2\epsilon/kT} = (e^{-\epsilon/kT})^2$$

i.e., proportional to the square of the probability of an energy ϵ. The best reason for accepting this distribution law is that it successfully predicts many different properties of molecules, not only thermodynamic properties but also velocities, etc.

According to quantum mechanics, any molecule is capable of having only certain discrete energies (and would radiate excess energy until it reached such a stable state or energy level). Suppose a system of N like molecules has

$$N_1 \text{ with } \epsilon = \epsilon_1$$
$$N_2 \text{ with } \epsilon = \epsilon_2$$
$$\cdot\ \cdot\ \cdot$$

Then

$$N = \text{total} = N_1 + N_2 + \cdot\ \cdot\ \cdot = \sum_i N_i$$

$$E = N_1\epsilon_1 + N_2\epsilon_2 + \cdot\ \cdot\ \cdot = \sum_i N_i\epsilon_i$$

The Boltzmann law tells us that

$$N_1 = xe^{-\epsilon_1/kT}$$
$$N_2 = xe^{-\epsilon_2/kT}$$
$$\cdot\ \cdot\ \cdot$$

So

$$N_1 + N_2 + \cdot\ \cdot\ \cdot = xe^{-\epsilon_1/kT} + xe^{-\epsilon_2/kT} + \cdot\ \cdot\ \cdot$$

$$\sum_i N_i = x \sum_i e^{-\epsilon_i/kT}$$

Then $N = xQ$, where $Q = \sum_i e^{-\epsilon_i/kT}$ is called the "partition function" since it represents the partitioning of probabilities of molecules' being in different energy states. Therefore

$$\frac{N_i}{N} = \frac{e^{-\epsilon_i/kT}}{Q}$$

since the x's cancel out. It is assumed that all these x's are equal for the various energy states, since no one energy level should have any particular special probability other than that resulting from its energy. It may be that some of the separate energy levels will have identical energy corresponding to the molecule's having two different stationary states with the same energy, and if so these separate states of the same energy are counted separately* (e.g., it might be that $\epsilon_1 = \epsilon_2 = \epsilon_3 \neq \epsilon_4$, etc.). The average energy $\bar{\epsilon}$ of one of the molecules is then, by the definition of an average,

$$\bar{\epsilon} = \frac{N_1\epsilon_1 + N_2\epsilon_2 + \cdots}{N} = \frac{1}{Q}\epsilon_1 e^{-\epsilon_1/kT} + \frac{1}{Q}\epsilon_2 e^{-\epsilon_2/kT} + \cdots$$

$$= \frac{\sum_i \epsilon_i e^{-\epsilon_i/kT}}{Q}$$

In terms of moles, the energy per mole must be just $N_0\bar{\epsilon}$, where N_0 is Avogadro's number. If we call $N_0\epsilon_i = E_i$ and remember that $N_0 k = R$, the gas constant,

$$E = \frac{\sum_i E_i e^{-E_i/RT}}{Q}$$

Note that

$$\frac{\partial \ln Q}{\partial T} = \frac{\partial}{\partial T}\left[\ln\left(\sum_i e^{-E_i/RT}\right)\right] = \frac{\sum_i E_i e^{-E_i/RT}}{RT^2 Q} = \frac{E}{RT^2}$$

The specific heat at constant volume is, according to classical thermodynamics,

$$C_v = \left(\frac{\partial E}{\partial T}\right)_v = \frac{\partial}{\partial T}\left[RT^2 \frac{\partial \ln Q}{\partial T}\right]$$

and the entropy is defined as

$$S - S_0 \equiv \int_0^T \frac{C_v}{T}\,dT = \int_0^T \frac{1}{T}\frac{\partial}{\partial T}\left(RT^2 \frac{\partial \ln Q}{\partial T}\right)dT$$

* Alternatively, we could use the equivalent definition

$$Q = \sum_i \omega_i e^{-\epsilon_i/kT}$$

where ω_i is the *degeneracy* of the state with energy ϵ_i.

The integral can be easily evaluated by integration by parts,

$$S - S_0 = \frac{1}{T} \mathbf{R} T^2 \frac{\partial \ln Q}{\partial T} + \mathbf{R} \int_0^T \frac{\partial \ln Q}{\partial T} \, dT$$

$$= \frac{E}{T} + \mathbf{R} \ln Q - \mathbf{R} \ln (Q)_{T=0}$$

The last term is independent of temperature and can be equated to S_0. The problem of evaluating S_0 is discussed in books on statistical mechanics (18). Usually Q is assumed equal to unity at $T = 0$, so $S_0 = 0$ (third law of thermodynamics). In any case, we find

$$S = \frac{E}{T} + \mathbf{R} \ln Q$$

From classical thermodynamics we know that the (Helmholtz) free energy $F = E - TS$, so

$$F = -\mathbf{R} T \ln Q \qquad \text{or} \qquad e^{-F/\mathbf{R}T} = \sum_i e^{-E_i/\mathbf{R}T}$$

the free energy simply being proportional to the logarithm of the partition function.*

It is customary among thermodynamicists to measure energies from the *lowest actual energy level* of each molecule. If this is done, the values of F and E calculated from partition functions are the same as those evaluated experimentally from thermochemical measurements. However, this definition of energy levels for partition functions is not useful in discussing isotope effects, an important part of physical organic chemistry. We shall therefore consistently measure energies from the *lowest point of the potential energy surface* for each molecule instead. Our energies do not go to zero at 0°K. for polyatomic

* The partition function *per molecule* Q is directly applicable for calculating the thermodynamic properties *per mole* only in the case of localized systems of non-interacting particles. For non-localized systems like a perfect gas, where the molecules are all indistinguishable, the correct expression is

$$F = -\mathbf{R}T[\ln (Q/N_0) + 1]$$

In this book we have neglected this extra complication throughout for simplicity even though, implicitly, we usually refer to perfect gases (*cf.* Appendix 1).

molecules but include the "zero-point" kinetic energies of molecular vibrations. The values of F and E calculated from our partition functions would then differ from the thermochemically measured functions by these "zero-point" energies, the difference in F being exactly the same as the difference in E. As long as the definition is used consistently, it does not affect the arguments or the thermodynamic definition of E. The meaning of this definition is further illustrated in this chapter and in Chapter 5.

At equilibrium, ΔF^0 is the free energy difference between reactants and products in the standard states (*e.g.*, 1 Molar). However, since we have said that partition functions shall be evaluated by calling the energy of the lowest point of *each molecule's* potential energy surface zero, we must correct the free energies calculated from partition functions for the fact that different kinds of molecules have energy zeros which are different. For a single kind of molecule A, the free energy is therefore

$$F_A^0 = -\mathbf{R}T \ln Q_A^0 + (E_0)_A$$

where $(E_0)_A$ is the energy difference (per *mole*) between the lowest point of molecule A's potential energy surface and any (arbitrary) zero of energy we wish to choose. The superscript zeroes mean that the partition function is evaluated for the standard state chosen. Exactly corresponding expressions hold for the free energies of other kinds of molecules, each E_0 being measured from the *same point* if we wish to compare free energies of different kinds of molecules.

For a reaction

$$aA + bB + \cdots \rightleftarrows mM + nN + \cdots$$

$$
\begin{aligned}
\Delta F^0 &\equiv mF_M^0 + nF_N^0 + \cdots - aF_A^0 - bF_B^0 - \cdots \\
&= m(-\mathbf{R}T \ln Q_M^0 + (E_0)_M) + n(-\mathbf{R}T \ln Q_N^0 + (E_0)_N) \\
&\quad + \cdots - a(-\mathbf{R}T \ln Q_A^0 + (E_0)_A) \\
&\quad\quad\quad - b(-\mathbf{R}T \ln Q_B^0 + (E_0)_B) - \cdots \\
&= -\mathbf{R}T \ln \left[\frac{(Q_M^0)^m (Q_N^0)^n \cdots}{(Q_A^0)^a (Q_B^0)^b \cdots} \right] + m(E_0)_M + n(E_0)_N \\
&\quad\quad\quad + \cdots - a(E_0)_A - b(E_0)_B - \cdots
\end{aligned}
$$

The differences in energy are simply, by definition, equal to ΔE_0. The energy difference can be included in the logarithmic term, giving

$$\Delta F^0 = -RT \ln \left[\frac{(Q_M^0)^m (Q_N^0)^n \cdots}{(Q_A^0)^a (Q_B^0)^b \cdots} e^{-\Delta E_0/RT} \right]$$

It is well known from classical thermodynamics that $\Delta F^0 = -RT \ln K$, where K is the equilibrium constant for the reaction. (Actually, we usually refer to equilibrium constants at constant pressure, in which case we should use the Gibbs free energy rather than ΔF^0, but in solution the two kinds of free energy are very nearly identical.) Hence

$$K = \left[\frac{(Q_M^0)^m (Q_N^0)^n \cdots}{(Q_A^0)^a (Q_B^0)^b \cdots} \right] e^{-\Delta E_0/RT}$$

Note that ΔE_0 is not the thermodynamic ΔE^0, since the former is measured from the bottoms of the potential energy curves, whereas the latter is measured from the lowest energy levels of the molecules (these differ by the zero-point energies).

It is usually found that, to a good approximation, the energy ϵ of a molecule can be separated into translational (ϵ_t), rotational (ϵ_r), vibrational (ϵ_v), and electronic (ϵ_e) contributions,

$$\epsilon = \epsilon_t + \epsilon_r + \epsilon_v + \epsilon_e$$

If this is substituted into the Boltzmann factor and factored,

$$e^{-\epsilon/kT} = e^{-(\epsilon_t + \epsilon_r + \epsilon_v + \epsilon_e)/kT}$$
$$= e^{-\epsilon_t/kT} e^{-\epsilon_r/kT} e^{-\epsilon_v/kT} e^{-\epsilon_e/kT}$$

Since each separate part of the energy can take on only discrete values such as $(\epsilon_t)_1$, $(\epsilon_t)_2$, $\ldots$; $(\epsilon_r)_1$, $(\epsilon_r)_2$, $\ldots$; etc., the molecule can have energy levels corresponding to every possible combination of these individual contributions. One such might be

$$\epsilon = (\epsilon_t)_6 + (\epsilon_r)_4 + (\epsilon_v)_2 + (\epsilon_e)_1$$

A little reflection, or the multiplication of a few terms, shows that the partition function itself can be factored:

$$Q = \sum_i e^{-\epsilon_i/kT}$$

$$= \sum_j e^{-(\epsilon_t)_j/kT} \sum_k e^{-(\epsilon_r)_k/kT} \sum_l e^{-(\epsilon_v)_l/kT} \sum_m e^{-(\epsilon_e)_m/kT}$$

Since each of the latter summations involves only one type of energy level, we might say that the total partition function can be factored into translational, rotational, vibrational, and electronic partition functions:

$$Q = Q_t Q_r Q_v Q_e$$

and we can attempt to evaluate each contribution independently.

If the container is large in volume compared with the volume of the molecule (18)*

$$Q_t = \frac{(2\pi mkT)^{3/2}V}{h^3}$$

where m is the weight of one molecule, V is the volume available to the molecule, and h is Planck's constant. This expression is for one isolated molecule, not a molecule in solution. However, for the transition-state theory we do not need an exact expression anyway, and when we consider isotope effects, the effect of the solvent very nearly cancels out between isotopic reactants.

At reasonably high temperatures (room temperature is high enough for almost all molecules), the rotational partition functions for linear and non-linear molecules are

$$\text{linear } Q_r = \frac{8\pi^2 IkT}{h^2\sigma}$$

$$\text{non-linear } Q_r = \frac{8\pi^2(8\pi^3 ABC)^{1/2}(kT)^{3/2}}{h^3\sigma}$$

* Simple derivations of Q_t and of Q_r for a linear molecule are given in Appendix 1.

where I is the principal moment of inertia (actually two equal ones) of a linear molecule; A, B, and C are the three principal moments of inertia of a non-linear molecule; and σ is the symmetry number, which is the number of indistinguishable orientations in space the molecule could assume (for H_2O, $\sigma = 2$; for H_3O^+, $\sigma = 3$; for HDO, $\sigma = 1$). There are only two principal moments of inertia for a linear molecule because angular momentum about the linear axis could not result from motion of the nuclei (they are all on the axis) but only from that of the electrons. However, we have arbitrarily decided to include electronic motions (energy levels) in the separate electronic partition function.

It is known from the quantum mechanics of vibrational motion that the energy levels of a simple harmonic oscillator are

$$\epsilon_i = (n + \tfrac{1}{2})\mathbf{h}\nu_i \qquad (n = 0, 1, 2, \ldots)$$

where the different energy levels of harmonic oscillator number i are found by using all integral values of the quantum number n and ν_i is the (classical) frequency of vibration,

$$\nu_i = \frac{1}{2\pi}\left(\frac{k}{\mu}\right)^{1/2} \qquad (3\text{--}3)$$

where k is the force constant and μ is the reduced mass for this vibration. The partition function for vibration i is therefore

$$\sum_n e^{-\epsilon_n/kT} = \sum_{n=0}^{\infty} e^{-(n+1/2)\mathbf{h}\nu_i/kT}$$

$$= e^{-\mathbf{h}\nu_i/2kT} \sum_{n=0}^{\infty} e^{-n\mathbf{h}\nu_i/kT}$$

The last summation can be shown to be a simple geometric series, the exact sum of which is well known:

$$\sum_{n=0}^{\infty} e^{-n\mathbf{h}\nu_i/kT} = e^0 + e^{-\mathbf{h}\nu_i/kT} + e^{-2\mathbf{h}\nu_i/kT} + \cdots$$

$$= \sum_{n=0}^{\infty} x^n = \frac{1}{1-x} = \frac{1}{1 - e^{-\mathbf{h}\nu_i/kT}}$$

It is a good approximation to divide up the vibration of a polyatomic molecule into a number of "normal vibrations" which can be treated as independent simple harmonic vibrations. This is exactly true if the force exerted on the nuclei is directly proportional to their displacement from their equilibrium positions, and is found to be very closely true in most molecules. Therefore the vibrational energy of the molecule can be expressed as the sum of the vibrational energy levels of the several normal vibrations. The vibrational partition function is then the product of the separate partition functions for each normal vibration by the same argument used in expressing the total partition function as the product $Q_t Q_r Q_v Q_e$:

$$Q_v = \prod^{i} \frac{e^{-h\nu_i/2kT}}{1 - e^{-h\nu_i/kT}}$$

where the product extends over all i vibrations of the molecule.* A linear molecule has $3N - 5$ vibrations, while a non-linear molecule has $3N - 6$ vibrations, where N is the number of nuclei in the molecule.

The lowest actual energy level of the molecule is $\sum_i h\nu_i/2$ since the lowest energy possible for any one vibration is $h\nu_i/2$ ($n = 0$). This is the so-called zero-point energy mentioned before. It is measured from the bottom of the potential energy surface for the molecule, *i.e.*, from the lowest electronic energy level of the molecule.

If we measure all energies from the lowest electronic energy level, as we said was most convenient, and therefore include

---

* Sometimes, especially in complex molecules, some of the $3N - 6$ internal degrees of freedom are *internal rotations* rather than vibrations. If the internal rotation is completely free (*e.g.*, rotation of the methyl groups in dimethylacetylene), the partition function is simply $(8\pi^3 I k T)^{1/2}/\sigma h$ where I is the moment of inertia for the internal rotation about its axis of rotation. For the case of *hindered* internal rotation (*e.g.*, rotation of the methyl groups in ethane) or more than one internal rotation in the same molecule, the partition function must frequently be evaluated numerically (see Pitzer (18)). Q_v will then include the i *vibrations*, times factors for the internal rotations.

the factor $e^{-\Delta E_0/\mathbf{R}T}$ in the expression for the equilibrium constant, this is equivalent to calling the energy of that lowest electronic level zero. Since the second electronic energy level of almost any molecule is of very high energy, it almost always turns out that the partition function

$$Q_e = \sum_m e^{-(\epsilon_e)_m/\mathbf{k}T}$$

has $(\epsilon_e)_1 = 0$ so that the first term in the sum is 1, while $(\epsilon_e)_2$ and all the higher (ϵ_e) are so large compared to $\mathbf{k}T$ at the ordinary temperatures of a few hundred degrees Kelvin that the rest of the terms in the sum are essentially zero. Therefore, usually,

$$Q_e = 1$$

and we normally do not need to consider Q_e at all in evaluating Q.

It is interesting to see just how different the energy level spacings in molecules usually are. Here are some average spacings between the lowest and the next highest energy level for different types of energy along with average partition functions *per degree of freedom:*[*]

TABLE 3–1

Energy Level Spacing and Partition Functions

	Energy Level Spacing	Partition Function (300°K.)
Electronic	5 e.v. or 115 kcal./mole	1
Vibrational	0.1 e.v. or 2.3 kcal./mole	10^{-4}–2
Rotational	10^{-4}–10^{-3} e.v. or 0.023–0.0023 kcal./mole	10–100
Translational	Much less than rotational	10^8–10^9

[*] The tremendous loss of probability associated with a bimolecular reaction can be seen from these approximate partition functions. Six translational degrees of freedom of the reactants are replaced by three translational and three vibrational and/or rotational degrees of freedom of the transition state. This adverse effect is compensated to a greater or lesser extent by the formation of a new bond. The vibrational partition functions include factors of *ca.* 1.0 to 2.0 for the non-zero-point energy part times *ca.* 10^{-4} to 0.8 for the zero-point energy part.

These are to be compared with $RT = 0.6$ kcal./mole at room temperature.

There is one other point we should mention, the vibrational partition function as $\nu_i \rightarrow 0$. If the vibrational frequency is very small,

$$e^{-h\nu_i/2kT} \rightarrow 1$$

$$1 - e^{-h\nu_i/kT} = 1 - \left(1 - \frac{h\nu_i}{kT} + \frac{h^2\nu_i^2}{k^2T^2} - \cdots\right)$$

$$= \frac{h\nu_i}{kT}$$

where we have used the infinite series expansion for the exponential but find that for very small ν_i the squared and higher terms are negligible. Then the partition function contribution from this vibration i of low frequency is

$$\frac{e^{-h\nu_i/2kT}}{1 - e^{-h\nu_i/kT}} = \frac{kT}{h\nu_i} \tag{3-4}$$

Transition-State Theory. The theory of absolute reaction rates, now usually called the transition-state theory, is derived by assuming that the rate of a reaction is dependent on an equilibrium between reactants and activated complexes (transition states) (13, 14):

$$A + B + \cdots \rightleftarrows M^{\ddagger} + N + \cdots$$

where $M^{\ddagger}$ is the transition state for the reaction.* We can then define an equilibrium constant:

$$K = \frac{(M^{\ddagger})(N) \cdots}{(A)(B) \cdots} \frac{\alpha^{\ddagger}\alpha_N \cdots}{\alpha_A\alpha_B \cdots}$$

$$= \frac{Q_{\ddagger}^0 Q_N^0 \cdots}{Q_A^0 Q_B^0 \cdots} e^{-\Delta E^{\ddagger}_0/RT} \tag{3-5}$$

* The product N in the above equation would not occur unless there were a rapid, equilibrium formation of an intermediate followed by a rate-determining transition state involving the intermediate, *e.g.*, a rapid reversible ionization of $RX \rightleftarrows R^+ + X^-$, followed by reaction of R^+ with solvent S to form product. Then $M^{\ddagger} = [R\text{---}S]^+$ and $N = X^-$.

where the α's are activity coefficients. The partition function $Q_{\ddagger}^0$ is for a metastable state, not a stable molecule. However, it is generally assumed that the translations and rotations are similar to those of a stable molecule. Also, all the normal vibrations of the transition state are assumed to be as for a stable molecule, except one. This one normal vibration corresponds to the process of decomposing the transition state into products. For example, in the reaction

$$A + B \rightarrow [A\text{---}B]^{\ddagger}$$

the transition state has only one normal vibration, the A---B stretching vibration, and this corresponds to forming products by bringing the nuclei together (the stretching vibration can also bring them apart, corresponding simply to decomposition back into reactants). This vibration is a metastable vibration in the sense that it has no restoring force (actually a negative one). Since the property of the activated complex is that it corresponds to the highest energy necessary to complete the reaction, if the A---B bond of the transition state is shortened, the system becomes *more stable*, and likewise, if it is lengthened, the system also becomes *more stable*. The reverse reaction, the decomposition of AB, must have this same transition state, a statement which is generally true for all reactions (at least all thermal reactions). It can be shown to be true by considering the thermodynamic relationships between reactants, products, and transition state. The mechanism will obviously involve the transition state of lowest possible energy which can be reached by putting thermal energy into the reactants. Since the number of transition states will depend on a Boltzmann distribution, any higher energy transition state would be much less probable. Since the energy of this lowest transition state is the same whether it is formed from reactants or from products, it will be the most favorable path for both the forward and the reverse reactions. This general result that the path (*i.e.*, transition state or transition states and intermediates if they occur) is the same for both forward and reverse reactions is called the *principle of microscopic reversibility*. Another example of the metastable vibration of a transition state is the displacement reaction

$$A + BC \rightarrow [A\text{---}B\text{---}C]^{\ddagger}$$

Here the transition state will have two stretching vibrations. One of these is a periodic (normal) vibration, something like:

$$\longleftarrow\text{---}A \quad\quad B\rightarrow \quad\quad C\longrightarrow$$

The other is an aperiodic (metastable) vibration, something like:

$$A\rightarrow \quad\quad \longleftarrow\text{---}B \quad\quad C\longrightarrow$$

The aperiodic vibration clearly corresponds to the formation of products (or reactants) from the transition state.

Generally these metastable vibrations should be of low "frequency." Actually the frequency is imaginary (involving $\sqrt{-1}$) because the force constant is negative (*cf.* Eq. (3–3)). In this case we will use the approximation Eq. (3–4) for the metastable vibration's contribution to the partition function,*

$$Q_{\ddagger}^{0} = Q^{\ddagger}\,\frac{\mathbf{k}T}{\mathbf{h}\nu^{\ddagger}} \tag{3–6}$$

where $Q^{\ddagger}$ includes all the contributions except that of the imaginary vibration $\nu^{\ddagger}$ (*i.e.*, the translations, rotations, and for a non-linear transition state $3N^{\ddagger} - 7$ vibrations, where $N^{\ddagger}$ is the number of nuclei in the transition state).

The rate is now equal to the concentration of transition states times the frequency with which these decompose:

$$\text{rate} = (M^{\ddagger})\nu^{\ddagger}$$

---

* There are numerous complications in this approximation. The partition function for the metastable degree of freedom cannot rigorously be equated to one for a normal vibration, because the "force constant" is negative. This approach is qualitatively justifiable even though it involves an imaginary partition function, because the same answer can be obtained in other ways, *e.g.*, by assuming that the top of the barrier is flat enough that the metastable degree of freedom can be treated as a *translation*. The rate problem can in principle be solved exactly by quantum mechanics, but the equations are prohibitively complex.

It works out well if we define an "equilibrium constant" $K^{\ddagger}$ which does not include the contribution of the imaginary vibration:

$$K^{\ddagger} \equiv \frac{Q^{\ddagger} Q_N^0 \; \cdots}{Q_A^0 Q_B^0 \; \cdots} \, e^{-\Delta E_0{}^{\ddagger}/RT}$$

In terms of K of Eq. (3–5),

$$K = K^{\ddagger} \frac{\mathbf{k}T}{\mathbf{h}\nu^{\ddagger}}$$

Solving Eq. (3–5) for $(M^{\ddagger})$ and using $K^{\ddagger}$, we obtain

$$(M^{\ddagger}) = K^{\ddagger} \frac{\mathbf{k}T}{\mathbf{h}\nu^{\ddagger}} \frac{(A)\alpha_A (B)\alpha_B \; \cdots}{\alpha^{\ddagger}(N)\alpha_N \; \cdots}$$

Note that the rate is assumed to be proportional to the actual number of transition states (*i.e.*, to $(M^{\ddagger})$) rather than to the thermodynamic activity $(M^{\ddagger})\alpha^{\ddagger}$. Using the value for $(M^{\ddagger})$ so obtained, we find*

$$\text{rate} = \frac{\mathbf{k}T}{\mathbf{h}} K^{\ddagger} \frac{(A)(B) \; \cdots \; \alpha_A \alpha_B \; \cdots}{(N) \; \cdots \; \alpha^{\ddagger}\alpha_N \; \cdots}$$

We can now define two rate constants. The observed rate constant, obtained by the usual procedure of measuring concentrations of reactants and/or products (*cf.* the first part of this chapter) is

$$k_{\text{OBS}} = \frac{\mathbf{k}T}{\mathbf{h}} K^{\ddagger} \frac{\alpha_A \alpha_B \; \cdots}{\alpha^{\ddagger}\alpha_N \; \cdots}$$

and depends on the medium through the activity coefficients.

---

* We could alternatively leave the "imaginary" frequency intact and write

$$\text{rate} = \nu^{\ddagger} K \frac{(A)(B) \; \cdots \; \alpha_A \alpha_B \; \cdots}{(N) \; \cdots \; \alpha^{\ddagger}\alpha_N \; \cdots}$$

where K is defined by Eq. (3–5), then attempt to evaluate $\nu^{\ddagger}$ and K. The metastable degree of freedom must make only a minor contribution to the energy E of the transition state, although it could make a substantial entropy contribution.

A thermodynamically constant rate constant, which is independent of the medium, is

$$k_{\text{THERMO}} = \frac{\mathbf{k}T}{\mathbf{h}} K^{\ddagger}$$

It can in some cases be evaluated experimentally by measuring k_{OBS} at very low concentrations where one is certain that all the activity coefficients are unity. Then by measuring k_{OBS} at higher concentrations and measuring all the activity coefficients except $\alpha^{\ddagger}$, which is experimentally inaccessible at present, one can calculate $\alpha^{\ddagger}$.

To make the transition-state theory more exact, it is necessary to take account of factors influencing the motion of activated complexes toward and away from the potential energy barrier. If the potential energy surface in the neighborhood of the transition state has a complicated shape, it might be that a transition-state molecule could sometimes pass over the barrier toward products and yet *return* before it loses any appreciable energy, to give reactants again. This possibility is exceedingly unlikely in solution, as opposed to the gas phase, because the transition-state complex, if surrounded by solvent molecules, is almost certain to be very rapidly deactivated to reactants or products by transfer of energy to solvent molecules in collisions (Chapter 5 of Ref. 19).

According to quantum mechanics, a particle may "tunnel" through a potential energy barrier and appear on the other side without ever possessing enough kinetic energy to pass over the top of the barrier. Also, a particle which has energy just a little greater than the necessary amount to pass over the top of the barrier may, according to quantum mechanics, be "reflected," *i.e.*, not allowed to pass. Any complete treatment of reaction rates must take account of these factors. Such a treatment introduces a *transmission coefficient* κ which is an average fraction of the transition-state complexes that actually become products. In fact, κ is more complicated than this because it must be evaluated by calculating the fraction of complexes of a certain energy which approach the barrier and pass through, and then averaging over all possible energies of such complexes, taking account of the probability that a complex will have a given energy. This kind of calculation is carried through in Appendix 2 and leads to a much more satisfying derivation of the transition-state rate equation, except that the rate derived in this section is multiplied by κ.

The tunneling correction is very small except for very light particles and/or very narrow barriers (narrow in the sense that the particle need not move very far to get from one side to the other). Although electrons can tunnel quite effectively, the probability of tunneling of a *nucleus* is likely to be small for any nuclei except hydrogen. Therefore, in most reactions, κ can be assumed to be very nearly unity. Some interesting results have been obtained for cases where tunneling may be important (20; 21; 22, page 57). There are very intricate problems in evaluating κ because tunneling can occur at points far enough from the transition-state configuration that the motions of the complexes are no longer separable into normal vibrations and calculations must be made for simultaneous motion in at least two dimensions.

We are now in a good position to derive the transition-state theory rate constant for the simple reaction

$$A + B \rightarrow [A\text{---}B]^{\ddagger} \rightarrow AB$$

and show that, for such simple reactions, the rate constants are the same from the two theories. The situation is more complex for cases where A and B are not monatomic, but it is possible that the two theories would give similar results in all cases if the probability factor P of the collision theory could be properly evaluated. The rate constant is, for perfect gases,

$$k = \frac{\mathbf{k}T}{\mathbf{h}} K^{\ddagger}$$

$$K^{\ddagger} = \frac{Q_{AB}^{\ddagger}}{Q_A^0 Q_B^0} e^{-\Delta E_0^{\ddagger}/RT}$$

Since the transition-state partition function $Q_{AB}^{\ddagger}$ has lost already its only vibrational contribution (*cf.* Eq. 3–6), only translational and rotational contributions must be included. Since A and B are atoms, only translational contributions must be included, because the rotations of the electrons of an atom are included in the electronic partition function Q_e, which was shown to be almost always equal to 1. Actually, if A and/or B were atoms with unpaired electron spins, the electronic partition functions would have to be included because there would be more than one energy level with zero energy, corresponding to the different possible orientations of electron spins. For a single unpaired electron, the spin can be either $+\frac{1}{2}$ or $-\frac{1}{2}$, so there are two levels of zero energy. Each of these levels would contribute unity to the electronic partition function sum, so in this case $Q_e = 2$. To avoid this complication, since we did not include it in discussing the collision theory, we assume that A and B have no unpaired electrons, *e.g.*, they may be one positive and one negative ion such as Li^+ and F^-.

We find, dividing each partition function by **V** to give units of molecules/cm.^{3},

$$K^{\ddagger} = \frac{[2\pi(\mathbf{m}_A + \mathbf{m}_B)\mathbf{k}T]^{3/2}8\pi^2 I_{AB}\mathbf{k}T\mathbf{h}^3\mathbf{h}^3}{\mathbf{h}^3\mathbf{h}^2\sigma_{AB}(2\pi\mathbf{m}_A\mathbf{k}T)^{3/2}(2\pi\mathbf{m}_B\mathbf{k}T)^{3/2}} e^{-\Delta E_0{}^{\ddagger}/RT}$$

$$= \mathbf{h}\left(\frac{\mathbf{m}_A + \mathbf{m}_B}{\mathbf{m}_A\mathbf{m}_B}\right)^{3/2}\frac{2^{3/2}\pi^{1/2}}{(\mathbf{k}T)^{1/2}}I_{AB}e^{-\Delta E_0{}^{\ddagger}/RT}$$

since $\sigma_{AB} = 1$. Now for a diatomic molecule,

$$I_{AB} = \mu_{AB}\mathbf{r}_{AB}^2$$

giving

$$K^{\ddagger} = \mathbf{h}\left(\frac{8\pi}{\mathbf{k}T\mu_{AB}}\right)^{1/2}\mathbf{r}_{AB}^2 e^{-\Delta E_0{}^{\ddagger}/RT}$$

$$k = \mathbf{r}_{AB}^2\left(\frac{8\pi\mathbf{k}T}{\mu_{AB}}\right)^{1/2}e^{-\Delta E_0{}^{\ddagger}/RT} \text{ cm.}^3/\text{molecule-sec.}$$

if r_{AB} is expressed in cm. To convert to liter-mole^{-1}-sec.$^{-1}$ units, this should be multiplied by N_0 molecules/mole and divided by 1000 cm.^{3}/liter, giving

$$k = \frac{N_0}{1000} r_{AB}^2 \left(\frac{8\pi kT}{\mu_{AB}}\right)^{1/2} e^{-\Delta E_0^{\ddagger}/RT}$$

identical with the expression from the collision theory if r_{AB}, the internuclear distance in the activated complex, is equal to $r_A + r_B$, the sum of the collision diameters of A and B, and E of the collision theory equals $\Delta E_0^{\ddagger}$ of the transition-state theory.

Thus it seems justifiable in some degree to talk of molecular collisions, an easy picture to conjure up, while making calculations based on the more thermodynamic than picturesque transition-state theory.

The activity coefficients of ions can be approximated by the simple Debye-Hückel theory in the form

$$\log \alpha = -aZ^2 \sqrt{\mu}$$

where α is the activity coefficient, a is a constant $= +0.509$ in dilute agueous solution at 25°, Z is the charge on the ion, and μ is the "ionic strength" of the solution:

$$\mu = \frac{1}{2} \sum_i C_i Z_i^2$$

where C is the concentration of ion i and the summation is taken over all the different kinds of ions in the solution. For the simple reaction of A + B (it is not necessary to restrict A and B to being monatomic),

$$k_{OBS} = \frac{kT}{h} K^{\ddagger} \left(\frac{\alpha_A \alpha_B}{\alpha_{AB}^{\ddagger}}\right)$$

The ionic strength should affect only the activity coefficient term, so that we can find out how k_{OBS} should change with ionic strength:

$$\frac{k_{OBS}}{k_{OBS}^0} = \frac{\alpha_A \alpha_B}{\alpha_{AB}^{\ddagger}}$$

where k_{OBS}^0 is the rate constant in highly dilute solution, all activity coefficients being one. The logarithmic form is

$$\log\left(\frac{\alpha_A\alpha_B}{\alpha_{AB}^\ddagger}\right) = -aZ_A^2\sqrt{\mu} - aZ_B^2\sqrt{\mu} + aZ_{AB}^2\sqrt{\mu}$$
$$= a\sqrt{\mu}\,(Z_{AB}^2 - Z_A^2 - Z_B^2)$$
$$= a\sqrt{\mu}\,[(Z_A + Z_B)^2 - Z_A^2 - Z_B^2]$$
$$= a\sqrt{\mu}\,2Z_AZ_B$$

This term is positive if Z_A and Z_B have like signs and negative if Z_A and Z_B have unlike signs; *i.e.*, the rate increases with ionic strength for reactions between ions with charges of the same sign and decreases with ionic strength for reactions between ions with charges of opposite sign. This theory explains some facts which were very difficult to understand before the transition-state theory, and generally experiments show that its predictions are reasonably accurate, at least with regard to sign even if not in absolute magnitude. The important feature is the inclusion of $\alpha^\ddagger$ in the denominator, for without $\alpha^\ddagger$ the predictions are completely different. The success of these salt effect predictions is good evidence that the fundamental assumption of the transition-state theory, that there is an equilibrium set up between reactants and activated complexes, is usually valid.

One can obtain a pseudothermodynamic picture of reaction rates by defining

$$\Delta F_0^\ddagger \equiv -\mathbf{R}T\ln K^\ddagger$$

The subscript zero denotes that this is the free energy difference between transition state and reactants in their standard states. Remember that $K^\ddagger$ is not a true equilibrium constant because it lacks the partition function contribution of the metastable vibration (sometimes called the reaction coordinate). Now

$$K^\ddagger = k_{OBS}\frac{\mathbf{h}}{\mathbf{k}T}\frac{\alpha^\ddagger}{\alpha_A\alpha_B}$$
$$-\mathbf{R}T\ln K^\ddagger \equiv \Delta F_0^\ddagger = 2.303\,\mathbf{R}T\log\left(\frac{\mathbf{k}T\alpha_A\alpha_B}{\mathbf{h}k_{OBS}\alpha^\ddagger}\right)$$

From the thermodynamic equation (assumed to apply to transition states as well as to ordinary molecules),

$$\Delta F_0^{\ddagger} = \Delta H_0^{\ddagger} - T\Delta S_0^{\ddagger}$$

we can by substitution show that

$$\log\left(\frac{k_{\mathrm{OBS}}}{T}\right) = \frac{-\Delta H_0^{\ddagger}}{2.303\mathrm{R}}\left(\frac{1}{T}\right) + \log\left(\frac{\alpha_A\alpha_B}{\alpha^{\ddagger}}\right) + \text{constant.}$$

If we assume (as should be usually so) that the ratio $\alpha_A\alpha_B/\alpha^{\ddagger}$ is essentially independent of temperature, then measurements of k_{OBS} at various temperatures will give $-\Delta H_0^{\ddagger}/2.303\mathrm{R}$ as the slope of a plot of $\log(k_{\mathrm{OBS}}/T)$ vs. $1/T$. From $\Delta F_0^{\ddagger}$ and $\Delta H_0^{\ddagger}$, $\Delta S_0^{\ddagger}$ can be easily calculated.* It will be interesting to look at some experimental values of these thermodynamic quantities of activation in Chapter 5.

A simple approximation to the effect of the solvent on reaction velocities is worth discussing, since it leads to the same qualitative conclusion stated in Chapter 2 (24). The activity coefficient of a non-ionic solute may be approximated as

$$\ln \alpha_x = \frac{\mathbf{V}_x}{\mathbf{R}T}(\delta_x - \delta_s)^2$$

where $\mathbf{V}_x$ is the molar volume of the solute X as a pure liquid, δ_x^2 is a parameter called the "internal pressure" or "cohesive energy density,"

$$\delta_x^2 = \Delta E_x/\mathbf{V}_x$$

where ΔE_x is the molar energy of vaporization of X. The cohesive energy density of the solvent, δ_s^2, is defined in the same way. Remembering that

$$\ln k_{\mathrm{OBS}} = \ln k_{\mathrm{THERMO}} + \ln\left(\frac{\alpha_A\alpha_B}{\alpha^{\ddagger}}\right)$$

we find

$$\ln\left(\frac{\alpha_A\alpha_B}{\alpha^{\ddagger}}\right) = \frac{\mathbf{V}_A}{\mathbf{R}T}(\delta_A - \delta_s)^2 + \frac{\mathbf{V}_B}{\mathbf{R}T}(\delta_B - \delta_s)^2 - \frac{\mathbf{V}^{\ddagger}}{\mathbf{R}T}(\delta_{\ddagger} - \delta_s)^2$$

* For a good discussion of thermodynamics of activation, see Ref. (23).

For the example of relatively non-polar reactants (low δ) and a polar transition state (high δ), the reaction should be slowed by non-polar solvents (δ_A, $\delta_B \sim \delta_s$; $\delta_{\ddagger} > \delta_s$) and speeded up by polar solvents (δ_A, $\delta_B < \delta_s$; $\delta_{\ddagger} \sim \delta_s$). The major conclusions of the rule of Chapter 2 can be derived from this approximate, empirical equation.

A rather interesting relationship between structure and the thermodynamics of activation is derived (25) by differentiating the equation

$$\Delta F_0^{\ddagger} = \Delta H_0^{\ddagger} - T\Delta S_0^{\ddagger}$$

with respect to a parameter λ representing a change in structure in the transition state of the reaction:

$$\frac{\partial \Delta F_0^{\ddagger}}{\partial \lambda} = \frac{\partial \Delta H_0^{\ddagger}}{\partial \lambda} - T\frac{\partial \Delta S_0^{\ddagger}}{\partial \lambda}$$

For an equilibrium, however, $\partial \Delta F_0^{\ddagger}/\partial \lambda = 0$ (this is frequently used as a definition of equilibrium), so that

$$\frac{\partial \Delta H_0^{\ddagger}}{\partial \lambda} = T\frac{\partial \Delta S_0^{\ddagger}}{\partial \lambda}$$

For wider structural changes, *e.g.* where we change one of the reactants by attaching substituents to it, these equations would not hold exactly, but it would not be surprising to find that (a) $\Delta F_0^{\ddagger}$ changed relatively little with structure and (b) the changes in $\Delta H_0^{\ddagger}$ and $\Delta S_0^{\ddagger}$ were in the same direction, so as to compensate each other in the free energy. In closely related reaction series, the heat and entropy of activation are frequently found to change by rather large amounts, but in the same direction, so that the free energy of activation is changed only slightly.

MOLECULAR ORBITAL CALCULATIONS

There are now a number of books which describe the applications of molecular orbital (MO) and other quantum mechanical theories to organic structures and mechanisms

(25–29), so it will not be necessary to discuss this subject in great detail. However, there are some simple approximations which are interesting in relation to solvolysis reactions.

Schrödinger Equation. The motion of electrons in molecules is described by a probability function rather than classical trajectories. For large numbers of molecules we are really interested only in average properties anyway, so the inability to use classical mechanics is no great disappointment. Electrons have been observed to undergo diffraction analogous to the diffraction of light. This leads into the probability treatment of electrons in that electrons *behave as if* they had an associated "wavelength" of their probability distribution given by

$$mv = \frac{h}{\lambda} \tag{3-7}$$

where m is the mass, v the velocity, λ the "wavelength," and **h** Planck's constant (we are here following Ref. (26)). A sine wave of wavelength λ has an amplitude ψ:

$$\psi = A \sin\left(\frac{2\pi x}{\lambda}\right)$$

as may be easily verified, where A is the maximum amplitude and x is the coordinate in space. Then

$$\frac{d^2\psi}{dx^2} = -\frac{4\pi^2}{\lambda^2} A \sin\left(\frac{2\pi x}{\lambda}\right) = -\frac{4\pi^2}{\lambda^2}\psi \tag{3-8}$$

The kinetic energy T is, from Eq. (3–7),

$$T = \frac{1}{2} mv^2 = \frac{1}{2m}\frac{h^2}{\lambda^2}$$

which, using Eq. (3–8), is

$$T = \frac{-h^2}{8\pi^2 m}\frac{1}{\psi}\frac{d^2\psi}{dx^2}$$

This applies to a particle which has kinetic energy only, but may be extended by noting that

$$T = E - V$$

where E is the total energy and V is the potential energy. Schrödinger's equation is then simply

$$\frac{d^2\psi}{dx^2} + \frac{8\pi^2 m}{h^2}(E - V)\psi = 0 \qquad (3\text{-}9)$$

for a particle moving in one direction only, where ψ will be some function of x.* For motion in three dimensions, ψ will be a function of three coordinates (as will V), and we must replace

$$\frac{d^2\psi}{dx^2} \quad \text{by} \quad \frac{\partial^2\psi}{\partial x^2} + \frac{\partial^2\psi}{\partial y^2} + \frac{\partial^2\psi}{\partial z^2}$$

The coordinates x, y, z can be transformed into polar coordinates or others if desirable, depending on the nature of the problem.

The peculiarity of Schrödinger's equation is that if (and only if, except in very special cases) we require ψ to be a "non-pathological" probability function, *i.e.*, to be finite, single-valued, and continuous as probabilities ought to be, there are only certain values of E for which the equation has any acceptable solution. This means that molecules have the very peculiar property of not being able to have energies other than certain discrete energy levels corresponding to the allowed values of E. If the molecule had any other energy content, it would be radiating light and would not stop radiating until it reached one of the stationary energy levels E.

Just as the square of the amplitude of a light wave measures the radiation intensity, so $[\psi(x, y, z)]^2$ for electrons measures the probability of finding the electron at some point (x, y, z). In order that ψ^2 equal this probability, we must have the sum

* It is customary to use E for the energy (*per molecule*) of a single state in Schrödinger's equation. This is not the same use as in the previous section, where E is the energy *per mole*. Schrödinger's equation can be arrived at by other procedures, but cannot be rigorously "derived." As with Newton's equations of motion, its best justification is that it works. For systems simple enough to be solved accurately, it agrees *exactly* with experiment.

of all individual probabilities equal to unity (the particle must be somewhere):

$$\int\int\int\psi^2\,dx\,dy\,dz\ =\ 1 \qquad\qquad (3\text{--}10)$$

where the integrals extend over all possible values of the coordinates.

If we could solve the Schrödinger equation for the values of E and ψ, we could call the lowest energy E_1 and the corresponding solution of the Schrödinger equation ψ_1, and so on, arranging the energies in order. Then, as with atoms, the lowest energy level could contain two and only two electrons (one of each spin), the next energy level two also, and so on until all the electrons the molecule possesses were assigned energy levels. The electronic energy of the molecule would then be the sum of the energies of the electrons, one energy for each electron. This method of assigning a separate energy to each electron is known as the molecular orbital approximation. Actually, of course, the energy of a molecule is not truly separable into parts contributed by individual electrons, because the electrons repel one another.

LCAO Approximation. Generally it is necessary to make the further approximation of expressing a molecular orbital as a sum of atomic orbitals φ:

$$\psi_1\ =\ c_{11}\varphi_1 + c_{21}\varphi_2 + c_{31}\varphi_3 + \cdot\ \cdot\ \cdot \qquad (3\text{--}11)$$

An atomic orbital is a wave function which is the solution of the Schrödinger equation for a particular atom of the molecule considered separated from the rest of the molecule. φ_1 is an atomic orbital centered on nucleus 1 of the molecule. These atomic orbitals may have different characteristic shapes.*

---

* *Orbitals* are simply functions which are stationary solutions of Schrödinger's equation for some system, *i.e.*, belong to a stationary state with a definite E. A complete diagram would somehow show the *value* of the wave function at each point in space. One way of doing this is to make a *contour diagram* of the locus of points of equal $\psi(x, y, z)$ or $\varphi(x, y, z)$. The most common way is to draw only a *single* one of these contours, such that 90 per cent of the electronic charge will be found inside the contour. None of the drawings here are to scale; they are rough indications of the *shape* of the contour.

Some are spherically symmetrical, and are known as s orbitals. Some are composed of two separate portions separated by a plane throughout which $\varphi = 0$ (a "nodal" plane), and are known as p orbitals (see Fig. 2). These two types of orbitals are all we are interested in here, although there are many other shapes labeled by d, f, ... Most atoms have an arrangement of orbitals very similar to that of the hydrogen atom. It is found that there is another important characteristic: the so-called "principal quantum number" n, which essentially determines the energy of the electron. The energy levels are as follows: when $n = 1$, there is a $1s$ orbital; this is the lowest energy (most stable) orbital of the atom. When $n = 2$, there are a $2s$ and three differently oriented $2p$ orbitals, $2p_x$, $2p_y$, and $2p_z$ when the nodal planes are the yz, xz, and xy planes, respectively, if the nucleus is at the origin. When $n = 3$, there are a $3s$, three $3p$, and five $3d$ orbitals. The pattern is similar throughout the periodic table. It turns out that for all atoms except hydrogen the $1s$ orbital is most stable, next the $2s$; only slightly less stable than $2s$ are the $2p$ orbitals (all three with equal energy), next $3s$, next $3p$, etc. (In hydrogen the energies of all $n = 2$ orbitals are equal, etc.) In common organic molecules there are two major types of bonds between atoms,

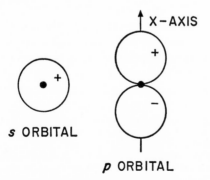

Fig. 2.   Approximate contours of equal value of φ for s and p_x orbitals, in a plane through the nucleus.

σ (sigma) and π (pi) bonds (corresponding with the Greek letters for the s and p atomic orbitals, respectively). Sigma bonds are cylindrically symmetrical about the axis of the bond. In the molecular orbital approximation, we can diagram bonds by showing a bond as resulting from the overlapping of atomic orbitals. Overlap of atomic orbitals leads to bonding because it tends to concentrate electrons (negative charge) between the nuclei, decreasing internuclear repulsions and leading to a "bonding energy" between those nuclei. Sigma bonds can be formed by overlapping s and/or p orbitals as shown in Fig. 3. Note that the two "lobes" of a p orbital have opposite signs. Although the absolute value of the sign, $+$ or $-$, has no physical significance (since electron probabilities are proportional to φ^2), the fact of opposite signs is important for bonding. Only when orbitals overlap with the same sign does overlap lead to bonding. This is because of the form of the molecular orbitals as LCAO's (Eq. (3–11)). If we add two positive (or two negative) orbitals, we increase the electron density between nuclei and get bonding; but if we add a positive and a negative orbital, we get a place between the nuclei where the sum is zero (a "nodal surface"), leading to decreased electron density between nuclei and repulsion, not bonding.

It is in many cases convenient to combine the atomic orbitals to form what are known as "hybridized orbitals," and then combine these hybridized orbitals to give the MO's. This does not change the results appreciably, but it does lead to simplifications and also to a better physical picture of bonding. The useful hybridized orbitals are those that are directed in such a way as to form multiple bonds easily. The carbon atom forms tetrahedral bonds in many molecules, and this type of bonding can be easily represented by four sp^3 hybridized orbitals, formed by combining the $2s$ and three $2p$ orbitals of carbon. Since carbon has four electrons in its valence shell, we can now combine the four $1s$ orbitals of four hydrogen atoms (each with one electron) with the four tetrahedral sp^3

hybrid orbitals of carbon, and get eight independent MO's. Of these MO's, four will be bonding (positive overlap) and four will be antibonding (negative overlap). We can put the eight bonding electrons into the four bonding MO's (one pair of opposite spins in each MO), leading to the methane mole-

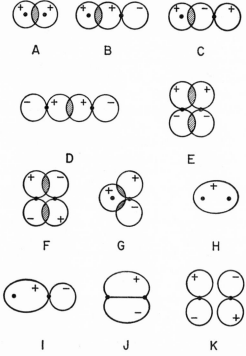

Fig. 3. Sigma and pi overlaps: (A) two s orbitals overlapping, σ-bond; (B) s and p orbitals overlapping, σ-bond; (C) negative sigma overlap leading to repulsion (antibonding); (D) two p orbitals overlapping, σ-bond; (E) two p orbitals overlapping, π-bond; (F) two p orbitals overlapping negatively, antibonding; (G) s and p orbitals overlapping, non-bonding because bonding and antibonding portions exactly cancel; (H) bonding MO corresponding to (A); (I) bonding MO corresponding to (B); (J) bonding MO corresponding to (E); (K) antibonding MO corresponding to (F).

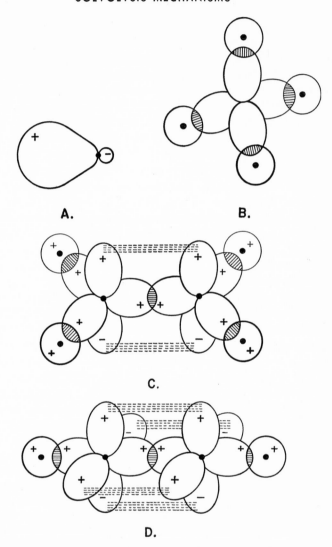

A.

B.

C.

D.

Fig. 4. Hybridized orbitals: (A) single sp^3 orbital (sp^2 and sp have similar shapes); (B) tetrahedral methane; (C) ethylene (σ- and π-bonds); (D) acetylene (σ- and two π-bonds).

cule. The two other common types of hybridization are sp^2, combining one s and two p orbitals to form three hybridized orbitals with their axes in a plane at 120° angles to one another, and sp, combining one s orbital and one p orbital to form two hybridized orbitals with their axes on a line at an angle of 180°.* In Fig. 4 are shown the rough, schematic atomic orbital diagrams which can be drawn for methane, ethylene, and acetylene. We draw only the positive overlaps which lead to bonding MO's. For a stable molecule, generally there are two electrons available to each overlapping pair of atomic orbitals, leading to a maximum amount of bonding. In ethylene there are a σ-bond formed by overlap of one sp^2 orbital from each carbon nucleus, a π-bond formed by overlap of the two unhybridized p orbitals (one from each carbon nucleus), plus the four carbon-hydrogen σ-bonds. In acetylene there are a sp-sp carbon-carbon σ-bond, two p-p carbon-carbon π-bonds (at right angles to each other), plus the two sp-s carbon-hydrogen σ-bonds. It is usually difficult to include the "rear," negative lobes of the hybrid orbitals in making such a diagram, so they are simply left out (they do not contribute to bonding anyway). Thus the double bond in ethylene is a $\sigma + \pi$ combination while the triple bond in acetylene is a $\sigma + 2\pi$ combination. Note that these diagrams are highly approximate; they merely indicate the nature and symmetry of the bonding MO's. More realistic sketches, showing the three-dimensional character of such atomic orbital diagrams are in Chapter 1 of Ref. (29).

Allyl Carbonium Ion. The procedure for making LCAO calculations can be made semiempirical by introducing certain parameters which allow us to solve the problem in part without ever specifying anything about the functional form of the φ_i or of the potential energy of the molecule. The energies E which are solutions of the Schrödinger equation can be sepa-

---

* These three kinds of hybridized orbitals are given as linear combinations of appropriate s and p orbitals in Appendix 3.

rated into two parts, the energies of the electronic motions and those of the nuclear motions. The latter, the vibrational energies of the molecule, are separate from the electronic energies to a good approximation, because the nuclei have mass so much greater than the electrons that they move very much more slowly. We can therefore consider the electronic motions, keeping the nuclei fixed at their equilibrium distance. We will write the Schrödinger equation (*cf.* Eq. (3–9)) as simply

$$\mathbf{H}\psi = E\psi$$

where $\mathbf{H}$ is the Hamiltonian operator for the molecule ($= T + V$ expressed in the differential form characteristic of our probability treatment). The MO's are then (*cf.* Eq. (3–11))

$$\psi_i = \sum_j c_{ji}\varphi_j$$

$$\mathbf{H} \sum_j c_{ji}\varphi_j = E \sum_j c_{ji}\varphi_j$$

$$= \sum_j c_{ji}\mathbf{H}\varphi_j$$

where we can put the $\mathbf{H}$ inside the summation sign since the c_{ji} are constants (to be determined). Now multiply both sides of the latter equation by φ_k and integrate the result over all space (*cf.* Eq. (3–10)):

$$\sum_j c_{ji} \iiint \varphi_k\mathbf{H}\varphi_j \, dx \, dy \, dz = E \sum_j c_{ji} \iiint \varphi_k\varphi_j \, dx \, dy \, dz$$

or

$$\sum_j c_{ji}\mathbf{H}_{kj} = E \sum_j c_{ji}\mathbf{S}_{kj}$$

The simplest approximation is to assume that

$$\mathbf{S}_{kj} = 0 \quad \text{if} \quad k \neq j$$

We know from Eq. (3–10) that

$$\mathbf{S}_{kk} = 1$$

so that

$$\sum_j c_{ji} H_{kj} = E c_{ki}$$

We also assume that, for a system made up of only $2p$ carbon orbitals which all have the same nodal plane (*i.e.*, a planar π-electron system),

$H_{kk} = H_{jj} = \alpha$

$H_{kj} = \beta$ if orbitals k and j overlap positively (*i.e.*, are on adjacent nuclei with proper signs)

$H_{kj} = 0$ if orbitals k and j are not on adjacent nuclei

We can also multiply through by one of the other orbitals instead of φ_k, obtaining for φ_m a new equation:

$$\sum_j c_{ji} H_{mj} = E c_{mi} \tag{3–12}$$

Let us solve these equations for the π-bonds of the allyl carbonium ion (Fig. 5), $C_3H_5^+$, which has three $2p$ orbitals of carbon overlapping in such a way that orbital 2 overlaps with both orbitals 1 and 3. Therefore,

$$H_{11} = H_{22} = H_{33} = \alpha$$
$$H_{12} = H_{21} = H_{23} = H_{32} = \beta$$
$$H_{13} = H_{31} = 0$$

where all these equalities come about because each of these orbitals is a p-orbital on carbon. We simply neglect the

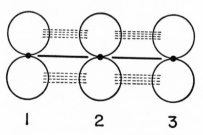

Fig. 5. The allyl carbonium ion.

σ-bonds, assuming that we can calculate the pi energy E_π of the ion separately from the sigma energy. We can multiply the Schrödinger equation through by φ_1, φ_2, or φ_3, giving three independent equations as follows:

$$c_{1i}\alpha \quad + c_{2i}\beta + c_{3i}\cdot 0 = Ec_{1i}$$
$$c_{1i}\beta \quad + c_{2i}\alpha + c_{3i}\beta \quad = Ec_{2i}$$
$$c_{1i}\cdot 0 + c_{2i}\beta + c_{3i}\alpha \quad = Ec_{3i}$$

or

$$c_{1i}(\alpha - E) + c_{2i}\beta = 0$$
$$c_{1i}\beta + c_{2i}(\alpha - E) + c_{3i}\beta = 0 \qquad (3\text{–}13)$$
$$c_{2i}\beta + c_{3i}(\alpha - E) = 0$$

These equations, since they all equal zero, can have a solution if and only if the determinant of the coefficients of the c_{ij}'s is zero:

$$\begin{vmatrix} \alpha - E & \beta & 0 \\ \beta & \alpha - E & \beta \\ 0 & \beta & \alpha - E \end{vmatrix} = 0$$

This equation is simplified by dividing each element of the determinant by β. The result still is 0, and if we define $x = (\alpha - E)/\beta$, we have

$$\begin{vmatrix} x & 1 & 0 \\ 1 & x & 1 \\ 0 & 1 & x \end{vmatrix} = 0$$

or

$$x^3 - 2x = 0$$

For x we have three solutions,

$$x = -\sqrt{2}$$
$$x = 0$$
$$x = +\sqrt{2}$$

corresponding to energies

$$E_1 = \alpha + \sqrt{2}\,\beta$$
$$E_2 = \alpha$$
$$E_3 = \alpha - \sqrt{2}\,\beta$$

where E_1 is the most stable energy level because α and β are negative quantities (corresponding to attraction energies of nuclei for electrons). It is easy to substitute E_1, E_2, and E_3 separately into the three Eqs. (3–13), finding for E_1: c_{11}, c_{21}, and c_{31}, etc., giving

$$\psi_1 = \frac{1}{2}\,(\varphi_1 + \sqrt{2}\,\varphi_2 + \varphi_3)$$

$$\psi_2 = \frac{1}{\sqrt{2}}\,(\varphi_1 - \varphi_3)$$

$$\psi_3 = \frac{1}{2}\,(\varphi_1 - \sqrt{2}\,\varphi_2 + \varphi_3)$$

after normalizing so that $\int\int\int\psi_1^2 = \int\int\int\psi_2^2 = \int\int\int\psi_3^2 = 1$. ψ_1 is a bonding MO ($E_1 < \alpha$); ψ_2 is a non-bonding MO or NBMO ($E_2 = \alpha$); and ψ_3 is an antibonding MO ($E_3 > \alpha$). Therefore the lowest electronic energy level of allyl carbonium ion is that in which ψ_1 is occupied by two electrons of opposite spin, so that

$$E_\pi = 2\alpha + 2\,\sqrt{2}\,\beta$$

It is simpler still to show that ethylene (2 overlapping carbon p orbitals) has MO's and E's

$$\psi_1 = \frac{1}{\sqrt{2}}\,(\varphi_1 + \varphi_2) \qquad E_1 = \alpha + \beta$$

$$\psi_2 = \frac{1}{\sqrt{2}}\,(\varphi_1 - \varphi_2) \qquad E_2 = \alpha - \beta$$

The delocalization energy or resonance energy is defined as the difference between E_π for the allyl carbonium ion (where the π electrons are delocalized over all three carbon nuclei) and E_π for the "localized" structure, a hypothetical structure in which the π electrons are all localized into ethylene-like π-bonds. The localized structure for allyl carbonium may be represented as

$$CH_2{=}CH - CH_2{}^+$$

and the delocalized structure as

$$[CH_2 \!=\! CH \!=\! CH_2]^+$$

The π energy of the localized structure is then the same as ethylene, $2\alpha + 2\beta$. The π delocalization energy is

$$
\begin{aligned}
DE_\pi &= 2\alpha + 2\sqrt{2}\,\beta - (2\alpha + 2\beta) \\
&= (2\sqrt{2} - 2)\beta = 2(\sqrt{2} - 1)\beta \\
&= 2(0.41)\beta = 0.82\beta
\end{aligned}
$$

The charges may be calculated from the coefficients of the molecular orbitals, since the probability of an electron's being on a certain atom is proportional to the square of the atomic orbital's contribution to the occupied ψ's. In allyl$^+$, only ψ_1 is occupied. The electronic charge surrounding nucleus 1 is therefore equal to

$$2\iiint [c_{11}\varphi_1]^2 \, dx \, dy \, dz$$

the factor 2 arising from the fact that two electrons occupy ψ_1. Since $S_{jj} = 1$, we have the charge q_1 on nucleus 1:

$$q_1 = 2c_{11}^2 = 2\left(\frac{1}{2}\right)^2 = \frac{1}{2}$$

This corresponds to half an electronic charge. Also,

$$q_2 = 2c_{21}^2 = 2\left(\frac{\sqrt{2}}{2}\right)^2 = 1$$

$$q_3 = 2c_{31}^2 = 2\left(\frac{1}{2}\right)^2 = \frac{1}{2}$$

If we consider the allyl$^+$ ion, but remove its two π-electrons, each carbon nucleus would bear unit positive charge. If we then fed these two π-electrons into the delocalized π system, the positive charge on nucleus 2 would be exactly neutralized by q_2 $(+1 - 1)$, while there would remain a charge of $+\frac{1}{2}$ on nuclei 1 and 3 $(+1 - \frac{1}{2})$.

Other quantities than charges can be calculated from the molecular orbital coefficients c_{ji} where

$$\psi_i = \sum_j c_{ji}\varphi_j$$

Two of the most interesting are the bond order and free valence. The π-bond order p_{rs} is

$$p_{rs} = \sum_j n_j c_{rj} c_{sj}$$

for the π-bond between atoms number r and s, where n_j is the number of electrons in molecular orbital number j. For example, in allyl$^+$, ψ_1 has $n_1 = 2$, and $n_2 = n_3 = 0$. Therefore, since $\psi_1 = \frac{1}{2}(\varphi_1 + \sqrt{2}\,\varphi_2 + \varphi_3)$, $p_{12} = 2(\frac{1}{2})(\sqrt{2}/2) = \sqrt{2}/2 = 0.707 = p_{23}$. These bond orders are useful in many cases to help estimate the bonding properties of π-electron systems. The free valence at a certain carbon atom is defined as the maximum possible bond order minus the sum of all the *actual* bond orders and is therefore a measure of the "residual bonding power" of the carbon atom. It is defined as

$$F_r = 4.732 - \sum p_{rs}$$

where $\sum p_{rs}$ includes all π-bonds to the carbon plus all sigma bonds ($p = 1$ for a sigma bond). Thus for allyl$^+$

$$F_1 = 4.732 - (0.707 + 3) = 1.025 = F_3$$
$$F_2 = 4.732 - (0.707 + 0.707 + 3) = 0.318$$

The number 4.732 can be shown to be the maximum possible value of $\sum p_{rs}$; it occurs for the central carbon atom of trimethylenemethane which has four π-electrons with each of the π bonds having an order $\sqrt{3}/3$. The atom-atom polarizability is just about what its name implies,

$$\pi_{rs} = \frac{\partial q_r}{\partial \alpha_s} = \frac{\partial q_s}{\partial \alpha_r}$$

where α_s is the coulomb integral H_{ss}. The value can be calculated from a rather complex formula:

$$\pi_{rs} = 4 \sum_{j=1}^{m} \sum_{k=m+1}^{n} \frac{c_{rj}c_{rk}c_{sj}c_{sk}}{E_j - E_k}$$

where m is the number of the highest *occupied* molecular orbital ψ_m (this orbital must be doubly occupied or the calculation cannot be made), and E_j is the energy corresponding to the MO ψ_j.

NBMO. The interesting point in solving the equation for allyl$^+$ is that it is a simple example of a system having a NBMO (non-bonding molecular orbital). These systems have been shown to have charge distributions and other properties which can be easily evaluated in the LCAO-MO approximation (30). It can be proved that alternant hydrocarbons and free radicals have in this approximation no charge on any carbon atoms ($(1 - q_i) = 0$). An alternant system is simply a set of conjugated π bonds (one p orbital per atom, all p orbitals having the same nodal plane) which does not involve any ring with an odd number of members. Further, it can be proved that odd-alternant hydrocarbons and radicals all have a NBMO. An odd-alternant system is an alternant system made up of an odd number of conjugated p orbitals. Thus the allyl free radical and the benzyl free radical are odd-alternant radicals.

Consider the allyl free radical. It has $(1 - q_1) = (1 - q_2) = (1 - q_3) = 0$, since it is alternant. It has (as we know from solving the Schrödinger equation) a NBMO, since it is an odd-alternant. Therefore, it has one electron in the NBMO. If we remove the electron from the NBMO we get the allyl carbonium ion. But the electron density will be removed from the radical in proportion to the squared coefficients of the atomic orbitals in the NBMO. We know

$$\psi_2 = \frac{1}{\sqrt{2}} (\varphi_1 - \varphi_3)$$

Therefore $(1/\sqrt{2})^2$ of a unit charge will be removed from carbon 1 and from carbon 3, and none (0^2) from carbon 2. So there is, in allyl$^+$, $+\frac{1}{2}$ on carbons 1 and 3, and 0 on carbon 2, as we found by solving for all the MO's. Since we can find these charge distributions solely from the atomic orbital coefficients of the NBMO, it is exceedingly interesting to find that we can calculate the NBMO coefficients without ever solving a determinant. This is especially valuable for large molecules where the determinants are very hard to solve (for allyl, 3×3; for benzyl, 7×7; etc.). We cannot find out about energies in this way, but in many cases, particularly in solvolysis reactions which may proceed through carbonium ions, it is of great interest to know how a positive charge will distribute itself.

The procedure involves, first, "starring" the molecule. Draw the structure and then star every alternate carbon nucleus so that (a) the maximum number of nuclei are starred and (b) no adjacent nuclei are starred. For allyl and benzyl,

We now use the facts that unstarred atoms have *zero* coefficients in the NBMO and that the sum of the NBMO coefficients around any unstarred atom must equal 0. Call the NBMO coefficients c_i^0 where the superscript denotes they are for a non-bonding MO and the subscript i refers to the atomic orbital φ_i. The NBMO is

$$\psi^0 = \sum_i c_i^0 \varphi_i$$

Suppose carbon 1 is unstarred. Then from Eq. (3–12) and the definitions of α and β

$$c_1^0(\alpha - E) + c_2^0 \beta_{12} + c_3^0 \beta_{13} + \cdots = 0$$

Now $\alpha - E = 0$ because for a NBMO $E = \alpha$. So

$$c_2^0 \beta_{12} + c_3^0 \beta_{13} + \cdots = 0$$
$$\sum_r c_r^0 \beta_{1r} = 0$$

If all β_{1r} are equal to β if carbon r is adjacent to carbon 1, and equal to zero if r is not adjacent to 1, as we assumed for allyl$^+$ before, then dividing by β,

$$\sum_r c_r^0 = 0$$

where the sum is over only those atoms adjacent to the unstarred atom 1.

For allyl$^+$, we call any one coefficient x and find all others in terms of x:

$$\overset{*}{C}\!-\!C\!-\!\overset{*}{C}$$
$$x -x$$
$$c_1{}^0 + c_3{}^0 = 0$$

Therefore

$$\psi^0 = x(\varphi_1 - \varphi_3)$$

Now, to normalize ψ^0, and so determine x, we have, abbreviating the integration over all coordinates of all electrons by a single integral sign,

$$\int (\psi^0)^2 = 1 = x^2 \int (\varphi_1 - \varphi_3)^2$$
$$= x^2 \int (\varphi_1^2 - 2\varphi_1 \varphi_3 + \varphi_3^2) = x^2(S_{11} - 2S_{13} + S_{33})$$

We assumed that $S_{ij} = 1$ if $i = j$, and 0 if $i \neq j$, so

$$x^2(1 - 2 \cdot 0 + 1) = 1$$

$$x = \pm \frac{1}{\sqrt{2}}$$

Since the sign of the orbital makes no particular difference, we choose $x = +1/\sqrt{2}$, giving

$$\psi^0 = \frac{1}{\sqrt{2}} (\varphi_1 - \varphi_3)$$

For benzyl⁺, we repeat the procedure:

$$\psi^0 = x(2\varphi_1 - \varphi_3 + \varphi_5 - \varphi_7)$$
$$\int (\psi^0)^2 = x^2(4 + 1 + 1 + 1) = 1$$
$$x = \pm \frac{1}{\sqrt{7}}$$

Choosing x positive, we obtain

$$\psi^0 = \frac{1}{\sqrt{7}} (2\varphi_1 - \varphi_3 + \varphi_5 - \varphi_7)$$

$$(1 - q_1) = \left(\frac{2}{\sqrt{7}}\right)^2 = \frac{4}{7}$$

$$(1 - q_3) = \left(\frac{-1}{\sqrt{7}}\right)^2 = \frac{1}{7} = (1 - q_7)$$

$$(1 - q_5) = \left(\frac{1}{\sqrt{7}}\right)^2 = \frac{1}{7}$$

$$(1 - q_2) = (1 - q_4) = (1 - q_6) = 0$$

Therefore in benzyl⁺, only $\frac{3}{7}$ of the positive charge is delocalized in this approximation, while in allyl⁺, $\frac{1}{2}$ of the positive charge is delocalized. This simple procedure can be used to calculate charges for very complex odd-alternant ions!

It is interesting to derive an approximation to the change in DE_π when two odd-alternant systems are joined together. Since in both odd-alternant systems all bonding MO's are doubly occupied, the interaction of the two NBMO's will approximately determine the change in DE_π (ΔDE_π). Suppose we have a benzyl carbonium ion and a methyl carbanion which we will join together to form styrene:

$$\left[\left\langle\!\!\!\bigcirc\!\!\!\right\rangle \!\!=\!\!=\!\!=\!\! CH_2 \right]^+ + CH_3^- \rightarrow \left\langle\!\!\!\bigcirc\!\!\!\right\rangle \!\!=\!\! CH \!\!=\!\!=\!\!=\!\! CH_2 + H_2$$

Of course, this reaction involves the removal of two H atoms and formation of a C—C σ-bond, but we are now interested in only the π energy. We neglect all changes in σ-bonding energy. We assume also that the unshared electron pair of CH_3^- occupies a NBMO ($E = \alpha$) which in this case is simply the atomic orbital φ_s, since there are no π bonds in CH_3^-. As we join the two atoms r and s, a π-bond will form between them which will change the energies of the NBMO's. If we denote the NBMO of benzyl by ψ^0 and that of methyl by φ^0, the two can combine to form a bonding MO (after normalization):*

$$\psi_B = \frac{1}{\sqrt{2}} (\psi^0 + \varphi^0)$$

and an antibonding MO:

$$\psi_{AB} = \frac{1}{\sqrt{2}} (\psi^0 - \varphi^0)$$

The two unshared electrons originally on CH_3^- can occupy the bonding MO ψ_B, thus stabilizing the combined system (styrene) relative to the odd-alternant starting materials (benzyl +

---

* We assume that the average energy of all other (occupied) π orbitals is approximately the same in benzyl as in styrene. ψ_B and ψ_{AB} represent the two possible ways in which ψ^0 and φ^0 can overlap.

methyl). Obviously the same change in DE_r would occur if we had benzyl⁻ and methyl⁺ or benzyl and methyl radicals, since the two electrons would be in NBMO's ($E = \alpha$) originally in any case.

The energy associated with ψ_B is then H_{BB}:

$$H_{BB} = \int \psi_B H \psi_B = \left(\frac{1}{\sqrt{2}}\right)^2 \int (\psi^0 + \varphi^0) H (\psi^0 + \varphi^0)$$

$$= \frac{1}{2} \int \psi^0 H \psi^0 + \frac{1}{2} \int \varphi^0 H \varphi^0 + \int \varphi^0 H \psi^0$$

since always

$$\int \varphi^0 H \psi^0 = \int \psi^0 H \varphi^0$$

for our systems. Now we must evaluate the integrals. The first two are simple because ψ^0 and φ^0 are NBMO's:

$$\int \psi^0 H \psi^0 = \alpha; \qquad \int \varphi^0 H \varphi^0 = \alpha$$

The form of ψ^0 will be

$$\psi^0 = c_1^0 \varphi_1 + c_2^0 \varphi_2 + \cdots + c_r^0 \varphi_r + \cdots$$

Since $\varphi^0 = \varphi_s$,

$$\int \varphi^0 H \psi^0 = \int \varphi_s H (c_1^0 \varphi_1 + c_2^0 \varphi_2 + \cdots + c_r^0 \varphi_r + \cdots)$$

$$= c_1^0 \int \varphi_s H \varphi_1 + c_2^0 \int \varphi_s H \varphi_2 + \cdots + c_r^0 \int \varphi_s H \varphi_r + \cdots$$

Now we assume as before that

$$\int \varphi_i H \varphi_j = 0$$

unless i and j are adjacent, in which case it equals β. Since, for our system (and for any other ions similar to benzyl), φ_r is the only orbital in ψ^0 which is adjacent to φ_s in the product, we have simply

$$\int \varphi^0 H \psi^0 = c_r^0 \cdot \beta$$

or

$$H_{BB} = \frac{1}{2} \alpha + \frac{1}{2} \alpha + c_r^0 \beta = \alpha + c_r^0 \beta$$

For two electrons we have for the π energy due to ψ_B,

$$E_B = 2\alpha + 2c_r^0\beta$$

The π energy of these two electrons before joining the systems together was 2α; therefore

$$\Delta DE_\pi = 2c_r^0\beta$$

Now consider the formation of styrene in a similar way, but from two even alternant hydrocarbons, benzene and ethylene:

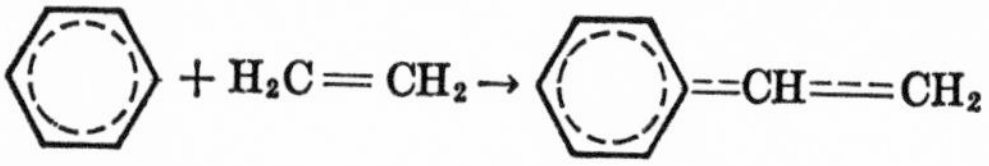

In this case both reactants have all their bonding MO's occupied, so that ΔDE_π is small and not much different for the above reaction than for the reaction of any other even alternant hydrocarbon with ethylene to produce the aryl-vinyl conjugated system.

A very interesting application of these ideas to solvolysis reactions has been made, and the above results plus those that follow have been derived more rigorously (31). The reaction rates of a series of arylmethyl chlorides such as benzyl chloride, 2-naphthylmethyl chloride, etc. have been investigated under various conditions. Suppose that the transition state for such a reaction in a highly ionizing solvent resembles the carbonium ion. We would like to find the ΔDE_π for the reaction:

$$ArCH_2{-}X \rightarrow ArCH_2^+ + X^-$$

It can be found from a cycle which uses quantities we can find from the properties of NBMO's. We want the ΔDE_π essentially for

$$ArH \rightarrow ArCH_2^+$$

since we are considering only π energies. This quantity can be evaluated from the energies for

$$ArH + CH_2{=}CH_2 \overset{1}{\rightarrow} ArCH{=}CH_2 \overset{2}{\rightarrow} ArCH_2^+ + CH_3^-$$

Quantity 1 is small and essentially constant for different Ar-groups. Quantity 2 is the negative of the quantity for the reverse reaction, analogous to the formation of styrene from benzyl + methyl, so it equals $-2c_r^0\beta$. Therefore

$$\Delta DE_\pi = \text{constant} - 2c_r^0\beta$$

where c_r^0 is the NBMO coefficient of the CH_2 carbon of $ArCH_2^+$, which can be found easily by the method of starring. The rate constant for the reaction is approximately

$$k = Ae^{-\Delta E^\ddagger/RT} \sim Ae^{-(\text{constant}-2c_r^0\beta)/RT}$$

or

$$2.3 \log k = \frac{2c_r^0\beta}{RT} + \text{constants}$$

i.e., the rate is slower if c_r^0 is greater (β is negative). For example, when Ar = phenyl, c_r^0 is $2/\sqrt{7}$, as we know from starring the $ArCH_2^+$ (benzyl+) ion. Thus the "reactivity index" for this compound is $2c_r^0 = 1.51$. For Ar = 2-naphthyl, $2c_r^0 = 1.46$, so that 2-naphthylmethyl should be more reactive than phenylmethyl, as has been found experimentally (31). If we had a SN2 reaction the transition state would have a bond partially formed to the attacking nucleophile and so would look less like the carbonium ion than in the case of a SN1 reaction. We might use the same reactivity index for the SN2 reaction, however, and then determine an "effective β" for the reaction by determining the slope ($\beta/2.3RT$) of a plot of $\log k$ *vs.* $2c_r^0$. The SN2 reaction should have a much smaller β than the SN1 reaction because a large part of ψ^0 would be used for bonding other than the π bonding of the $ArCH_2$ system in the SN2 transition state (ψ^0 would be involved with both the entering and leaving groups). Solvolysis (31) of $ArCH_2$—Cl in formic acid 0.38 M in H_2O at 25° gave $\beta = -33$ kcal./mole; solvolysis of $ArCH_2$—Cl in 80% aqueous ethanol (v/v) at 50° gave $\beta = -9.5$ kcal./mole; and SN2 reaction of $ArCH_2$—Cl with iodide ion in acetone at 25° gave $\beta = -5$ kcal./mole. By this criterion, then, it seems probable that the solvolysis in formic acid is SN1-like, while the solvolysis in ethanol-water is SN2-like. MO theory gives us an interesting criterion of mechanism in this case.

ω-Technique. It is undoubtedly true that the presence of charge on a nucleus changes the value of the integral α for that nucleus from the value for the case in which there is no net charge on the nucleus. In allyl carbonium ion carbon atoms 1 and 3 have approximately $+\frac{1}{2}$ charge and carbon atom 2 has approximately zero charge. The ω-technique is a simple means of allowing for the change in α resulting from the presence of charge on carbon atoms 1 and 3. It is assumed (32) that the change in α is linearly related to the charge:

$$\alpha_i = \alpha_0 + (1 - q_i)\omega\beta$$

where α_i is the new α integral, α_0 is the original α integral, q_i is the charge for atom i calculated from the LCAO-MO method described above for allyl$^+$, ω is a constant of proportionality, and β is the standard β integral. The method consists of calculating the charge distribution on the assumption that all α's are equal, from the q_i so obtained calculating new α_i, again calculating the charge distribution using the new α_i (the same standard value for the β integral is kept throughout), and repeating the process until the results are "self-consistent," *i.e.*, until the new values of q_i are the same as the previous set. Using the value of 1.4 for ω (33), greatly improved charge distributions and energy values can be calculated for organic cations. For allyl$^+$, we start with $(1 - q_1) = (1 - q_3) = 0.500$, $(1 - q_2) = 0.000$; after self-consistency is reached $(1 - q_1) = (1 - q_3) = +0.429$, $(1 - q_2) = +0.142$.

Non-planar Systems. Without going into any details, it is worthwhile mentioning that calculations have been made for systems where the overlapping orbitals are "tipped" with respect to one another by the geometrical requirements of the σ-bonds. Promising results have been obtained, for example, in calculations of DE_π for certain "non-classical" carbonium ion structures (29, 34, 35). Calculations have also been made of the ease of forming intermediates with bridged phenyl rings or alkyl groups (corresponding to 1, 2 rearrangements) in carbonium ions, free radicals, and carbanions. It was found (36) that 1, 2 migration of alkyl groups in carbanions should be relatively unfavorable, but that similar migration of phenyl groups should be quite favorable.

A number of references to the use of MO predictions in correlating and predicting structures and reactivities of unsaturated systems are given in a recent paper (37).

LCBO Approximation. In the solution of the Schrödinger equation for allyl$^+$ we never needed to know anything about the atomic orbitals φ or the Hamiltonian H, because we evaluated all integrals involving them in terms of the parameters α and β. The same technique can be applied to using, instead of a linear combination of atomic orbitals (LCAO), a linear combination of "bond" orbitals (LCBO). A bond orbital is simply a wave function which describes the electron probability in a given bond (e.g., a C—H or a C—C bond) of a molecule. The molecular orbitals ψ are then found in terms of the bond orbitals, which we call χ to distinguish them from atomic orbitals φ:

$$\psi_j = \sum_i c_{ij}\chi_i$$

The procedure is then exactly the same as for LCAO, leading to a determinant which must equal 0. The only difference is that the parameters for the bond orbitals will not be equal to the parameters for the atomic orbitals. Nevertheless we can find energies in terms of these parameters. Delocalization energies will turn out to be in units, not of the parameter β, but of some new parameter, say γ. The LCBO technique is especially useful for aliphatic compounds, e.g., the hydrocarbons and their radicals and carbonium ions (38). For example, it predicts that the cleavage of a carbon-carbon σ-

bond in **2** should be more favorable than in **1** by some 6.4 kcal./mole:

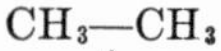

$$
\begin{array}{ccc}
& & \text{CH}_3 \\
& & | \\
\text{CH}_3\text{—CH}_3 & & \text{CH}_3\text{—C—CH}_3 \\
\textbf{1} & & | \\
& & \text{CH}_3 \\
& & \textbf{2}
\end{array}
$$

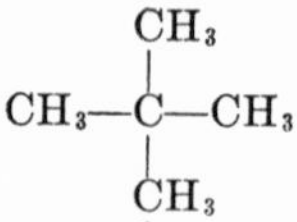

In the SN2 reaction of $ArCH_2Cl$ with iodide ion in acetone solution, the transition state would probably have the two hydrogen nuclei of the CH_2 group in the plane of the nuclei of the aromatic group, while the C—Cl and I—C bonds would probably be perpendicular to the plane:

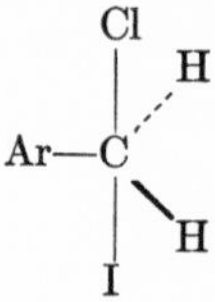

$$
\begin{array}{c}
\text{Cl} \\
| \quad \text{H} \\
\text{Ar—C}^{'} \\
| \quad \diagdown \text{H} \\
\text{I}
\end{array}
$$

If we consider the Ar group separately from the ICH_2Cl group, there will be π MO's in the Ar group, while in the ICH_2Cl group we may use a LCBO, the bond orbitals being χ_1 for the C—Cl bond and χ_2 for the C—I bond (39). It is easy to see that the MO's will then be approximately

$$\psi_1 = \frac{1}{\sqrt{2}}\,(\chi_1 + \chi_2)$$

$$\psi_2 = \frac{1}{\sqrt{2}}\,(\chi_1 - \chi_2)$$

(This would be exactly true only if the entering and leaving groups were identical.) The four electrons (2 from the C—Cl bond plus an unshared pair from I^-) can then occupy these MO's, two in each. Now if we consider the interaction of ψ_1 and ψ_2 with the MO's of the Ar group, ψ_1 has the wrong symmetry (+ on both sides of the carbon atom) and therefore has an antibonding interaction with the MO's of Ar. On the other hand, ψ_2 has the right symmetry (+ on one side, − on the other side, of the carbon atom) and can overlap strongly to produce bonding with the MO's of the Ar group. Thus of the four electrons associated with the I—C—Cl bonds, two are quite localized and two can be extensively delocalized through the aryl group. Good correlation with experimental rates for different Ar groups was obtained by calculating such energies, assuming "reasonable" values for the overlap integral of the "quasi-π" orbital ψ_2 with the p-orbital of the aryl group and for the coulomb integral (α') for ψ_2.

STERIC EFFECTS

Considerable effort has been put into calculations of steric effects, *i.e.*, interactions between groups or atoms which are not actually bonded together, with encouraging success. Experimentally as well as theoretically, molecules or non-bonded groups are attracted to one another mildly, but start to repel strongly if they get too close together. The facts that gases form liquids, but that liquids are not very compressible, illustrate the attraction and repulsion of molecules. The same effects can occur on an intramolecular level.

Because chemical bonds are so strong, it turns out that excessive energy is necessary to stretch them appreciably, much less energy being required to bend them. Therefore, in molecules containing intramolecular repulsions, the geometry of the molecule will adjust itself so that the energy is lowest, by mainly bending various bonds. The bond lengths will not be changed much from unstrained counterparts (40). The importance of bending and unimportance of stretching is fundamental in understanding steric effects.

The potential energy of bending or stretching a bond is given approximately by

$$ E = \frac{1}{2} kq^2 $$

where k is a force constant and q is the change in a coordinate, a distance in the case of stretching and an angle in the case of bending.   We have assumed the bending or stretching is adequately approximated as a harmonic oscillator, although clearly for large q (large displacements from equilibrium) this will not be true.   Stretching force constants are usually of the order of 3×10^5 to 12×10^5 dynes/cm. while bending force constants for C-H bonds are about 0.3–0.9×10^{-11} erg/radian^2.   The effect of non-bonded interactions may be approximated by an energy of the form

$$E = -\frac{\mu}{r^7} + \frac{\lambda}{r^{11}}$$

where r is the distance between the interacting atoms.   The parameters μ and λ must of course be determined by experiment.   The total energy of the molecule can be found as a function of the positions of all the nuclei by summing the stretching and bending energies for each bond along with the interaction energies between the various non-bonded nuclei in the molecule.   The result will be a complicated expression involving a large number of q_i plus r_i.   Some of these will not be independent, so they must be expressed in terms of coordinates which are independent (*e.g.*, r_i will be a function of several q_i because, as the q_i change, so will r_i).   Then the minimum energy can be determined by the usual procedure of setting the derivatives equal to 0:

$$\frac{\partial E}{\partial q_i} = 0; \qquad \frac{\partial E}{\partial r_i} = 0$$

where the q_i and r_i are the independent coordinates.   The result is one equation for each q_i and for each r_i, or n equations in the n unknown coordinates.   These can be solved in principle for the n coordinates of the conformation which has minimal energy, thus completely determining the structure (*i.e.*, equilibrium nuclear positions) of the molecule.   The major problem is the lack of accurate force constants or empirical means of estimating them.

Calculations of energies for cyclopentane (41) show the possibility of two conformations, the *envelope* and *half-chair*

(42). Such calculations have also been applied to cyclo-pentane rings fused to other rings, as in steroids (43). The important conclusion of this work is that cyclopentane and its derivatives are nowhere near to being planar, as might be expected from consideration of carbon bond angles alone. The repulsions of eclipsed hydrogen atoms make the energy of the planar conformation too high.

The results of an extensive quantitative study of steric effects in SN2 reactions of alkyl halides with halide ions in acetone have been beautifully summarized (44). Account was taken of bond stretching and bending and of non-bonded interactions, to find the most favorable theoretical structure for the transition states of these backside displacement reactions. All the carbon-halogen bonds are stretched in the transition states because of the steric repulsions of the substituents on the central carbon atom. In Table 3–2 (44) are listed

TABLE 3–2

Calculated Positions of Iodine Nuclei in the SN2 Displacement Transition States for Reactions $I^- + RI \rightarrow IR + I^-$

R	Amount of Stretching of Each C---I Bond (Å)	Deviation of I---C---I Bond Angle from 180°
CH_3-	0.36	0.0°
CH_3CH_2-	0.37	3.8°
$(CH_3)_2CH-$	0.38	5.0°
$(CH_3)_3C-$	0.40	0.0°
$CH_3CH_2CH_2-$	0.37	3.8°
$(CH_3)_2CHCH_2-$	0.39	5.0°
$(CH_3)_3CCH_2-$	0.43	17.6°

the results for the reaction of isotopic iodide ions with alkyl iodides, a symmetrical exchange reaction (45). Thus the generalization that for molecules the stretching of bonds is unimportant in steric effects is certainly not true for transition states. Here stretching and bending are both important. In some cases the deviation from the idealized model of the SN2 transition state, which assumes that the entering and leaving nuclei are collinear with the central carbon nucleus, is considerable. There appears to be, as yet, no way of experimentally verifying this non-collinearity. The relative rates of reaction were also calculated and agree very well with the experimental relative rates, considering that the experimental relative rates range up to a factor of 5,000,000. There may be side reactions of olefin formation which make the experimental rates somewhat in error. Nevertheless, the approach may be judged a tremendous success. The arithmetic involved is terribly complex; however, it would appear to be very worthwhile to make calculations for solvolytic reactions. This apparently has not been done.

CONCLUSION

Although making theoretical calculations for complex systems involves gigantic computational difficulties or severe approximations or large numbers of empirical parameters (or a combination) in most cases, the results are worth the effort. Theoretical interpretations of structure and reactivity provide an understanding of the physical principles involved which cannot be gained through qualitative arguments alone.

It may be confidently predicted that the technique of using theoretical predictions to suggest new experiments will be more and more used in conjunction with chemical intuition to solve problems which we cannot even see clearly today.

REFERENCES

Many of the topics in this chapter are discussed in a text on theoretical organic chemistry, K. B. Wiberg, *Physical Organic Chemistry* (John Wiley and Sons, Inc., New York, 1964).

The classical book on collision theory of reactions in solution is the one by Moelwyn-Hughes (12), which contains a great deal of theory as well as data and has a useful appendix summarizing the relationship of collision theory with transition-state theory.   The classical book on transition-state theory is Glasstone, Laidler, and Eyring (13), which contains many details, especially about calculation of potential energy surfaces.   For the chemist interested in the application of chemical kinetics to reaction mechanisms, Frost and Pearson (14) is a good, introductory work.   It contains a chapter which discusses in detail the present status of several interesting mechanistic problems.   Along the same line in many respects, but on a more advanced level, is S. W. Benson, *Foundations of Chemical Kinetics* (McGraw-Hill Book Company, Inc., New York, 1960).

For statistical mechanics, the easiest book is the nice little volume by Dole (18), which starts at the very beginning and tells the reader how to make his own calculations for many systems, by treating selected topics. Pitzer's book on *Quantum Chemistry* (18) covers the wide range its title implies and is especially good on chemical bonding, infrared spectra, and the relationship of spectra to thermodynamic quantities. Rushbrooke's book (18) is less practical than the other two, but is a *very* satisfying introduction to the theory behind statistical thermodynamics.   The interesting discussions of Leffler and Grunwald (19) and of Kreevoy (23) are introductory, at about the same level as this chapter.

Bell's book on the proton (20) is a very complete treatment of acids and bases and their quantitative properties.

There are now a number of good books on the application of quantum chemistry to organic structures and mechanisms (25, 26, 27, 28, 29), whereas a few years ago there were none. Streitwieser is really complete on MO theory. Linnett is introductory, but is especially good on electron correlation. Coulson is an excellent, largely qualitative, discussion of valence.   Daudel, *et al.*, is an excellent comprehensive book on both MO and valence bond methods and is divided into a first section on semiempirical methods and a second (advanced) section on non-empirical methods.   Roberts is a rapid introduction to the methods of actually performing simple calculations, including the use of simple group theory. More advanced books include H. Eyring, J. Walter, and G. E. Kimball, *Quantum Chemistry* (John Wiley and Sons, Inc. New York, 1944), and W. T. Simpson, *Theories of Electrons in Molecules* (Prentice-Hall, Inc., Englewood Cliffs, N.J., 1962). The paper by Swain and Thorson (37) is a good one for applications of simple group theory.

Westheimer's chapter (40) is a very good summary of the quantitative treatment of steric effects.

I. Prigogine, *The Molecular Theory of Solutions* (North-Holland Publishing Company, Amsterdam, 1957), is a good source on the statistical theory of solutions.

4

Mechanisms

STRUCTURAL EFFECTS IN TRANSITION STATES

It is interesting to discuss the activated complexes for different types of reactions in terms of whether they resemble the products or the reactants. In a SN2 process, if the nucleophile has not formed a very strong bond to carbon, and the leaving group's bond to carbon has not been broken extensively at the transition state, the transition state is reactant-like. If the new bond is extensively formed and the old bond extensively broken at the transition state, the transition state is product-like. It is also interesting to compare the effects of various substituents on transition state structure. A certain substituent might be found to make its transition state more product-like than the transition state for the same reaction carried out under exactly the same conditions except without the substituent in question. The most common examples of such effects occur as the result of introducing substituents into a phenyl ring. We might compare the transition state structures for the ethanolysis (solvolysis in ethanol) of a series of substituted benzyl chlorides, and try to determine whether electron-supplying substituents tend to make the transition states more product- or reactant-like than electron-withdrawing substituents. Two qualitative arguments for predicting the effects of structural changes in reactants on the structures of transition states have been published, and will be discussed in turn.

In 1955, the "Hammond postulate" was advanced (46). It relates the energy contents of reactants, intermediates, and products to the expected geometry of the transition states:

> If two states, as for example, a transition state and an unstable intermediate, occur consecutively during a reaction process and have nearly the same energy content, their interconversion will involve only a small reorganization of the molecular structures. (46)

This postulate can be applied to SN1 and SN2 type reactions. In a SN1 reaction which has the formation of a carbonium ion as its rate-determining step, the carbonium ion has a much higher energy content (is much less stable) than the reactant. The postulate predicts that the transition state should be more product-like (carbonium ion-like) than reactant-like, *i.e.*, that the bond between carbon and the leaving group will be extensively ruptured at the transition state. That this is probably correct is indicated by the success of predictions of relative rates in such solvolysis reactions on the basis of such factors as relative resonance energies (DE_π) of ions produced and the relief of steric strain which accompanies conversion of the tetrahedral reactant into the planar carbonium ion (46). SN2 reactions may have transition states varying all the way from reactant-like to product-like. The postulate predicts that a highly exothermic SN2 process (a) should have a reactant-like transition state, since the reactants are much less stable than the products and therefore should provide a better model for the transition state. A highly endothermic SN2 process (b) should have a product-like transition state. Intermediate situations (c), where the reactants and products have similar energies (by similar we mean of the order of 0–5 kcal./mole difference), should have transition states for which neither reactants nor products would be a good model. Cases (a), (b), and (c) above are illustrated in Fig. 6, where the reasonable assumption that the curvature of

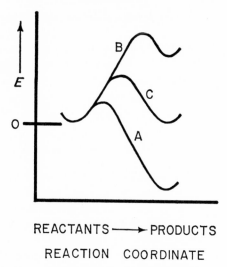

REACTANTS ⟶ PRODUCTS

REACTION COORDINATE

Fig. 6. Energy diagrams for exothermic (A), endothermic (B), and intermediate (C) SN2 processes. Energy of reactants arbitrarily set equal to zero for all three cases.

the reaction energy profile in the area of the transition state is similar for cases (a), (b), and (c) leads to the transition state structures predicted by the postulate. Theoretical calculations for hydrogen atom transfer reactions (21) are in accord with the predictions.

This beautifully simple postulate correlates a large amount of information about solvolysis as well as other reactions. The simplicity is a result of the use of almost entirely thermodynamic terminology, and therein lies not only its wide scope but also its possibility of being incorrect when applied to reactions that are not exceedingly endo- or exothermic. It should be emphasized that the conclusions about SN1 and SN2 reactions which Hammond arrived at are very likely valid. The possible trouble comes in applying the postulate to finer details than Hammond ever intended it for, such as the mere change of a substituent in a reactant. Such a small change of structure could lead to a change in energy of reaction (difference between products and reactants) of only a few kcal./mole at most.

The second argument is a rule which was advanced to explain certain experimental observations which appeared to be opposite from the predictions of the Hammond postulate applied to fine details (47). The rule is mainly meant to deal with small structural changes in contrast with the Hammond postulate. In order to be unambiguous, the rule had to be couched in somewhat esoteric language. If we restrict ourselves temporarily to systems which do not have π overlap, the rule can be stated very simply: *Electron-supplying substituents tend to lengthen transition-state bonds which are being made or broken.* Applied to a simple SN1 ionization, the rule predicts that in RX,

$$RX \rightarrow R^+ + X^-$$

an electron-supplying substituent in R would tend to make the R---X bond longer in the transition state than for the unsubstituted compound. An electron-supplying substituent in X is also predicted to make the R---X bond longer in the transition state than for the unsubstituted compound. These predictions do not take account of differences in solvation or steric effects, so these two effects might modify the prediction of the rule in some cases. The situation can be pictured for an electron-supplying substituent Z as follows:

$$RX \; \rightarrow \; [\overset{\delta^+}{R}\text{----}\overset{\delta^-}{X}]^{\ddagger}$$
$$ZRX \rightarrow [\overset{\delta^+}{ZR}\text{------}\overset{\delta^-}{X}]^{\ddagger}$$
$$RXZ \rightarrow [\overset{\delta^+}{R}\text{------}\overset{\delta^-}{XZ}]^{\ddagger}$$

These effects can be explained by the fact that the bonds being made or broken in the transition state are much longer than ordinary covalent bonds. Since they are much longer,

the overlap is much less, and they may be considered to be electron-deficient. Supplying electrons to an electron-deficient
bond should tend to strengthen that bond by decreasing the
repulsion between the nuclei at either end. A bond which is
potentially stronger should require more stretching before the
transition state can be reached; *i.e.*, supplying electrons to a
bond being broken should increase the length of that bond in
the transition state. The formation of a bond which is
potentially stronger should require less bond-formation before
the transition state can be reached; *i.e.* supplying electrons to
a bond being formed should increase the length of that bond in
the transition state. This reasoning based on electron-deficient transition state bonds is different from the analogous
situation with ordinary molecules. A normal covalent bond,
e.g., a C—Cl bond,

$$\overset{\delta^+ \quad \delta^-}{\text{C—Cl}}$$
$$\longleftarrow \longrightarrow \text{Dipole moment}$$

is strengthened by supplying electrons to the negative end of
the dipole (Cl) and weakened by supplying electrons to the
positive end of the dipole (C). A useful way of thinking of a
transition-state bond being made or broken is as pictured:

$$\longleftarrow \longrightarrow$$
$$\text{C----Cl}$$
$$\Leftarrow \quad \Rightarrow$$

Even though the over-all dipole moment is in the same direction as for a neutral molecule, it may be thought of as being
composed of two smaller dipoles, so that the bond is electron-
deficient in the area between the nuclei and therefore tends to
be strengthened by electron supply from either end.

In a SN2 reaction, we have one bond forming as the other
bond is breaking. Supplying electrons to X is predicted to
lengthen the X----C bond at the transition state:

$$\text{X} + \text{CY} \rightarrow [\text{X----C----Y}]^{\ddagger} \rightarrow$$

But there are two opposing effects on the C----Y bond. First, supplying electrons at X should certainly also tend to supply electrons to the C----Y bond. However, this first effect should be smaller than the second effect—that the lengthened X----C bond should tend to polarize the electrons into the region between X and C, leaving C with less electron density. The lessened electron density at C should make the C----Y bond shorter. This second effect should be more important than the first because the first is transmitted from X to C to the C----Y bond while the second is felt directly at C, a shorter distance from the C----Y bond. Thus an alternating effect is predicted. We may diagrammatically summarize these effects as follows, where Z is an electron-supplying substituent:

$$X + CY \rightarrow [X\text{----}C\text{----}Y]^{\ddagger}$$
$$ZX + CY \rightarrow [ZX\text{------}C\text{--}Y]^{\ddagger}$$
$$X + CYZ \rightarrow [X\text{--}C\text{------}YZ]^{\ddagger}$$
$$X + CZY \rightarrow [X\text{------}CZ\text{------}Y]^{\ddagger}$$

When there are π systems present which can be conjugated with the transition state bonds, it becomes necessary to postulate that the bond-lengthening effects are not associated with a given single bond but with a *reacting orbital*. A reacting orbital is considered to be a type of orbital which contains electrons but no nuclei. It can be considered to be made up of atomic orbitals and/or portions of atomic orbitals. The reason for using reacting orbitals as the fundamental unit of bonding is that, as we have discussed above, the electrons are polarized toward or away from the nuclei by substituents. There seems to be nothing theoretically wrong with defining such orbitals, and they seem to be useful. The original postulate was the following (47):

In a simple atomic orbital diagram of the transition state, locate all *reacting bonds*, bonds which are present in the transition state but entirely absent in either the reactants (for bonds being made) or the products (for bonds being broken). A *reacting orbital* defines an electron cloud, bounded by nuclei but containing no nuclei, which includes one reacting bond. Identify the reacting orbitals, each composed of the atomic orbital portions of a reacting bond plus all other atomic orbital portions which overlap with them at the transition state, each portion bounded by nuclei but with no interposed nuclei; *i.e.*, halves of a *p*- or *s*-orbital belong to different reacting orbitals. Starting at the point of structure change, star (*) the nearest reacting orbital(s) and *alternate* more remote reacting orbitals. Wavemark (∼) other reacting orbitals. The rule is that bonds utilizing starred orbitals are lengthened at the transition state by electron-supplying substituents and shortened by electron-attracting substituents; the opposite is true for bonds utilizing waved orbitals. A more electron-supplying substituent is one which is more basic toward a proton.

For a reacting bond in which the substituent change changes one atom (*e.g.*, from CCl to CBr), the predicted change is for the *difference* between transition state and reactant or product lengths. Because it is more basic toward a proton, Cl is more electron-supplying than Br. When there is more than one reacting orbital in an even-membered ring, the effect along the shortest path should prevail.

An example of the application of the hypothesis to solvolysis is the solvolysis of cumyl chlorides

in methanol, ethanol, and 2-propanol at 25°. The sensitivity of the rate to changes in solvent polarity is larger for *m*-methyl and *p*-phenyl but smaller for *m*- or *p*-chloro, *p*-carbomethoxy, or *p*-trifluoromethyl substituents. In agreement with prediction, electron-supplying substituents appear to cause more complete ionization (longer C—Cl bond in the transition state) than electron-withdrawing substituents. The transition state may be pictured as follows, the star on the reacting orbital which contains the C—Cl bond indicating that that bond should be lengthened by electron-supplying substituents:

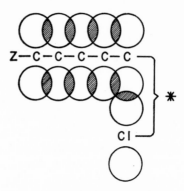

This postulate only predicts the *direction* of effects, not the magnitude. In some cases the effect might be too small to measure, although very small changes can be studied by kinetic isotope effects (Chapter 6). However, the postulate's main use is probably the correlation of data. If any apparent or real exceptions turn up, it will be exceedingly interesting to explore the reasons for the exceptional behavior.

NON–SOLVOLYTIC REACTIONS

Since there is a possibility of nucleophilic attack by solvent in solvolysis reactions, we will now discuss some results in reactions which involve nucleophiles other than the solvent. In such cases, changes in mechanism can be demonstrated kinetically by finding out whether the rate is dependent upon, or independent of, the concentration of the nucleophile.

Although, in polar solvents, tertiary halides are well known to react by the SN1 mechanism even in the presence of large concentrations of good nucleophiles, there is some evidence that they may react by the SN2 mechanism in less polar solvents. In this case one might find instances in which a mixture of SN1 and SN2 reactions occurs simultaneously or even ones in which the SN2 mechanism is the exclusive reaction path.

For a time, it appeared as if this were what happens when *tert*-butyl halides react with lithium halides in anhydrous acetone. In the extensive investigation of branched and unbranched alkyl halides referred to before (44, 45), the reactions appeared to be mainly kinetically second-order. In the three cases in which a first-order component occurred, it appeared to lead to elimination (olefin), not to alkyl halide, product. These beautiful results are apparently not valid for *tert*-butyl derivatives, however, because it was found (48a) that *tert*-butyl bromide reacts with lithium chloride in acetone to give nearly quantitative elimination and only *ca.* 3% *tert*-butyl chloride. The second-order rate constants were shown to be possibly the result of a salt effect on a SN1 reaction rather than a mixture of SN1 and SN2. The observed rate constant for the latter case should be

$$k_{\text{OBS}} = k_1 + k_2(S) \qquad (4\text{--}1)$$

where k_1 is the first-order rate constant for the SN1 reaction, k_2 is the second-order rate constant for the SN2 reaction, and (S) is the concentration of the reactive nucleophile. In the case of salts dissolved in acetone, this concentration probably must be corrected for ion pairing. Apparently the lithium salts are unreactive as ion pairs, only the dissociated halide ions having appreciable nucleophilic reactivity. If the observed effect were a salt effect, the observed rate constant should be

$$k_{\text{OBS}} = k_1^0[1 + b(\text{MY})] \qquad (4\text{--}2)$$

where k_1^0 is the first-order rate constant in the absence of added salt, (MY) is the salt concentration and b is the parameter which expresses the sensitivity of the reaction in question to salt effects. Since Eqs. (4–1) and (4–2) have the same form, it is impossible, from a kinetic study alone, to determine whether the reactions in acetone are simply a mixture of SN1 and SN2 or are complicated by salt effects. From data on other reactions in acetone, it appears probable that salt effects are important (48a), but it is possible that the *tert*-butyl halide reactions have some SN2 component as well. Salt effects can be very large in non-polar solvents, as evidenced by a b value of *ca.* 2×10^6 for lithium perchlorate in ether (48b).

A recent investigation of mixed kinetics appears to demonstrate that SN1 and SN2 mechanisms occur simultaneously (49). The reactions of *p*-phenoxybenzyl chloride and of *p*-methoxybenzyl chloride in 70% aqueous acetone (v/v) at 20.08° were studied in the absence and presence of various salts. The communication (49) does not give complete details, but the results indicate that with no salt present the reaction is SN1 with the solvent; with nucleophilic anions present there is, in addition to the reaction with solvent, a SN2 reaction with the anions. The results are in Table 4–1.

TABLE 4–1

Rate Constants for Second-Order Reactions of p-Phenoxybenzyl Chloride (1) and p-Methoxybenzyl Chloride (2) with Anions (X⁻) in 70% Aqueous Acetone (v/v) at 20.08°

X^-	$10^4 k_2(1)$; l. mole⁻¹sec.⁻¹ (std. error, $\pm 0.2 \times 10^{-4}$)	$10^6 k_2(2)$; l. mole⁻¹sec.⁻¹ (std. error, $\pm 0.2 \times 10^{-6}$)	$\dfrac{k_2(1)}{k_2(2)}$
$PhSO_3^-$	2.0	1.6	125
NO_3^-	3.2	2.3	139
F^-	4.2	4.9	86
*Cl^-	6.6	7.6	87
Br^-	7.9	50.9	15.5
N_3^-	34.5	710.3	4.9

$(H_2O; SN1)$ $k_1 = 2.306 \times 10^{-4}$ sec.⁻¹ $k_1 = 1.708 \times 10^{-6}$ sec.⁻¹

$$\frac{k_1(1)}{k_1(2)} = 135$$

* Exchange with radioactive Cl^-.

The reaction without added salts has the characteristics of a typical SN1 reaction—its salt, solvent, and common-ion effects are similar to those of benzhydryl chloride (Ph_2CHCl). The SN2 reaction is possible with these benzylic chlorides, presumably because there would be so much less steric hindrance to nucleophilic attack than with secondary or tertiary halides. Nevertheless, SN1 reaction also occurs because of the possibility of stabilizing the transition state for ionization by the powerful electron-donating delocalization effect of the *p*-oxygen atom. Part of the developing positive charge can be stabilized by delocalization of an unshared pair of electrons from oxygen into the ring.

The rate constants were obtained by following the rate of production of chloride ions, then correcting for the rate of the solvent reaction in the presence of the dissolved salt. This latter correction cannot be measured directly, but a good estimate of its magnitude was obtained from control experiments using benzhydryl chloride. The latter compound appears not to undergo any SN2 reaction (steric hindrance), but showed a certain rate enhancement with added salts. Also the salt effects on the *p*-substituted benzyl chlorides could be obtained along with benzhydryl chloride when very weak nucleophiles were used—ions such as ClO_4^- and BF_4^-. The accelerations caused by adding salts of these anions were similar for all three substituted alkyl halides but differed by small factors which were independent of the nature of the electrolyte, *i.e.*, dependent only on electrolyte concentration. It was assumed that these differences were specific salt effects rather than the result of intrusion of SN2 attack, which seems reasonable since the nucleophiles were so much weaker than water itself. The same small differences between salt effects on the three reactions were assumed to apply also in the case of more nucleophilic anions. The rates of SN1 reaction in the presence of such nucleophiles could then be calculated from the measured salt effects on benzhydryl chloride. This SN1 component was subtracted from the over-all rates of formation of chloride ions to give the SN2 reaction rates of the nucleophiles, and these rate constants are listed in Table 4–1. They increase in the expected order of nucleophilic activity of the anions. The ratio $k_2(1)/k_2(2)$ may be considered to be a measure of the charge distribution of the transition state. This is a vague concept, but at least we might expect that a strong nucleophile such as azide ion (N_3^-) would have a transition state with a longer N—C bond and a shorter C—Cl bond than a weaker nucleophile such as $PhSO_3^-$ or even H_2O (*cf.* page 82). We might then expect that the effect on rate of substituting a *p*-methoxy group for a *p*-phenoxy group would be smaller for a more reactant-like transition state, *i.e.*, for N_3^-, as observed. The similarity of $k_2(1)/k_2(2)$ for $PhSO_3^-$ and NO_3^- to $k_1(1)/k_1(2)$ for the solvolytic reaction seems significant. It would be expected if water is acting as a nucleophile in the solvolytic reaction just as $PhSO_3^-$ and NO_3^- do in their SN2 reactions, but the similarity should not exist if water is not acting as a nucleophile. Unless the results are similar for purely fortuitous reasons, one can conclude that water is attacking as a nucleophile, at least to some extent, in the SN1 reaction. This point will be discussed in more detail later in this chapter. It was shown that in these reactions the nucleophiles participate in the SN1 reaction as well as the SN2, by determining the products and showing that, in the cases of N_3^-, Cl⁻, Br⁻, and NO_3^-, more substituted benzyl azide, chloride, bromide, or nitrate product, respectively, was formed than could be accounted for by the SN2 rate constants. Therefore some of these products must have arisen by competition of the anions with water for the carbonium ion produced in the SN1 component of the reaction. In these cases, SN1 and SN2 reactions of the nucleophile occur simultaneously. It seems possible that such mixtures of mechanisms may occur in solvolysis reactions too, but of course we cannot use the criterion of kinetic orders to unravel the results in solvolysis reactions.

There is still lingering doubt in some minds about the SN1 and SN2 classifications, because many reactions appear to have both SN1 and SN2 characteristics. This has led to a question of whether mechanisms which are neither SN1 nor SN2 may not be "hybrid mechanisms," somewhere between. The problem has been discussed in some detail (50), and it is worthwhile to emphasize one conclusion here. The real criterion of SN1 or SN2 mechanism is kinetic order. If we adhere to this criterion, there can be no hybrid mechanism, because there is no intermediate case between one molecule and no molecule. Either a nucleophile is present in the transition state (SN2) or it is absent (SN1). This is a result of the quantization of matter into fundamental particles, atoms, and molecules, and cannot be denied without changing the theoretical basis of chemical structure, thermodynamics, and statistical mechanics. A nucleophile cannot be "partially present" in the transition state. A transition state where a nucleophile is present is SN2, where a nucleophile is absent is SN1, and if both types are present in solution at the same time, the mechanism is properly described as consisting of simultaneous SN1 and SN2 mechanisms.

This conclusion appears to be sound, yet when we come to discuss solvolysis in the same terms, the problem arises again, because solvent molecules seemingly must always be "present" in (and around) the transition state.

There are certainly differences between nucleophiles added to the solution and solvent molecules as nucleophiles. One major problem has been the effect of the surrounding solvent molecules on the nucleophile. Anions, especially, must be strongly solvated or they would never even be soluble. It is therefore of interest to discuss solvent effects on nucleophilicity. In polar solvents, the nucleophilicity of halide ions generally falls in the order $I^- > Br^- > Cl^- > F^-$. This is partially illustrated by the reactivity of CH_3I in water at $25°$ (51), the relative rates being I^- (160); Br^- (14); Cl^- (1.0). The reaction of CH_3Br with nucleophiles in water at $25°$ gives I^- (140); Cl^- (1.0). However, in anhydrous acetone, the reaction of n-butyl brosylate $(CH_3(CH_2)_3OSO_2C_6H_4Br-p)$ with 0.04 M tetra-n-butylammonium salts at $25°$ gives Cl^- (18);

Br^- (4); I^- (1.0); under the same conditions isopropyl bromide ((CH_3)$_2$CHBr) gives Cl^- (11); Br^- (5); I^- (1.0). The order has been completely reversed by the change from a polar to a non-polar solvent! The rates in acetone are complicated by ion pairing, some salts (such as lithium halides) existing largely as anion-cation pairs and higher aggregates. It seems probable that the ion pairs are much less reactive as nucleophiles than free, solvated anions. In arriving at the rates in acetone it was necessary to correct for the different amounts of ion pairing with different anions. The concentration of free anions was determined conductimetrically and it was assumed that these were the only reactive nucleophiles. From the observed rate of reaction and the concentration of free anions, the rate constants could be evaluated. The ammonium salts are, however, almost completely dissociated in acetone, the observed relative rates (before correction for ion pairing) being Cl^- (18); Br^- (5); I^- (1.0) for n-butyl brosylate.

The interpretation of these results is not complete, but there are two similar interpretations, which may in fact mean the same thing. It is said (51) that a non-specific solvent effect could account for the results. The solvent sensitivity of the halide ion reactions should be smaller if the charge is less concentrated, $i.e.$, if the ion is larger. The reversal would then be expected if a sufficiently large solvent change were made. This idea says nothing about the direction of the change, however. A more specific explanation, for which there is no experimental proof, is that there is a specific solvation effect. The fluoride ion, being small and therefore having a highly concentrated negative charge, should be a better nucleophile than chloride, chloride better than bromide, bromide better than iodide (in basicity $F^- > Cl^- > Br^- > I^-$ even in water). This is the nucleophilic order observed in acetone. The reversal of this expected order in water may then be a result of the strong hydrogen bonds between water molecules and the anion. The magnitude of the solvation energy should be in the order of increasing charge concentration in the anion, $F^- > Cl^- > Br^- > I^-$. In order for the anion to attack carbon as a nucleophile, it may be necessary for a water molecule to be dissociated from it, the dissociation of a water molecule being much more difficult for fluoride than for chloride, etc. The nucleophilic order in water would then possibly reflect the ease of removal of solvating water molecules, this solvation effect outweighing the inherently greater reactivity of free fluoride.

It is well known that, in SN2 reactions, rates with a given nucleophile and leaving group depend also on the carbon atom in between. For SN2 reactions the rates for various alkyl groups R in the reactions $X + RY \rightarrow XR + Y$ fall in the order methyl > ethyl > isopropyl > *tert*-butyl. For SN1 reactions the rates are in the exact reverse order. It is usually assumed that the SN2 order represents the effect of steric hindrance to approach of the nucleophile, large R groups slowing the rate. The SN1 order is considered to represent the increased stability of secondary and tertiary carbonium ions, which are partially formed in the SN1 transition state. In solvolysis reactions, the order of the R groups is usually the same as in SN1 reactions. This does not mean that all the solvolysis reactions have SN1 mechanisms, however. A SN2 reaction with solvent may have a number of features which make it not completely analogous to a SN2 reaction with a nucleophile solute. For the moment, we may use the vague concept that a nucleophilic solute probably must be desolvated before it can attack, whereas the solvent is always adjacent to the substrate, *i.e.*, in its immediate solvation shell.

The hypothesis that steric effects may have profound effects upon rates or even mechanisms is summed up in the "F.B.I. strains," three effects which should affect the relative energies of reactants and transition states (52). F-strains, or Front strains, are steric inhibitions of bond formation. For example, the reaction of 4-*tert*-butylpyridine with methyl iodide to give the corresponding N-methylpyridinium salt in nitrobenzene solution at 30° is about 10^4 times faster than the reaction of

2-*tert*-butylpyridine under the same conditions. The electrical effects of the alkyl substituent should be similar in the 2- and 4-positions, but the steric interference to attack of the lone pair of electrons of the nitrogen atom on the carbon atom of methyl iodide should be negligible for the 4-substituent, yet very large for the 2-substituent. The 2-*tert*-butyl group interferes with the approach of the methyl iodide molecule to the nitrogen atom of the amine.

B-strains, or Back strains, are the steric effects associated with the "crowding" of substituents in a molecule. For example, in *tert*-butyl chloride, the methyl groups are at *ca.* 109.5° angles, and the hydrogen atoms of these methyl groups are probably close enough together to interfere with one another, a destabilizing influence. However, if *tert*-butyl chloride underwent SN1 cleavage to a carbonium ion, some of the Back strain would be relieved; the methyl groups would be at 120° angles, further apart, in the (presumably) planar trimethylcarbonium ion. The relief of B-strain may be an important driving force in many SN1-type reactions. The relative rates of solvolysis in 80% aqueous ethanol (v/v) at 25° of alkyl chlorides illustrate this (53): $(CH_3)_3CCl$, 1.0; $(CH_3)_2[(CH_3)_3CCH_2]CCl$, 21; $CH_3[(CH_3)_3CCH_2]_2CCl$, 580.

I-strains, or Internal strains, are steric effects associated with angle deformations in compounds containing rings. For example, in cyclopropyl bromide, where the bromine atom is attached to a tetrahedral carbon atom of the ring, the bond angles of the ring are 60°, strained from the tetrahedral angle of 109.5°. If this compound undergoes either SN1 or SN2 reaction, the hybridization of the ring carbon atom attached to the bromine atom should be approximately sp^2 in the transition state. The normal sp^2 bond angle is 120°, but the internal angle of the ring is still 60°. Therefore the strain induced by the ring will be greater in the transition state than in the reactant, and such reactants should be much slower than would otherwise be expected. In fact cyclopropyl bromide is completely unreactive towards potassium iodide in acetone at

100°, whereas isopropyl bromide reacts at a reasonable rate under these conditions (54).

One fundamental difference between the usual models of SN1 and SN2 reactions is that the SN1 reaction is thought to proceed via a carbonium ion intermediate, while the SN2 reaction is thought to involve no intermediate. There appears to be no known case where the existence of an intermediate in a SN2 reaction has been proved, but there is one case where some circumstantial evidence exists. The reaction of *trans*-4-*tert*-butylcyclohexyl tosylate with lithium bromide in acetone at 75° is second-order and leads partly to substitution, partly to elimination (55). The formation of the olefin needs to be explained. The authors felt that an E2 elimination (*i.e.*, a second-order attack of nucleophile (base) on the β-proton) is precluded by the conformation of the substrate and by the fact that the fraction of elimination is equal (0.25 ± 0.01) for lithium bromide and for *tetra-n*-butylammonium bromide, the latter precluding any involvement of the cation in some cyclic *cis* elimination transition state. A SN2 reaction to give the 4-*tert*-butylcyclohexyl bromide followed by an E2 reaction of this (presumably) *cis* bromide is ruled out by the fact that the intermediate bromide is known to be too unreactive by a factor of at least 100. An E1 reaction (*i.e.*, a unimolecular ionization to carbonium ion, followed by elimination from the carbonium ion) might be thought to explain the results, the second-order nature of the reaction being explained as a salt effect on the rate of ionization. However, lithium bromide reacts much faster than lithium perchlorate, whereas in ordinary SN1 reactions lithium perchlorate gives rate enhancements as high as, or higher than, the bromide.

The original substrate's most stable form will be a chair (*cf.* page 11) with both tosylate and *tert*-butyl groups equatorial. We might say that the elimination is E2, but performed only on the small fraction of the substrate molecules which have the tosylate grouping axial (there are a boat form and a chair form). The tosylate should be in a favorable position for elimination when axial. However, we know from rough estimates of the energy involved (40, Chapter 1), that probably between 6 and 14 kcal./mole is necessary to effect conversion into these axial forms, so that it is difficult to see how enough substrate molecules could get into either form to compete with the SN2 attack of bromide. It was suggested that the rate-determining step is attack of bromide on carbon to give an *intermediate* with both bromide and tosylate partially bonded to carbon, and that this intermediate can subsequently decompose into the bromide and the olefin.

There is a report that the rates of reaction of allyl chloride with hydroxide ions at 64.9° in dioxane-water mixtures are in an unexpected order (56). In 40% water-dioxane (v/v), with 0.17 M KOH, the second-order rate constant for attack of hydroxide ion is 3.64×10^{-2} l. mole^{-1} min.$^{-1}$, while in 60% water-dioxane (v/v), with 0.16 M KOH, the second-order rate constant is 7.39×10^{-2} l. mole^{-1} min.$^{-1}$ The reaction involves HO$^-$ in the transition state, since it is second-order. We would therefore expect that increasing the per cent water (*i.e.*, the polarity) of the solvent should decrease the rate of reaction since the negative charge should be delocalized in the transition state, but localized on the oxygen atom of HO$^-$ in the reactant. Experimentally the rate is greater in the *more polar* solvent. This result indicates that the transition state is more polar than the reactants, possibly having a structure similar to a carbonium ion associated with two negative ions,

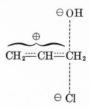

i.e., a large degree of charge separation. Before accepting this conclusion completely, we should know whether all of the KOH is dissociated into hydroxide and potassium ions in both solvents, because if some K^+HO^- ion pairs were present, there might be different amounts in the two solvents, which could account for the difference in rates. Tentatively, however, these experiments point to the possibility of SN2 transition states with a high degree of carbonium ion (SN1) character.

SOLVOLYSIS MECHANISMS

The major problem in discussing solvolysis mechanisms is the lack of the mechanistic criterion of kinetic order which clearly differentiates SN1 and SN2 mechanisms when the nucleophile is not the solvent. Other criteria must be used for solvolyses. The use of other criteria, however, cannot establish the kinetic order. We are left with a confusing circular path because, as we have seen, many possible mechanisms may have some characteristics of SN1 type and some characteristics of SN2 type.

The molecularity of the *rate-determining* step is supposed to differentiate the SN1 and SN2 mechanisms—if unimolecular, the mechanism is SN1; if bimolecular, SN2. According to our kinetic discussions in Chapter 3, the kinetics may be complicated by reversibility, *e.g.*, the common-ion effect, so there may be no single step which really determines the rate of product formation. To be precise, therefore, we should consider the composition of the transition state(s) on the reaction path. Of primary importance is the transition state of *greatest free energy;* it is the one which largely determines the rate of product formation. Each elementary step should be considered separately, the questions of whether an *intermediate* subsequently forms and what properties an intermediate has being largely irrelevant to the discussion of prior transition states. Most of the confusion about solvolysis mechanisms is cleared up by considering the "rate-determining" transition state separately.

The "rate-determining" transition state for a SN2 substitution by a nucleophile which is not the solvent has a composition which is abundantly clear—there must be significant bonding between nucleophile and substrate in the transition state. The composition of the rate-determining transition state for a SN1 reaction is not so clear. We know it does not involve bonding between a nucleophile which is not the solvent and the substrate, but we do not know whether it involves *no* nucleophilic assistance or significant nucleophilic assistance by *solvent* molecules but not by the added nucleophile.

In solvolysis reactions the situation is similar to that in SN1 reactions with added nucleophiles. We cannot distinguish kinetically between "rate-determining" transition states which do or do not involve significant nucleophilic assistance by a solvent molecule. In fact a continuously variable series of transition-state structures is possible and undoubtedly exists, depending on the solvent and the substrate. The energy of interaction between the carbon nucleus and a solvent molecule at the backside from the leaving group can vary from zero to the strength of an ordinary covalent bond (50–100 kcal./mole).

The analysis of the problem therefore involves deciding where the dividing line between significant and insignificant nucleophilic assistance should be drawn. Realistically, the distinction should be made at the point where the energy of interaction between solvent molecule and substrate is $\sim RT$ (*ca.* 0.6 kcal./mole at room temperature). Any "bond" stronger than $\sim RT$ could in principle be detected by suitably refined techniques. A bond much weaker than RT could not be specifically detected because of the thermal agitation of the molecules. It is only at this dividing line that we can legitimately speak of a "mixed mechanism" in the sense of one mechanism which "partially" involves nucleophilic assistance. The reason is that there will be a Boltzmann distribution of transition states with various nucleophilic assistance energies above and below RT, so that in one sense this could be called a "mixed mechanism." In reality, however, all transition states are of one type or the other—involving nucleophilic assistance which is either significant or insignificant.

When bonding energy is as weak as RT, it is difficult to draw any meaningful distinction between solvation (non-specific) and covalent bonding (specific). In fact, many bonds which are normally classified as solvation are *much* stronger than 0.6 kcal./mole. Nevertheless, we should not think of a "mixed" mechanism as a fuzzy concept used to explain results that appear not to be distinctly with or without nucleophilic assistance. Every mechanism must involve one or more distinct kinds of transition states, and must not do violence to our knowledge of the structure of matter. We should think in terms of the average properties of large numbers of individual transition states, rather than trying to think of a single transition state possessing all of these average properties simultaneously. The situation is analogous to speaking of "the average chemist," which is a useful concept, but we all know that it is a composite of many real chemists, none of whom has all the characteristics of the average.

This dividing line is at such a small bond energy that probably nearly every reaction would have nucleophilic assistance in the transition state amounting to more than RT. We should therefore look for a more meaningful way of thinking about solvolysis mechanisms. One possibility is to realize that all such reactions probably involve significant nucleophilic assistance and then attempt to evaluate the *relative amounts* in each reaction. The amount of bond-breaking is fully as significant as the amount of bond-making (nucleophilic assistance). There are several extreme types of transition states which are conceivable, all intermediate types between these extremes being possible as well:

$$S\text{------}R\text{--}X$$
$$S\text{------}R\text{------}X$$
$$S\text{--}R\text{------}X$$
$$S\text{--}R\text{--}X$$

The second is carbonium-ion-like, probably typical of SN1 reactions, while the fourth is probably typical of SN2 reactions. The SN1 and SN2 types may be considered as extreme mechanistic types, but there are really two other extremes as well.

At this point, the obvious question is this: Even if all solvolysis mechanisms do involve significant nucleophilic assistance in the "rate-determining" transition state, what would be the point of mechanistic change *if* we could measure kinetic order with respect to solvent molecules? The answer to this question must be found, not in the properties of single molecules, but in the statistics of large numbers of molecules. Unfortunately, it must be different for each and every reaction. It is possible that in a given reaction, products could form in two ways—with and without nucleophilic assistance. If the free energy barrier for one path is significantly higher than that for another path, the path with the lowest barrier will largely account for the formation of products. But a *finite number* of reactant molecules will decompose by the other path, although this number may be very small because a difference in barrier heights of merely 1.37 kcal./mole would make one process ten times more favorable (at 300°K.); 8.22 kcal./mole, a million times. If the difference in barrier heights approached zero, both mechanisms would contribute substantially to the rate of product formation. The actual amount of nucleophilic assistance is not exclusively important in determining the point of kinetic changeover, but rather the relative heights of the two barriers. And the less favorable path could in many cases require an "activated complex" which is merely an "excited state" of the transition state for the more favorable path; this excited structure would then be unstable, not metastable, and there would be only a single mechanism. If, on the other hand, *two metastable structures* (transition states) existed, one involving a solvent molecule as nucleophile and the other, none, then there would be two separate mechanisms. If the free energies of activation for these two mechanisms were similar, then both mechanisms could contribute significantly to the formation of products. In this case the two activated complexes would differ in many ways besides the relative amounts of nucleophilic assistance; their differences would come into their partition functions. Probably a case which involves two significant mechanisms is very exceptional, most solvolysis reactions (except in mixed solvents) probably having only one significant mechanism. If so, we are back to the situation mentioned in the previous paragraph, that the most meaningful thing would be to try to evaluate the relative amounts of nucleophilic assistance in different reactions.

If a solvolysis reaction proceeds by a direct displacement of leaving group by solvent, without the intervention of carbonium ion type intermediates, the solvent molecule which is providing nucleophilic assistance in the transition state is inevitably the same one which is attached to the substrate in the final product. In reactions of this type with a hydroxylic solvent, it is thought that the initially formed product is an oxonium ion:

$$\text{RX} + \text{R'OH} \xrightarrow{\text{slow}} \text{R'}\overset{+}{-}\text{O}\underset{\text{H}}{\overset{\text{R}}{<}} + \text{X}^-$$

$$\text{R'}\overset{+}{-}\text{O}\underset{\text{H}}{\overset{\text{R}}{<}} \underset{\text{fast}}{\rightleftharpoons} \text{R'}-\text{O}-\text{R} + [\text{H}^+]$$

which rapidly loses a proton to the solvent. This type of intermediate is usually ignored when we say that such a solvolysis has a SN2-like mechanism, with no intermediates. The reason is that chemists feel that such an intermediate is of very low energy relative to the transition state (*i.e.*, much more stable than the transition state), and that it could not lead to rearranged products, but must inevitably lose a proton and form product. And if the product ever becomes reprotonated, it can do nothing but lose the proton again. A detailed study of this question would be interesting, but in most cases it is undoubtedly justifiable to assume that this protonated intermediate can do nothing other than lose a proton. An interesting criterion of "significant" nucleophilic assistance in the transition state might therefore be whether the nucleophile of the transition state inevitably ends up in the product or not. If some intermediate forms after the "rate-determining" transition state which can exchange one solvent molecule for another, then even though nucleophilic assistance be present in the transition state, it might be considered to be only weak assistance. Knowing, for a given reaction, whether the transition-state nucleophile always ends up in the product would be exceedingly interesting, but as a criterion of nucleophilic assistance it is complicated by the fact that it really depends on the properties of the *intermediate* rather than the *transition state*.

Intermediates have been detected in many solvolysis reactions, and they usually seem to have carbonium-ion-like properties. Just as with the transition states, a continuous range of intermediates with variable amounts of bond-making and of bond-breaking is conceivable. If there is essentially no nucleophilic assistance in the transition state, it would be possible to have an ion pair R^+X^- or a free carbonium ion R^+ as the initial product (intermediate), and these could react with solvent in various ways. If there is significant nucleophilic assistance in the transition state, the initial product might be an ion pair SR^+X^- (S being a solvent molecule) or possibly SR^+, but the latter should rapidly collapse to product by loss of a proton. A final type of intermediate would be a solvated carbonium ion, possibly SR^+S, which might be formed by attack of solvent on SR^+X^- or other intermediates. SR^+S could conceivably be formed by direct attack of *two* solvent molecules on RX, which would give a rather unusual transition state. It should be remembered that various intermediates, such as R^+X^-, could be formed in a rapid equilibrium followed by "rate-determining" reaction of the intermediate with solvent. It is possible that several of these intermediates could be involved in a single reaction mechanism, but we should not invoke several intermediates unless experiment requires them.

Another way of looking at the problem would be to try to distinguish between solvation and strongly covalent bonding. If a solvated carbonium ion-anion pair can exchange rapidly

$$S' + S\text{---}R^+\text{---}X^- \underset{k_1}{\overset{k_1}{\rightleftharpoons}} S'\text{---}R^+\text{---}X^- + S$$
$$\downarrow k_2 \qquad\qquad \downarrow k_2$$
$$S\text{---}R + X^- \qquad S'\text{---}R + X^-$$

one solvent molecule, S, for another, S', $(k_1 \gg k_2)$, the solvation bond could be considered non-specific. On the other hand, if no exchange of S can occur once the S---R^+ bond is formed $(k_2 \gg k_1)$, the solvation bond could be considered specific (covalent). This distinction is based on rates and is not necessarily dependent on the actual strength of the bond. Attempts to evaluate the relative rates represented by k_1 and k_2 would be more interesting and useful than attempts to find out whether the solvation bonds have energies greater or less than RT.

There are two kinds of experimental evidence which would contribute to our knowledge of the mechanism of a reaction: (1) evidence distinguishing between the necessity and absence of nucleophilic participation in the transition state, or showing the *relative amount* of nucleophilic assistance, and (2) evidence distinguishing between the presence and absence of an intermediate and between the various possible reactions of an intermediate if formed.

Much of the confusion about solvolysis mechanisms can be avoided by considering the possibilities in these terms, but such consideration also suggests many problems which must be solved before we can really understand which category is involved in any reaction. Probably the most important question to be answered is whether nucleophilic assistance is involved or not. All experiments known to the author can be explained by assuming that SN1 reactions, even with externally added nucleophiles, do involve some nucleophilic assistance by solvent molecules, which can be replaced by molecules of added nucleophile before the product is formed. We will next turn to the experimental evidence relating to the nucleophilic participation question.

NUCLEOPHILIC ASSISTANCE

A number of investigations are concerned with the importance of nucleophilic assistance in the transition state, but there still appears to be no conclusive evidence. One problem is that if nucleophilic assistance is relatively unimportant in determining the energy of the transition state, as it probably is in some cases, it is very difficult to find criteria to determine whether it is important at all.

Lyate Ion. One criterion of sensitivity of the substrate to nucleophilic assistance is to compare the rate of solvolysis with the rate of reaction with the conjugate base of the solvent. Both a solvent molecule and a molecule of conjugate base have very similar structures (especially as far as steric effects), differing only by the presence or absence of a proton. Some such data are listed in Table 4–2 (57). The rate constants

TABLE 4–2

Effect of Lyate Ion on Solvolysis of Methyl, Ethyl, and Isopropyl Benzensulfonates in Dry Ethanol at 70°

Rate Constant	Base	Methyl	Ethyl	Isopropyl
$k_1 \times 10^4$ sec.$^{-1}$	—	0.705	0.306	1.02
$k_2 \times 10^4$ l. mole^{-1} sec.$^{-1}$	0.02 M	10300	401	70

are derived by correcting the rate in the presence of base for solvolysis where necessary. The ratio k_2/k_1 is very large for methyl, smaller for ethyl, and smallest for isopropyl. If data were available for a tertiary system, such as *tert*-butyl, the ratio would undoubtedly be less than 1, as it is for several other tertiary systems, k_2 being too small to measure. These ratios are dependent on solvent, temperature, and leaving group, as might be expected. Ratios less than 1 indicate an extraordinary insensitivity to the several powers of ten difference in basicity between a solvent molecule and its conjugate base. Substrates with such insensitivity would seem to require little nucleophilic assistance in the transition state, otherwise the base should have a large effect on the rate. Because of solvation effects, the lyate ion being much more tightly hydrogen-bonded to solvent than a solvent molecule is hydrogen-bonded to solvent, and because of the steric effect of changing the substrate group from CH_3 to $(CH_3)_3C$, we cannot conclude that nucleophilic assistance is unimportant in tertiary systems. What we can conclude is that nucleophilic assistance is generally much *less* important for tertiary than for primary substrates, but *may* be important for both.

Solvent Effect. A study of the rates of solvolysis of three chlorides which commonly undergo SN1 reactions indicates that nucleophilic assistance is important in the transition states for the solvolysis reactions. The data are in Table 4–3

TABLE 4–3

Relative Rates of Solvolysis in Formic Acid (k) and in 80% Aqueous Ethanol (v/v) (k_0) at 25°

Compound	$\log\left(\dfrac{k}{k_0}\right)$
$(CH_3)_3C$—Cl	2.08
$C_6H_5CHClCH_3$	2.35
$(C_6H_5)_2CHCl$	2.61

(58). If all three substrates solvolyze with transition states which involve no nucleophilic assistance by solvent molecules, it is hard to explain the order of rate ratios. The compound which ionizes most easily ($(C_6H_5)_2CHCl$) should be least sensitive to changes in dielectric constant or other specific properties of the solvent, whereas in fact benzhydryl chloride is most sensitive to the change in solvent from 80% aqueous ethanol to formic acid.   Benzhydryl chloride should require less "help" from the solvent than *tert*-butyl chloride (*cf.* the Hammond postulate).   On the other hand, the results are easily explained if nucleophilic assistance is important in these transition states. That the rates are faster in formic acid is explained by the fact that the dielectric constant of formic acid is greater than that of 80% aqueous ethanol.   That the rates are faster in formic acid by a larger amount for benzhydryl chloride than for *tert*-butyl chloride is explained by the fact that the nucleophilic assistance in the transition state is greater for *tert*-butyl chloride than for benzhydryl chloride.   Thus *tert*-butyl chloride, requiring more "help" from solvent in its transition state, could be less sensitive to the ionizing properties of the solvent if the transition state were less polar.   This conclusion is not completely rigorous, because steric effects on solvation might be complicating the observed rate ratios for the different substrates, but it does indicate that nucleophilic assistance may be of importance in the solvolysis of some substrates such as *tert*-butyl chloride which generally react by a SN1 mechanism even with powerful nucleophiles present.

From data such as the above, it might be concluded that really all reactions were SN2 in the sense of requiring nucleophilic assistance.   Those that are SN1 in kinetic order might simply be using solvent as nucleophile in the transition state, since solvent is present in so much higher concentration than any added nucleophile ($10-55.5$ M *vs.* $0.01-1.0$ M).   After the transition state was reached, an intermediate would form which would react rapidly with added nucleophile (or with solvent) to give the observed product(s).   It is difficult to disprove such a suggestion because even 1.0 M nucleophile must change the properties of the solution so that one no longer has the same solvent as with low nucleophile concentrations.   Therefore rate effects produced by adding such large amounts of nucleophiles cannot be interpreted: one would not know whether they were a result of nucleophilic interaction or simply of the change in medium.

In fact, there is some quantitative indication that the above explanation is realistic. Using the equation

$$\log\left(\frac{k_i}{k_0}\right) = sn$$

(for discussion and reference see p. 162), where k_i is the rate constant for reaction of a certain nucleophile with a given substrate, k_0 is the rate constant for reaction of water with the same substrate, s is a constant characteristic of the substrate, and n is a constant characteristic of the nucleophile, one can determine the relative rate for attack by water or some nucleophile on a substrate such as *tert*-butyl bromide. The value of s is by definition 1.00 for methyl bromide. Iodide ion is 10^5 times better than water as a nucleophile towards methyl bromide. However, the factor is much less for *tert*-butyl bromide, being calculated to be about 20 for acetone solution, using the rates for LiCl, LiBr, and LiI discussed previously (44, 45, 48). Admittedly the *tert*-butyl reactions were found to lead mainly to elimination and may have been SN1, not SN2; nevertheless, the observed rates may suggest some order of magnitude of the sensitivity of the *tert*-butyl system to nucleophilic properties. The calculated factor of 20 may even be too large. But if we assume that salts are usually in concentrations of 0.1 M or less, and use the concentration of 55.5 M for water, we can calculate that only about $20 \times 0.1/55.5 \approx 0.04$ of the reaction would ordinarily proceed by attack of iodide. This calculation is exceedingly crude, but it does give some idea that the low sensitivity of certain substrates to differences in nucleophilicity may explain the tendency towards SN1 reaction mechanism, even though both SN1 and SN2 mechanisms might involve nucleophilic assistance, one by solvent, the other by added nucleophile. The mixed mechanism observed (49) for $C_6H_5OC_6H_4CH_2Cl$, both SN1 and SN2, may be explained if this substrate is of intermediate sensitivity, utilizing nucleophilic assistance from both solvent and nucleophile.

Bridgehead Ions. There is some evidence which seems inconsistent with nucleophilic assistance's assuming an important role in the solvolysis of such compounds as *tert*-butyl halides (59). A model of 1-bromobicyclo[2.2.2]octane:

shows that it would be virtually impossible for a solvent molecule to approach the bromine-bearing carbon atom from the rear as in a typical SN2 reaction; there are too many CH_2 groups in the way. Yet the compound solvolyzes, albeit very slowly, in aqueous ethanol, formic acid, and acetic acid (60). In addition, its rates of solvolysis change from solvent to solvent in very nearly the same way that *tert*-butyl bromide's rates do. The mY treatment (see Chapter 5) indicates that the sensitivities of both the *tert*-butyl and the bicyclic compound to changes in the "ionizing power" of the solvent are nearly equal. Since the bicyclic compound cannot have backside nucleophilic assistance in the transition state, it might be concluded that no nucleophilic assistance exists for *tert*-butyl bromide either. The product from the bicyclic bromide is reported to be the unrearranged alcohol, so that the results cannot be explained by some rearrangement of the carbon skeleton. Aside from the possibility that the similarity of solvolysis behavior of the two compounds is fortuitous or that the calculated sensitivities to solvent ionizing power are relatively insensitive to mechanistic changes, we could seemingly only invoke some kind of frontside nucleophilic assistance in the bicyclic system. The similarity to *tert*-butyl could then be explained if *tert*-butyl, too, involved frontside nucleophilic assistance, presumably because the three CH_3 groups of the *tert*-butyl group sterically hindered backside nucleophilic assistance. Such a mechanism for the solvolysis of *tert*-butyl

bromide is highly improbable, because solvolysis reactions usually lead to more inversion than retention of configuration in
optically active systems. Frontside attack would seem
exceedingly likely to lead to net retention of optical configuration. Therefore, we probably must conclude that nucleophilic
assistance is not important enough in *tert*-butyl bromide to
make its solvent sensitivity much different from that of the
bicyclic compound. Nucleophilic assistance could still be
important, but certainly not as important as in the solvolysis
of methyl or ethyl bromide. A more detailed comparison of
these reactions would be very interesting. If the bicyclic
system does in fact react without nucleophilic assistance, either
frontside or backside, then of course it is reasonable that
nucleophilic assistance should be unimportant in many other
systems. Since the rate is much slower for the bicyclic system, it is conceivable that some mechanism other than SN1 or
SN2 may operate, such as a concerted four-center rearrangement involving a water molecule at the frontside and producing directly alcohol and hydrogen bromide:

There is no evidence for such a mechanism.

The appearance potentials of strained carbonium ions from
bicyclic systems have been measured in a mass spectrometer
(61). The carbonium ions

formed from the corresponding bromides have appearance
potentials of 10.66 and 9.98 e.v. (electron volts), respectively.
These numbers are the energies for the reaction

$$R—X \rightarrow R^+ + Br\cdot + electron$$

To convert them to the energies for the reaction

$$R—X \rightarrow R^+ + Br^-$$

the electron affinity of $Br\cdot$, 82 kcal./mole (see Ref. (3), p. 181),
must be subtracted. Since 1 e.v. corresponds to 23.06 kcal./
mole, the ionizations of the two bicyclic bromides into R^+ +
Br^- have energy changes of 163 and 148 kcal./mole, respectively. The corresponding energies for some other ions are
(Ref. (3), p. 181): $(CH_3)_3C^+$, 146; $(CH_3)_2CH^+$, 162; $CH_3CH_2^+$,
184; CH_3^+, 216; $C_6H_5CH_2^+$, 148 kcal./mole. The 1-bicyclo-
[2.2.1]heptyl ion is much less stable than the 1-bicyclo[2.2.2]-
octyl ion or the *tert*-butyl ion. The instability probably
occurs because the positive carbon atom cannot assume sp^2
hybridization in the more strained bicyclic ion. The results
for the bicyclic ions should be checked by measuring the ionization potentials of the corresponding free radicals, as was
done with the other ions mentioned. It is possible that the
ions formed from the bicyclic bromides are rearranged in some
way so that the charge is not at the bridgehead. Further
study of these strained structures, and of the even more
strained structures now available, could be very interesting.

MO Calculations. We should also mention again (see
Chapter 3) the MO calculations (31) for arylmethyl chlorides,
which indicated that these compounds may react by a SN1-like
mechanism in moist formic acid, but by a more nearly SN2-like
mechanism in 80% aqueous ethanol.

Stereochemistry. One other important way of learning
about the question of nucleophilic assistance is to study
stereochemical results in the solvolysis of compounds where the

central carbon atom, the one on which displacements occur, is optically active. Starting with an optically pure substrate, it is possible from the optical purity of the product to compute how much racemization occurs during the course of the reaction. Such racemization experiments must be carefully controlled, because one needs to be sure whether racemization occurs prior to, during, or after solvolysis. We have pointed out previously that simple solvolysis reactions usually lead to partial racemization, *i.e.*, to more inversion than retention of optical configuration.

A particularly interesting stereochemical study was the reaction of the hydrogen phthalate of 2,4-dimethyl-4-hexanol

with refluxing methanol (62). The product was entirely the methyl ether, formed by attack of methanol on the carbon atom which was optically active, displacing the hydrogen phthalate anion. This resulting ether, recovered from the reaction mixture, had an optical rotation corresponding to 54 per cent net inversion and 46 per cent racemization, in other words 77 per cent inversion and 23 per cent retention. The reactant ester did not racemize under the experimental conditions, and the product ether racemized slowly, the above percentages having been corrected for the slow racemization of product. This tertiary alkyl compound, a type of structure thought to form reasonably stable carbonium ions, underwent surprisingly little racemization on solvolysis in the rather polar solvent methanol! The results were rationalized on the basis of a mechanism which involves more than one intermediate:

$$R_3C\!-\!X \rightarrow \left[\begin{array}{c} R \\ | \\ S\text{---}C\text{---}X \\ \diagup \quad \diagdown \\ R \qquad R \end{array} \right] \xrightarrow{k_i} \begin{array}{c} \text{inverted} \\ \text{product} \end{array}$$

$$\downarrow k_r$$

$$\begin{array}{c} \text{racemic} \\ \text{product} \end{array} \xleftarrow[\text{fast}]{} \left[\begin{array}{c} R \\ | \\ S\text{---}C\text{---}S \\ \diagup \quad \diagdown \\ R \qquad R \end{array} \right]^{+} + X^{-} \qquad (4\text{--}3)$$

The first intermediate formed can be thought of as an ion pair (carbonium ion $+ \ X^-$) solvated by one solvent molecule, S, on the backside of the central carbon atom. This intermediate would then lose X^- and form product at a rate k_i, or alternatively lose X^-, simultaneously gaining another solvent molecule to give the symmetrical intermediate solvated by two solvent molecules, at a rate k_r. The symmetrical intermediate could then lose one solvent molecule and form product, with equal probability of inversion or retention since either S molecule could be lost. The fraction of net inversion would be $k_i/(k_i + k_r)$ and the fraction of racemization would be $k_r/(k_i + k_r)$. The fraction of total inversion would be $(k_i + \frac{1}{2}k_r)/(k_i + k_r)$ and the fraction of retention would be $\frac{1}{2}k_r/(k_i + k_r)$.

A detailed study of the acetolysis of optically active 2-octyl p-toluenesulfonate revealed that this secondary alkyl system leads to almost complete inversion of configuration (63). A substantial amount of product acetate is racemized, but most of this apparent racemization is actually racemization of the starting material by attack of the p-toluenesulfonic acid (or its anion) produced as the reaction proceeds. It was also found that 2-octyl p-nitrobenzenesulfonate, which solvolyzes faster than 2-octyl p-toluenesulfonate, simultaneously reacts with lithium p-toluenesulfonate to produce 2-octyl p-toluene-sulfonate with practically complete inversion of configuration. The results were explained by a 2-octyl carbonium ion–p-

toluenesulfonate ion pair, which could react with solvent or with added anion. From the fact that n-butyl and benzyl p-nitrobenzenesulfonates do not seem to react a great deal more rapidly with added lithium p-toluenesulfonate than 2-octyl p-nitrobenzenesulfonate, it was concluded that the exchange mechanism could not involve simple nucleophilic attack by salt on substrate, since the primary systems should be much more sensitive to nucleophilic attack than the secondary one. However, the primary systems do appear to be somewhat faster, so that nucleophilic attack is not ruled out.

There have been a few other investigations of solvolysis stereochemistry. The results range from almost complete inversion to almost complete racemization, depending on the substrate and solvent.* It is clear from the results for 2-octyl p-toluenesulfonate above (63) that some of these results may have indicated more racemization than actually occurred via solvolysis. But a few generalizations can be drawn, subject to more experiments (see Ref. (3), pages 59–60). Polar solvents tend to enhance racemization (*e.g.*, more in water than in methanol), presumably by stabilizing ionic intermediates, giving them more time to racemize. Substrates which could form very stable carbonium ions (*e.g.*, $(C_6H_5)_2CH$—Cl where the carbonium ion charge is predicted by the NBMO method to be only 0.4 on the central carbon atom, the rest being delocalized into the two phenyl rings) usually lead to considerable racemization. Solvents such as dioxane which could lead to intermediates of the type

$$RX + \bigcirc \rightarrow \left[\bigcirc^{+} \text{---}R\text{---}X \right]$$

---

* There are two very recent reports of solvolyses with partial *retention* of configuration (81b). These results, observed in optically active diarylmethyl and triarylmethyl systems, seem consistent only with *frontside* attack of solvent on either RX or an ion pair intermediate such as $[R^+\text{---}X^-]$ or $[S\text{---}R^+\text{---}X^-]$. It is possible that a solvent molecule ROH which solvates the X^- portion of the intermediate ion pair may be aided in forming a bond to the R^+ portion by simultaneous transfer of a proton to the X^-.

tend to lead to extra racemization (*e.g.*, in dioxane-water mixtures), because the intermediates containing dioxane could not lead to stable products and would eventually react with a water molecule.

INTERMEDIATE FORMATION

Knowing whether an intermediate forms is also necessary in order to understand solvolysis mechanisms. It is difficult to be sure whether an intermediate forms, in many cases. An intermediate is known to be formed in a number of reactions. But we have no way of showing experimentally that an intermediate does *not* form! The fact that no intermediate has been detected in a reaction does not necessarily mean that none is formed. Therefore, the experimental situation at present is that we have some reactions in which an intermediate is known to form, and others in which an intermediate is not known to form.

Trapping. A very useful way of detecting an intermediate is to trap it. Numerous examples of such trapping experiments exist, but we will discuss only three recent ones.

Sodium borohydride has been used as a trapping agent (64). The reaction of sodium borohydride ($Na^+BH_4^-$) with alkyl halides and sulfonates has typical SN2 characteristics, including Walden inversion at the reaction center, rate decreases in the order primary > secondary > tertiary alkyl, and predominant olefin formation from tertiary halides. The reaction of 0.25 M $(C_6H_5)_2CHCl$ and 1.80 M $NaBH_4$ in diglyme solution at 45° gave a 6% yield of $(C_6H_5)_2CH_2$ after 4 hr. However, in 20% water–80% diglyme (v/v) solution, the reaction rate was 60-fold faster. In 4 hr. at 45° a 72% yield of $(C_6H_5)_2CH_2$ was isolated. The rate constant (first-order) for solvolysis of the substrate in the aqueous solvent at 45° in the absence of $NaBH_4$ was 1.34×10^{-4} sec.$^{-1}$, while in the presence of $NaBH_4$ the rate constant (still first-order) was 2.1×10^{-4} sec.$^{-1}$. The slight increase in rate is presumably a salt effect caused by $NaBH_4$, and cannot explain the fact that the product is mostly the hydrocarbon $(C_6H_5)_2CH_2$ instead of the alcohol $(C_6H_5)_2CHOH$. The only reasonable explanation of the results is that an intermediate forms which can then react with either borohydride or water. Otherwise we would have to say that the rate of the reaction with water is slowed by a factor of 3 or 4 by the presence of $NaBH_4$. This is unreasonable because, if anything, added salt should speed up the reaction. Probably the intermediate is some type of solvated carbonium ion, but the fact that it was trapped only demonstrates its existence, not its structure.

In the solvolysis of optically active 2-octyl brosylate

in 75% dioxane–25% water (v/v) at 65°, the alcohol formed was found to be 77 per cent inverted and 23 per cent racemized (65). Upon addition of N_3^- ions, some of the product was R—N_3 (partially racemized), but the alcohol formed in competition with azide appeared to be 100 per cent inverted. The 2-octyl azide was found to be formed with net inversion; at high N_3^- concentrations it was largely inverted, while at lower N_3^- concentrations it was largely racemized. The *rates* were increased substantially by N_3^-, so this reaction does not involve entirely trapping of an intermediate by N_3^-. In pure methanol at 65°, the solvolysis product was 100 per cent inverted. In 25% dioxane–75% water (v/v) at 65°, 2-octyl mesylate (methanesulfonate) gave 2-octanol with 95 per cent inversion. Upon addition of 0.04 M N_3^- ions, 21.7 per cent of the product was 2-octyl azide formed with 83 per cent inversion. The remainder of the product was 2-octanol formed with 97 per cent inversion. The rate constant (measured at 38.6°) for the reaction was the same with 0.04 M N_3^- as in its absence, so this reaction is an example of trapping of an intermediate by N_3^-. In pure H_2O at 65°, 2-octyl mesylate gave

2-octanol with 100 per cent inversion.   Upon addition of 0.1 M N_3^- ions, 2-octyl azide was formed with 99 per cent inversion, and 2-octanol was formed with 98 per cent inversion.

These data form a consistent picture if it is assumed that 2-octyl brosylate and 2-octyl mesylate solvolyze by the same mechanisms.   The results in 75% dioxane are consistent with formation of an intermediate oxonium ion by nucleophilic attack of dioxane:

This intermediate could react with water to form alcohol of retained configuration (by double Walden inversion).   In the presence of N_3^- the oxonium ion could be completely trapped by N_3^- to form 2-octyl azide with retained configuration.   The alcohol could then be formed with 100 per cent inversion by nucleophilic attack of H_2O on the substrate, possibly through some ion-pair intermediate such as $[H_2O\text{---}R^+\text{---}X^-]$, as in Eq. (4–3).   In the absence of N_3^-, alcohol would be formed via attack on both oxonium ion and substrate, thus leading to partially racemized alcohol.   The formation of completely inverted product in the methanolysis of 2-octyl brosylate and in the hydrolysis of 2-octyl mesylate indicates that the race-mized alcohol formed in 75% dioxane is not formed through a carbonium ion or ion-pair intermediate; racemized alcohol should certainly form in the pure solvents then also.   There-fore the oxonium ion intermediate seems more reasonable. The trapping experiment in 25% dioxane shows that an *inter-mediate* which can react with N_3^- must be formed in this reaction, and that this intermediate must be optically active since it leads to largely *inverted* 2-octyl azide.   It is very prob-able that this intermediate is not the oxonium ion, since it should lead to 2-octyl azide of *retained* configuration.   Thus a second type of intermediate is implicated and this seems likely to be an ion pair, either $[R^+\text{---}X^-]$ or $[S\text{---}R^+\text{---}X^-]$.   It is not certain that this ion pair is involved in the reaction in 75% dioxane, but for simplicity it is reasonable to assume that the reaction in 75% dioxane involves the ion pair and the oxonium ion.

The acetolysis of optically active (deuterated) 1-butyl-1-d p-nitrobenzenesulfonate in 55% dibutyl ether–45% acetic acid (v/v) results (66) in 71% 1-butyl-1-d acetate with $97 \pm 6\%$ net inversion of configuration and 29% undeuterated butyl acetate. In addition to these acetolysis products (62 per cent of the total product), butyl acetate (38 per cent of the total product) is produced by a side reaction of dibutyl ether with the p-nitrobenzenesulfonic acid produced in the solvolysis. The excess undeuterated butyl acetate over that formed by the side reaction is presumably produced through a tributyl-oxonium ion intermediate formed by attack of solvent on the substrate:

$$CH_3CH_2CH_2CHD{-}OSO_2{-}\langle\bigcirc\rangle{-}NO_2 + (CH_3CH_2CH_2CH_2)_2O \rightarrow$$

$$CH_3CH_2CH_2CHD{-}\overset{+}{O}(CH_2CH_2CH_2CH_3)_2 + O_2N{-}\langle\bigcirc\rangle{-}SO_3{}^-$$

The fact that the deuterated butyl acetate formed was essentially completely inverted indicates that a further rapid equilibrium with excess butyl ether is set up so that the deuterated oxonium ion leads mainly to deuterated ether plus undeuterated acetate:

$$CH_3CH_2CH_2CHD\overset{+}{O}(CH_2CH_2CH_2CH_3)_2 \xrightleftharpoons{\quad(CH_3CH_2CH_2CH_2)_2O\quad}$$

$$(CH_3CH_2CH_2CH_2)_3\overset{+}{O} + CH_3CH_2CH_2CHDOCH_2CH_2CH_2CH_3$$

$$\downarrow\ CH_3CO_2H$$

$$CH_3CH_2CH_2CH_2O\overset{\|}{\underset{O}{C}}CH_3 + (CH_3CH_2CH_2CH_2)_2O$$

The idea that such intermediates as [S---R---X] and [S---R---S]$^+$ may exist points out a fundamental problem which needs solution: How could [S---R---X] react with solvent to form [S---R---S]$^+$? There cannot be an ordinary nucleophilic displacement by solvent. Two possible transition states are diagramed.   They have octahedral structures in analogy with the structures of certain complex inorganic ions:

However, their bonding is quite different because carbon has no low-lying d-orbitals to participate in bonding.   New experimental approaches are needed to find out whether such transition states exist in solution, and if so, to study their structure. The other possibility would be a stepwise reaction in which X^- dissociates from R before the second S molecule attacks.   The problem with such a process is that it is difficult to see why $[S\text{---}R]^+$ would not simply collapse simultaneously to a tetrahedral product without ever forming $[S\text{---}R\text{---}S]^+$.

External Return. We have already mentioned external return briefly. Its most common manifestation is in a common-ion effect. If a compound RX reacts to form an intermediate I plus X^-

$$RX \underset{k_{-1}}{\overset{k_1}{\rightleftarrows}} I + X^-$$
$$H_2O + I \overset{k_2}{\rightarrow} product(s)$$

we showed in Chapter 3 that the rate is given by

$$rate = \frac{k_1(RX)}{\dfrac{k_{-1}(X^-)}{k_2(H_2O)} + 1}$$

Therefore, if added X^- has an effect on the rate of reaction different from the effect of salts not containing X^-, we say that a mass law effect is probably operating to drive the initial reaction to the left, *i.e.*, to decrease the concentration of I. For easily ionizable substrates, the addition of a common-ion salt usually slows the reaction, while the addition of a non-common-ion salt usually speeds the reaction as expected for a simple ionic strength effect. The presence or absence of a common-ion effect depends on the mechanism in two ways. First, if the effect exists, it shows that an intermediate necessarily exists (really a special kind of trapping), which can react with either solvent or X^-. Second, the effect may exist in different magnitudes depending on the ratio $k_{-1}/k_2(H_2O)$. The larger the ratio, the more retarding effect is brought about by a given concentration of X^-. The value of the ratio may be determined experimentally, and is characteristic of the structure of the intermediate since it is really the ratio of the susceptibility of the intermediate to attack by X^- ions *vs.* solvent molecules. Thus by measuring the *extent* of trapping we may hope to gain information about the structure of the intermediate. If the ratio is 10 or more, it may be evaluated from kinetic studies using added X^-, but if it is less than about 10, it cannot be evaluated accurately from kinetics alone. For trityl chloride ($(C_6H_5)_3C$—Cl) the ratio is about 400 (67), while for benzhydryl chloride ($(C_6H_5)_2CHCl$) it is 11.5 (68), both in aqueous acetone. Compounds which form stable carbonium ions appear to have k_{-1} quite a bit larger than k_2 when X^- is chloride. This seems fairly reasonable, since Cl^- should be a somewhat better nucleophile than H_2O, and stable intermediates (solvated carbonium ions?) should show a preference for reacting with a better nucleophile.

A more subtle technique was used (69) to determine the amount of internal return for *tert*-butyl chloride solvolysis in methanol-water mixtures. The rate of trapping of intermediate by *radioactive* chloride ions was studied, unreacted alkyl chloride being recovered and analyzed for radioactivity.

This extremely sensitive tool demonstrated that *ca.* 10 per cent of the intermediate (carbonium ions?) was captured by 0.5 M Cl⁻ ions in 75:25 (v/v) methanol:water solvent at 35° with a 0.085 M initial concentration of *tert*-butyl chloride. This implies that chloride ions are only slightly more effective (when relative concentrations are taken into account) than solvent at reacting with the intermediate. It was also found that 0.5 M N₃⁻ traps *ca.* 13 per cent of the intermediate under the same conditions.

The different effects of various kinds of salts in such reactions are sometimes confusing. Basically, there is no clear-cut distinction between a common ion and other ions. If a good nucleophile such as N₃⁻ is added to a solution, it can trap an intermediate to form R—N₃, which compounds are usually stable and do not react further. If a poor nucleophile such as ClO₄⁻ is added, it probably cannot compete with the solvent for the intermediate because its rate of reaction is so slow. Even if it did compete successfully, the product R—ClO₄ would be so reactive that it would react immediately with solvent. Therefore such a salt would affect the rate only by a salt effect but could not produce any significant amount of trapped product such as R—ClO₄. A good nucleophile which is also a much better leaving group than that in the substrate, *e.g.*, I⁻ with RCl, could trap the intermediate to form RI but the trapped iodide would be so reactive that it would disappear much faster than the rate of the reaction of RCl. The difference between I⁻ and N₃⁻ is simply that RI would be quite unstable under solvolytic conditions and would not accumulate, while RN₃ would normally be stable under such conditions and would therefore accumulate in the reaction mixture at the expense of solvolysis products. Finally, if a common ion is added, such as Cl⁻ with RCl, the situation is intermediate between N₃⁻ and I⁻. The trapped product RCl happens to be identical with the substrate and is therefore neither much less reactive (as RN₃ is) nor much more reactive (as RI is). This is the only reason why the effect of a common ion may be thought of as unique. However, it is obvious that we might find a non-common ion which had the same reactivity as the common ion, and that its effect on the rate of solvolysis would be the same as the effect of a common ion. There are various intermediate cases and no distinct dividing line between common and non-common ion effects. If a common ion could react with [S---R---S]$^+$ or even [R—S]$^+$ to form R—X (*cf.* Eq. (4–3)), a common-ion effect would exist. A number of possible detailed mechanisms may therefore lead to a common-ion effect, so that we cannot necessarily (as has been frequently supposed) assume that a common-ion effect proves that R$^+$ + X$^-$ exist as free ions in solution, although this remains the most reasonable mechanism if we allow R$^+$ to be strongly solvated.

Since the values of k_{-1}/k_2 differ widely with the structure of RX, we might try to interpret them in terms of the possible intermediates formed. The usual interpretation is that a free carbonium ion forms in all these cases, and that large values of the ratio correspond to more stable carbonium ions, which can therefore be more selective in preferring attack by X$^-$ over attack by solvent. On the other hand, if nucleophilic assistance is present in the transition state, we would predict that it would be more important in the case of substrates which cannot form very stable carbonium ions, *i.e.*, more important for *tert*-butyl than for trityl. Then the difference between trityl and *tert*-butyl could be explained by assuming that the intermediate [S---R---X] (*cf.* Eq. (4–3)) were more stable for *tert*-butyl and therefore led much of the time directly to products, although in some cases it might be converted back to RX through [S---R---S]$^+$. In the former case, we assume *tert*-butyl to form a less stable intermediate and so be very unselective; in the latter case, we assume *tert*-butyl to form a more stable intermediate involving S, which prevents much competition by X$^-$. Thus the values of these ratios, although interesting, still cannot be interpreted as evidence about the structure of the intermediate. More information is needed.

Product Ratios. A third way of detecting intermediates is to determine product ratios in competing reactions. If one gets the *same* mixture of products with *different* leaving groups, it is assumed that the step in which the leaving group is lost, usually the rate-determining step, is different from the product-forming step, such a mechanism of necessity involving an intermediate between the rate-determining and product-determining transition states.

It was shown that when the two compounds $(C_6H_5)_2CH$—Cl and $(C_6H_5)_2CH$—Br solvolyze in 90% aqueous acetone (v/v) at 50° in the presence of 0.10 M NaN_3, the bromide reacts 33 times faster than the chloride. But very nearly 66% $(C_6H_5)_2CHOH$ and 34% $(C_6H_5)_2CHN_3$ are formed from both the chloride and the bromide (70). It was concluded that the same intermediate forms in each case and this common intermediate leads to the same product ratios. This seems very reasonable, since coincidence is unlikely. However, it is still entirely possible that the intermediate [S---R---X] forms first but does not react to product before it exchanges with solvent to form $[S---R---S]^+ + X^-$.

Another example is in a solvolysis reaction which leads partially to olefins (71). The following results were obtained in solvolysis in 80% aqueous ethanol (v/v) for reactions which gave both elimination and substitution:

$$(CH_3)_3C\text{---}Cl \xrightarrow{65.3°} 36\% \text{ elimination}$$
$$(CH_3)_3C\text{---}S^+(CH_3)_2 \xrightarrow{65.3°} 36\% \text{ elimination}$$
$$CH_3CH_2C(CH_3)_2\text{---}Cl \xrightarrow{50°} 40\% \text{ elimination}$$
$$CH_3CH_2C(CH_3)_2\text{---}S^+(CH_3)_2 \xrightarrow{50°} 48\% \text{ elimination}$$

The similar amounts of elimination from both R—Cl and R—$S^+(CH_3)_2$ imply that the product-determining transition state should not involve the leaving group. The difference between 40 and 48 per cent may be ascribed to a small part of the elimination's occurring from [S---R---X] in one or both cases, the major amount still occurring from an intermediate like [S---R---S]⁺.

In less ionizing solvents, product ratios for such eliminations are dependent on the leaving group (72):

$$(CH_3)_3C—Cl \xrightarrow[C_2H_5OH]{75°} 44\% \text{ elimination}$$

$$(CH_3)_3C—S^+(CH_3)_2 \xrightarrow[C_2H_5OH]{75°} 18\% \text{ elimination}$$

$$(CH_3)_3C—Cl \xrightarrow[CH_3CO_2H]{75°} 73\% \text{ elimination}$$

$$(CH_3)_3C—S^+(CH_3)_2 \xrightarrow[CH_3CO_2H]{75°} 12\% \text{ elimination}$$

These facts were interpreted to mean (72) that ion pairs are formed and that elimination occurs from the ion pair rather than from a free carbonium ion. These ion pairs could exist as [R---X] or [S---R---X]. Possibly the anion Cl⁻ removes the proton in the case of the chloride; this would explain the large change with leaving group (72).

Such product-ratio experiments do not prove that an intermediate exists, but they do tell something about the likely structure of the intermediate *if* it exists.

It still seems possible to rationalize solvolysis mechanisms on the basis of Eq. (4–3). A combination of evidence may allow us to categorize some mechanisms even further. For example, we have the evidence for nucleophilic assistance in the solvolysis of *tert*-butyl chloride (58), plus the stereochemical evidence in an analogous tertiary system (62), plus the internal-return experiments with radioactive Cl⁻ (69), plus the experiments on per cent elimination (71).

ELECTROPHILIC PARTICIPATION

In a solvolysis reaction in which nucleophilic assistance is not of overriding importance, some other factors must operate to make the reaction energetically feasible. Logically, one might suppose that the solvent could exert a solvation effect on the leaving group which would help to break the RX bond, *i.e.*, "pull" the leaving group away. Some evidence for such an effect is found in the ethanolysis of $(C_6H_5)_2CH$—Cl (73). The rate is independent of added base $(C_2H_5O^-)$. Addition of small amounts of H_2O (0–2 M) increases the rate considerably, yet the *product* is still mainly $(C_6H_5)_2CH$—OC_2H_5. The results are presented in Table 4–4. The discrepancy between

TABLE 4–4

Reaction of Benzhydryl Chloride ($(C_6H_5)_2CH$—Cl) with Ethanol in the Presence of Small Amounts of Water

| (H_2O), M | $k \times 10^5$, sec.$^{-1}$ | Mole % Benzhydrol | |
		Found	Calculated
0.0	5.72	—	0
0.600	7.90	1.8	27.7
1.320	10.57	11.8	46.0

amounts of alcohol formed and amounts calculated on the basis of the rate increase is large. The effect of water on the rate is too large to be attributed to a simple medium effect on addition of such small amounts of water. In fact nitrobenzene produces an opposite rate effect, yet both nitrobenzene and water increase the dielectric constant of the medium. Therefore water appears to exert a specific effect on the rate, probably a hydrogen-bonding effect on the leaving chloride ion, water being more effective than ethanol at "pulling" the leaving group away.

The study of the reactions of trityl chloride $(C_6H_5)_3C$—Cl under various conditions led to the idea that both a "push" (nucleophilic assistance) and a "pull" (electrophilic assistance) are necessary in any nucleophilic displacement reaction (9). A series of kinetic studies was presented to show that kinetic order cannot really determine the mechanism of a reaction (74):

$$(C_6H_5)_3C—Cl + H_2O \xrightarrow[\text{1st order}]{H_2O} \left[H_2O\text{---}\overset{\displaystyle |}{C}\text{---}Cl\text{---}H_2O \right]^{\ddagger}$$

$$C_6H_5CH_2—Cl + Hg(NO_3)_2 \xrightarrow[\text{2nd order}]{H_2O} \left[H_2O\text{---}\overset{\displaystyle |}{C}\text{---}Cl\text{---}\overset{\displaystyle |}{Hg} \right]^{\ddagger}$$

$$(C_6H_5)_3C—Cl + CH_3OH + C_6H_5OH \xrightarrow[\text{3rd order}]{C_6H_6}$$

$$\left[\overset{\displaystyle CH_3}{\underset{\displaystyle H}{\diagdown}} O\text{---}\overset{\displaystyle |}{C}\text{---}Cl\text{---}HOC_6H_5 \right]^{\ddagger}$$

$$CH_3Br + H_2O \xrightarrow[\text{1st order}]{H_2O} \left[H_2O\text{---}\overset{\displaystyle |}{C}\text{---}Br\text{---}H_2O \right]^{\ddagger}$$

$$CH_3Br + \underset{}{\text{⬡N}} \xrightarrow[\text{2nd order}]{C_6H_6} \left[\text{⬡N}\text{---}\overset{\displaystyle |}{C}\text{---}Br\text{---}HC_6H_5 \right]^{\ddagger}$$

$$CH_3Br + \underset{}{\text{⬡N}} + HgBr_2 \xrightarrow[\text{3rd order}]{C_6H_6} \left[\text{⬡N}\text{---}\overset{\displaystyle |}{C}\text{---}Br\text{---}Hg \diagup \right]^{\ddagger}$$

The kinetic results can be interpreted with the hypothetical transition states shown, each utilizing both nucleophilic and electrophilic assistance from either solvent or added reagents. Mercuric (and silver) ions are well-known electrophilic reagents.

The study of ionic reactions in benzene solution is exceedingly complex and pertains only indirectly to solvolysis reactions. However, there are some interesting results for methanolysis of $(C_6H_5)_3C—Cl$ in benzene solution (75). Using tritium-labeled (radioactive) methanol, the rate of reaction was found to be first-order in methanol, even at methanol concentrations of 10^{-6} M. At higher methanol concentrations the rate became second-order in methanol (always first-order in trityl chloride).

In some cases it is thought that reactions of trityl compounds with hydroxylic reagents actually proceed by prior equilibrium formation of an *ion pair* R^+X^- followed by nucleophilic attack on the ion pair.   It is difficult to establish such a mechanism in the case of solvolysis, because other mechanisms are very similar.

Another entirely different piece of evidence for the necessity of more than one solvent molecule in a solvolysis reaction exists, the fact that many esters can be readily steam-distilled without hydrolysis (76).   In hot water *solution* many esters are rapidly hydrolyzed.   The association of one (or a few?) water molecules with the compound in the vapor phase apparently cannot lead to hydrolysis at temperatures where hydrolysis occurs easily in solution with many water molecules available.

ION PAIRS

If *external return* (the common-ion effect) exists, why not *internal return* as well?   As a matter of fact, internal return does exist.   For example, solvolysis of α,α-dimethylallyl chloride in acetic acid gives, in addition to solvolysis products, a rearranged chloride (77):

$$CH_2{=}CH-\underset{\underset{CH_3}{|}}{\overset{\overset{CH_3}{|}}{C}}-Cl \rightarrow Cl-CH_2-CH{=}C\overset{CH_3}{\underset{CH_3}{\diagup}}$$

There is no common-ion effect, so the rearrangement cannot be a result of formation of a free carbonium ion which can react with chloride ion at either of two carbon atoms to form the two alkyl chlorides:

$$CH_2{=\!=}CH{=\!=}C\overset{CH_3}{\underset{CH_3}{\diagup}}$$
$$Cl^-$$

The cause must be either an intermediate *ion pair* (R^+Cl^-) which can rearrange internally, *i.e.*, by internal return, or a concerted rearrangement, chloride leaving one carbon atom as it forms a bond to the other. The rate of internal return is speeded up by increasing ionizing power of the medium, so the transition state must be quite polar. Therefore the hypothesis of an ion pair intermediate seems more reasonable.

A review on ion pair return has been published and can be consulted for more examples (78). Some of the studies have been very complex, involving measurement of rates of racemization, rates of product formation, and the effect of added salts on each of these rates separately. The results have been interpreted by a mechanism which involves two kinds of ion pairs (79) in addition to free ions:

$$\text{RX} \rightleftarrows [\text{R}^+\text{X}^-] \rightleftarrows [\text{R}^+\| \text{X}^-] \xrightarrow{\text{S(solvent)}} \text{RS}$$
$$\mathbf{1} \qquad \mathbf{2} \quad \Big\downarrow \text{Z}^-$$
$$\text{RZ}$$

Species **1** was called an *intimate ion pair*, and species **2** was called a *solvent-separated ion pair*. These two species would explain why racemization is faster than solvolysis.

It has been pointed out (80a) that instead of **1** and **2**, two ion pairs of the same type, namely $[\text{R}^+\text{X}^-]$ and $[\text{R}^+\text{Z}^-]$, would explain the results without the necessity of two types of ion pairs. Evidence was presented that only one type of ion pair is necessary to explain the oxygen isotopic equilibration of trityl benzoate-carbonyl-O^{18} (RX) in dry acetone at 60°:

$$(C_6H_5)_3C—OCC_6H_5 \rightleftarrows (C_6H_5)_3C—O^{18}CC_6H_5$$
$$\overset{\|}{O^{18}} \qquad\qquad\qquad \overset{\|}{O}$$

The equilibration has a rate constant of 3.8×10^{-6} sec.$^{-1}$. With 0.020 M RX and 0.006 M LiN$_3$, the initial rate of equilibration is zero (after RN$_3$ + C$_6$H$_5$CO$_2^-$ start forming, the rate of equilibration is greater than zero, presumably on account of reaction of C$_6$H$_5$CO$_2^-$ (X$^-$) with RX). The rate constant for reaction of azide ion is 4.4×10^{-6} sec.$^{-1}$, little different from that in the absence of azide. The product is RN_3. Since the *rate* is not appreciably affected by azide, N_3^- cannot be attacking RX, but must be trapping an intermediate formed in the equilibration reaction. Since the rate of equilibration is zero with azide, the intermediate captured by it is logically the same one which would have otherwise led to equilibration of O^{18}. The intermediate is probably an ordinary ion pair $[R^+X^-]$, within which equilibration of O^{18} easily occurs in X^-. In the absence of N_3^-, the ion pair will recombine to form RX, with oxygen equilibration. In the presence of N_3^-, RN_3 is presumably formed from every ion pair, so that none can recombine to RX. These results should be compared with the analogous reactions of trityl 2-methylbenzenesulfinate (80b).

We must await more evidence to see whether two *types* of ion pairs are really required in any mechanism. Much work on this problem remains to be done.

Another recent O^{18} "scrambling" experiment is of especial interest (81). In the solvolysis of benzhydryl and of *tert*-butyl *p*-nitrobenzoates in 90% and 80% aqueous acetone respectively,

$$(C_6H_5)_2CH\!-\!O\!\!\underset{\underset{O^{18}}{\|}}{C}C_6H_4NO_2\text{-}p$$

$$(CH_3)_3C\!-\!O\!\!\underset{\underset{O^{18}}{\|}}{C}C_6H_4NO_2\text{-}p$$

it was found that O^{18} scrambling is just about 3 times as fast as solvolysis with the former substrate, but that no O^{18} scrambling occurs with the latter. An intermediate ion pair would account for the results with the benzhydryl compound, but if an analogous intermediate forms with the *tert*-butyl compound, either it must be incapable of returning to reactant (internal return) or it must have a structure in which the two ester oxygen atoms are not equivalent. Since *p*-nitrobenzoate is not a particularly good leaving group, it is possible that this *tert*-butyl derivative requires considerable nucleophilic assistance at the transition state, thus making internal return difficult.

NEIGHBORING GROUPS

The problem of solvolysis mechanisms is complicated enough when we restrict ourselves to molecules containing only one functional group (the leaving group). But if we add another functional group near the reaction site, things can be considerably more complicated! When a nucleophilic group is placed on a carbon atom adjacent to that holding the leaving group, *neighboring-group participation* may occur. One such example is the formation of α-hydroxypropionate ion from α-bromopropionate ion. In acid solution optically active α-bromopropionic acid gives the inverted hydroxy acid:

$$\underset{\overset{|}{Br}}{CH_3CHCO_2H} \rightarrow \underset{\overset{|}{OH}}{CH_3CHCO_2H}$$

In basic solution, a second-order reaction of the α-bromopropionate anion with hydroxide ion gives inverted hydroxy-acid anion. But in dilute base, the α-bromopropionate anion undergoes a first-order reaction to give the α-hydroxypropionate anion of *retained* configuration! A mass-law (common-ion) effect exists in this latter reaction, in that the reaction is speeded by non-reactive salts, but slowed by bromide ions (82). The common-ion effect indicates that an intermediate must exist which retains optical activity in such a way as to lead to net retention on attack by water. Since we know that nucleophilic reactions usually proceed by inversion, we might look for a double inversion which would give the same product as retention or double retention. Since the retention occurs with the anion, but not with the acid, it seems likely that the CO_2^- group is involved. An intermediate α-lactone seems to explain the results and seems possible since β-lactones have actually been isolated but are very reactive:

$$CH_3CHCO_2^- \xrightleftharpoons[\text{inversion}]{} CH_3CH\underset{}{\overset{O}{\diagup\diagdown}}C{=}O + Br^-$$

$$\Big\downarrow H_2O, \text{inversion}$$

$$\underset{CH_3\overset{|}{C}HCO_2^-}{\overset{OH}{|}}$$

with Br below the first structure.

Nucleophilic attack with inversion by O^-, displacing Br^-, gives the α-lactone. Nucleophilic attack by water on the α-carbon atom of the lactone, with inversion, gives the α-hydroxypropionate anion with net retention.

Other groups such as sulfide, bromine, oxide, and acetoxy can also give neighboring group participation:

$$R{-}\underset{\underset{\overset{|}{O}{-}CCH_3}{\overset{|}{O}}}{CH}{-}\overset{\overset{X}{|}}{C}HR' \rightarrow X^- + R{-}CH\underset{\underset{CH_3}{\overset{+}{C}}}{\overset{\diagup\diagdown}{O \,\,\, O}}CHR' \xrightarrow{\text{fast}}$$

$$RS{-}CH_2CH_2Cl \rightarrow Cl^- + CH_2\underset{\underset{R}{\overset{|}{S^+}}}{\overset{\diagup\diagdown}{}}CH_2 \xrightarrow{\text{fast}}$$

$$R\underset{\overset{|}{Br}}{CH}{-}\overset{\overset{X}{|}}{C}HR' \rightarrow X^- + RCH\underset{\underset{+}{\overset{|}{Br}}}{\overset{\diagup\diagdown}{}}CHR' \xrightarrow{\text{fast}}$$

$$R\underset{\overset{|}{O}{-}CH_3}{CH}{-}\overset{\overset{X}{|}}{C}HR' \rightarrow X^- + RCH\underset{\underset{CH_3}{\overset{|}{O^+}}}{\overset{\diagup\diagdown}{}}CHR' \xrightarrow{\text{fast}}$$

These intermediates are thought to exist, mainly because of rate enhancement (*cf.* Chapter 5) and stereochemical results. There is no rigorous proof for some of them, especially for the "bromonium ion" type.

Hydrocarbon groupings can also exhibit neighboring group effects. One of the most prominent of such groups is the phenyl group, which is thought to give "phenonium ion" intermediates:

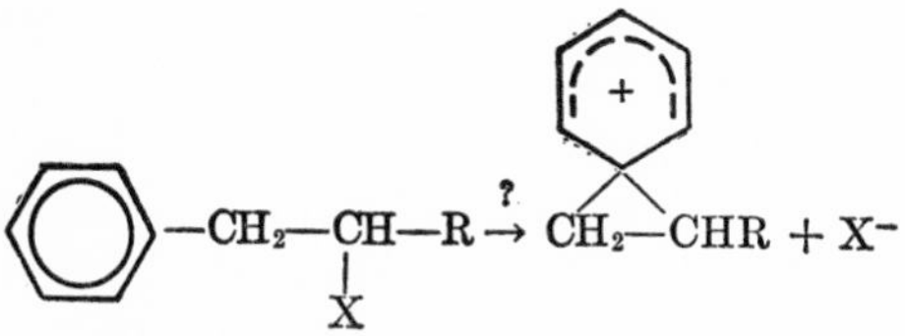

It seems as if every solvolysis reaction with a phenyl group on the β-carbon atom has been said to involve participation. In my opinion, such participation has been really proved in few, if any, cases. One of the most convincing (and earliest) investigations is the solvolysis of optically active 1-phenyl-2-tosyloxypropane (83)

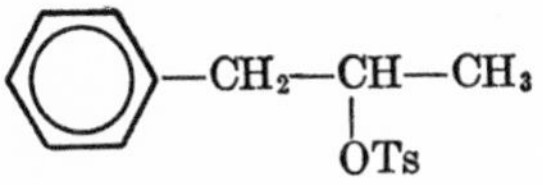

in three solvents. The product is essentially entirely unrearranged. The amounts of inversion and retention of the products are listed in Table 4–5. The results can be nicely explained by a competition between nucleophilic attack by

TABLE 4–5

Stereochemistry of Solvolysis of 1-Phenyl-2-tosyloxypropane

Solvent	Product	Inversion	Retention
C_2H_5OH	$C_6H_5CH_2CHCH_3$ $\mid$ OC_2H_5	93%	7%
CH_3CO_2H	$C_6H_5CH_2CHCH_3$ $\mid$ $OCOCH_3$	65%	35%
HCO_2H	$C_6H_5CH_2CHCH_3$ $\mid$ $OCHO$	15%	85%

solvent (giving inversion), and neighboring-group participation by phenyl (with inversion) followed by attack by solvent (with inversion again, giving net retention). Ethanol should be most nucleophilic and therefore should lead to most inversion by the assumed mechanism. The results could be easily explained by non-bridged ion pair intermediates (Eq. (4–3)) if it were not for the result in formic acid; schemes like Eq. (4–3) cannot explain net retention, but only net inversion or complete racemization. In order to explain the results without phenyl participation, we should have to invoke some kind of steric shielding of the carbonium ion intermediate such that solvent prefers to attack the side leading to retention. It would be conceivable that the phenyl group, rather than forming any real bond, merely prevents backside solvent attack, and that the carbonium ion is so reactive that it reacts with formic acid to give retention in most cases before it can get into conformational equilibrium by rotation about the C_1—C_2 bond. We cannot be sure whether *intermediates* which involve neighboring groups' bonding to carbon exist or not, although we do know that *transition states* involving such bonding do exist, because in some cases rearrangement of the phenyl group from one carbon to another occurs (84).

NON-CLASSICAL IONS

Although a controversy is raging about whether "non-classical" carbonium ions exist, indeed about what a "non-classical" carbonium ion *is*, we should discuss the question briefly. Those charged intermediates involving neighboring group participation are the type of ions usually considered to be non-classical. A number of such possibilities were listed in the preceding section, *e.g.*, the bromonium ion and the phenonium ion. Generally an ion is thought to be non-classical if its bonding does not correspond to structural types which have been isolated. Thus the cyclic, 3-membered ring sulfonium and oxonium ion intermediates mentioned in the preceding paragraph are *classical* because stable sulfonium and oxonium ions are known. A simple bromonium ion has never been isolated but nevertheless seems quite classical by analogy with the sulfonium and oxonium ions. Stable bromonium ions with bromine bonded to two aryl groups are known (85). A phenonium ion is somewhat of a borderline case because the following reaction allows the isolation of an uncharged species with a structure very similar to that proposed for a phenonium ion (86):

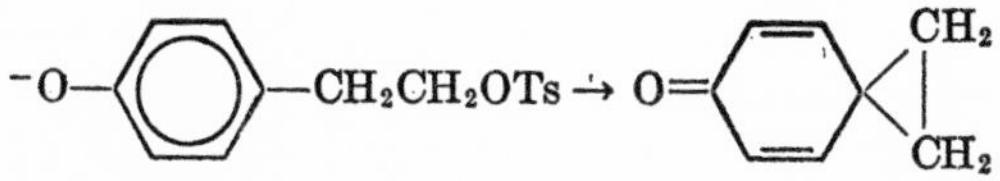

However, in the absence of O^-, we do not know for sure whether the symmetrical 3-membered ring has more or less energy than the "classical" carbonium ion.

Another type of ion which is thought to exist in some systems is of the type called *homoallylic*, corresponding to the following reaction:

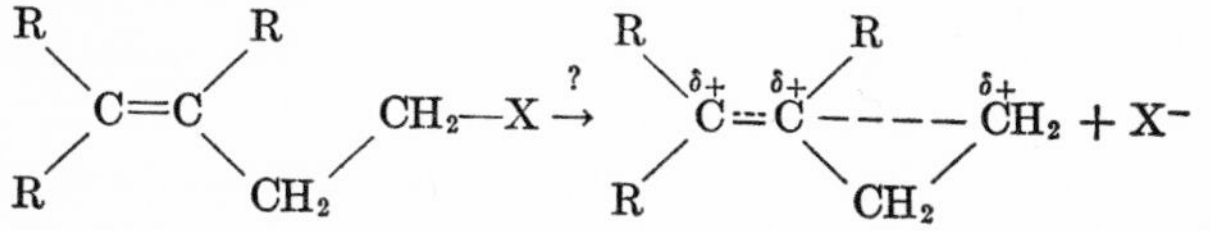

The name arises because it is a homolog of allyl$^+$, a CH_2 group being interposed between two of the carbon atoms which are supposedly conjugated. In the absence of the neighboring vinyl group, this ion would be a primary carbonium ion and should be very unstable. If, however, the charge could be delocalized through overlap of the vacant p-orbital of the CH_2 group with the p-orbitals of the vinyl group, the resulting ion should be stabilized considerably, although probably less so than the allyl$^+$ ion. MO calculations (*e.g.*, see Ref. (29)) indicate that overlap should occur, resulting in a considerable DE_π. In my opinion, such an ion should not be considered to be non-classical. Anyone would agree that such a structure would have some delocalization if it existed. The only question is how much delocalization. It is significant that the best evidence for such delocalization comes from rigid ring systems where the double bond and the carbonium ion carbon are held in positions which are geometrically favorable for maximum overlap.   For example, solvolysis of *anti*-7-norbornenyl *p*-toluenesulfonate (**1**) has been carefully examined (87).

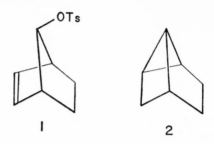

Trapping experiments with sodium borohydride in aqueous diglyme solution (*cf.* page 112) show that an intermediate is present which reacts with high concentrations of BH_4^- to form largely tricyclic hydrocarbon **2**.   In the absence of borohydride, the product is the *anti*-7 alcohol (unrearranged). The two groups of investigators (87) differ in their interpretation of the results, but since the reaction seems to be greatly accelerated by the presence of the double bond (*ca.* 10^{11} times), this may possibly be a case of homoallylic-type participation, or if the ion is symmetrical, "bishomocyclopropenyl" participation (87b).

A third type of ion which really seems to have no classical analogy, at least in organic systems, is a structure with a bridged alkyl group, a type which has been invoked to explain some kinds of rearrangement.   For example, we might have a structure with a bridged methyl group:

$$
\begin{array}{c}
CH_3 \qquad R \quad R \qquad \overset{CH_3}{\underset{+}{\diagup \diagdown}} \quad R \\
R-C-C-X \rightarrow^{?} \quad C === C \quad + X^- \\
R \qquad R \quad R \qquad R
\end{array}
$$

This is the only kind of ion for which I think the term *non-*

classical is justified.   It involves, really, a carbon atom with 5 σ bonds (the CH_3 carbon atom), a stable organic analog of which has never been isolated.   The dimer of trimethylaluminum is known to have a bridged structure involving two stable pentavalent carbon atoms:

$$
\begin{array}{ccccc}
CH_3 & & CH_3 & & CH_3 \\
\diagdown & \diagup & & \diagdown & \diagup \\
& Al & & Al & \\
\diagup & & \diagdown & \diagup & \diagdown \\
CH_3 & & CH_3 & & CH_3
\end{array}
$$

However, the dimer is stable only in the gas phase or in inert solvents; in diethyl ether only the monomeric etherate $(CH_3)_3Al$—$O(C_2H_5)_2$ is present.   In such bridged structures, one (sp^3 ?) carbon orbital is participating in two bonds.   A bromonium ion, for example, is quite different because bromine has unshared electron pairs, *i.e.*, non-bonding orbitals, which should be reasonably available for bonding.   Bromonium ions therefore would have two bromine orbitals participating in two bonds (one in each) and are therefore quite classical (although quite unstable, apparently).

The real question is to try to decide experimentally whether such structures correspond to intermediates or transition states:

$$
\underset{1}{R_2\overset{\displaystyle \overset{CH_3}{|}}{C}-CR_2-X} \xrightarrow{-X^-} \underset{1}{R_2\overset{\displaystyle \overset{CH_3}{|}}{C}-\overset{+}{C}R_2} \rightarrow \underset{2}{R_2C \overset{CH_3}{=\!\!\overset{+}{=\!\!=}} CR_2}
$$

$$\downarrow$$

$$\text{product(s)} \leftarrow \underset{3}{R_2\overset{+}{C}-\overset{\displaystyle \overset{CH_3}{|}}{C}R_2}$$

or

$$
\underset{1}{R_2\overset{\displaystyle \overset{CH_3}{|}}{C}-CR_2-X} \xrightarrow{-X^-} \underset{1}{R_2\overset{\displaystyle \overset{CH_3}{|}}{C}-\overset{+}{C}R_2} \rightarrow \left[\underset{4}{R_2C \overset{CH_3}{=\!\!\overset{+}{=\!\!=}} CR_2} \right]^{\ddagger}
$$

$$\downarrow$$

$$\text{product(s)} \leftarrow \underset{3}{R_2\overset{+}{C}-\overset{\displaystyle \overset{CH_3}{|}}{C}R_2} \qquad (4\text{-}4)$$

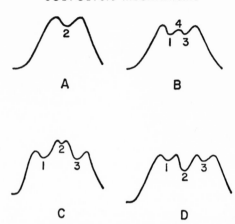

Fig. 7.   Free energy diagrams for possible mechanisms involving alkyl group participation.   Numbers correspond to structures in Eq. (4–4).

In Fig. 7 are pictured some possible free energy diagrams corresponding to the structural changes in Eq. (4–4).   In situations (A) and (D) the non-classical ion is definitely an important intermediate.   In situation (B) the non-classical structure is not an intermediate but merely a transition state connecting the two classical structures.   Part (C) is a borderline case in which the non-classical ion is an intermediate, but of higher energy than the classical structures.   We do not know which type should in principle be most favorable because the increased delocalization in 2 should stabilize it, while the angle strain of forming the 3-membered ring should destabilize it.

The decision between these extremes is difficult indeed, and most (if not all) results can be reasonably explained on the basis of carbonium ions which do not involve such non-classical bridging.

The ideas that rapidly equilibrating classical carbonium ions can explain the stereochemistry and isotopic labeling experiments and that steric hindrance in the reactants may have the effect of rate acceleration have been discussed (Ref.

(22), page 140). Attention was called to the fact that, since alternative interpretations do exist, experiments which seem to call for non-classical ions should be carefully scrutinized. The stereochemistry of solvolysis of 3-phenyl-2-butyl tosylate in acetic acid at 49.6° seems to imply backside participation by the phenyl group, yet the rate constant, 2.38×10^{-6} sec.$^{-1}$, is less than that for the same compound without the phenyl group (2-butyl tosylate), 4.3×10^{-6} sec.$^{-1}$. The phenyl group could be participating after the transition state, however.

In an interesting review article (88) on carbonium ion structure, much pertinent data has been summarized. The authors also point out the interesting analogy between boron compounds (BR_3) and ions (CR_3^+), in that boron has a vacant p-orbital (see also Ref. (22), page 159).

One of the reactions which may involve alkyl-bridged ions is the solvolysis of cyclopropylcarbinyl derivatives, *e.g.*,

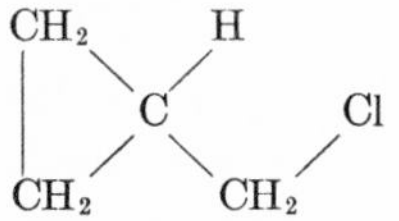

The products of hydrolysis include the following (89):

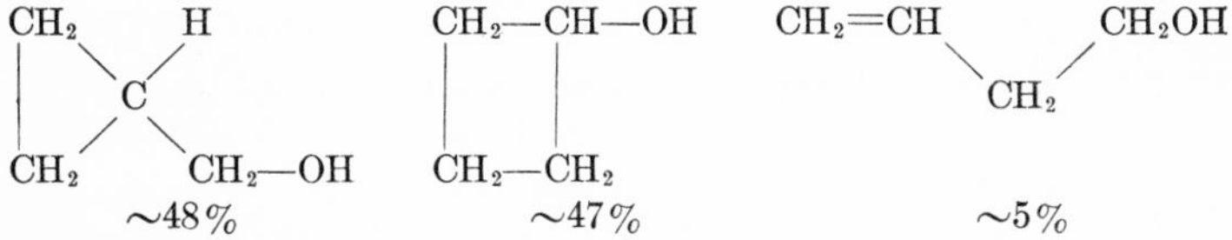

The same product mixture is formed in very nearly the same proportions from cyclobutyl chloride. There is rearrangement of isotopic labels during the course of hydrolysis:

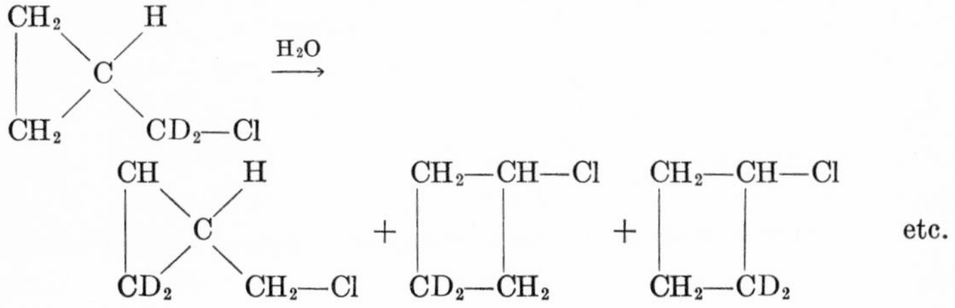

The product and isotopic scrambling studies, together with the fact that the rate of reaction of these chlorides is greater than can be easily explained on the basis of analogies with ethyl chloride, cyclopentyl chloride, etc., led to the formulation of a "bicyclobutonium" structure for the carbonium ion intermediates which probably occur in the reaction:

$$\text{[structure diagram]}$$

Possible atomic orbital diagrams of the non-classical bonding of the proposed intermediate and the completely symmetrical transition state are in Fig. 8.   The results can be explained on

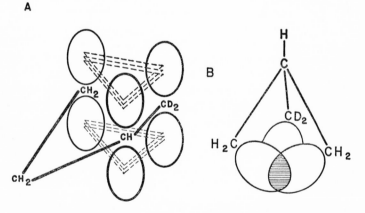

Fig. 8.   Possible atomic orbital diagrams of (A) bicyclobutonium ion and (B) tricyclobutonium transition state.

the basis of many rapidly equilibrating classical carbonium ions, but it should be possible to prove experimentally which scheme is correct.

Alkyl-bridged structures are also thought to be responsible for the stereochemistry and other properties of reactions such as the acetolysis of *exo*-norbornyl brosylate (*p*-bromobenzene-sulfonate) (90):

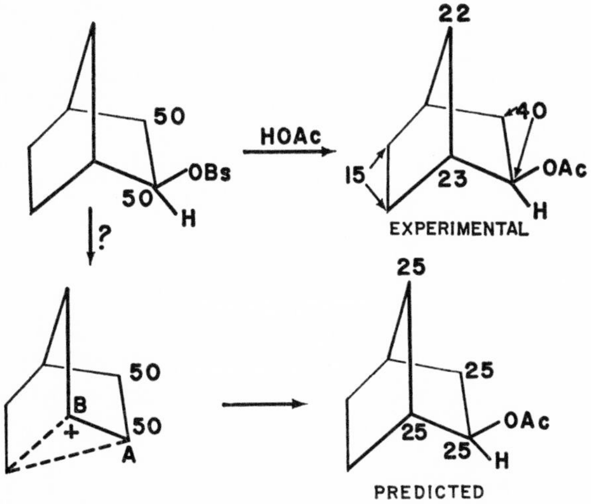

The numbers at various carbon atoms are percentages of the C^{14} radioactive isotope label which are at these positions.* If the non-classical ion were formed as pictured, attack by acetic acid would occur equally at positions A and B, leading to the same product in either case, and the label would be equally distributed at four carbon atoms in the product. The experimental results show somewhat more scrambling than predicted and must result from some hydride shift in the intermediate.

---

* Although the drawing shows only one optical isomer in each step, the experiment was done with racemic starting material, so that each of the four formulas in the drawing should be thought of as a racemic mixture of the formula pictured and its mirror image.

However, some recent work (91a) with the systems (where An = $-C_6H_4OCH_3\text{-}p$):

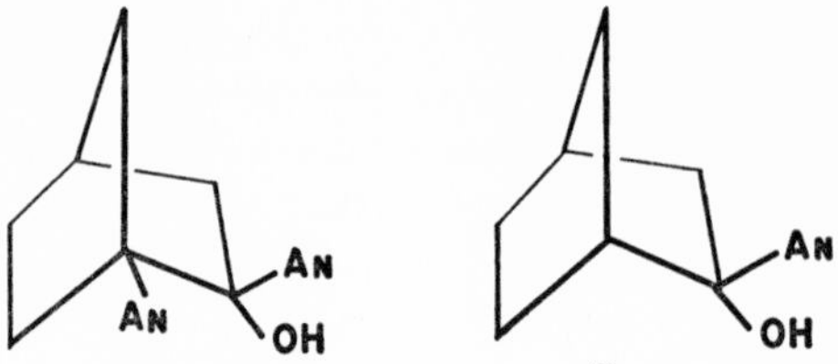

shows that these alcohols, when dissolved in sulfuric acid, produce carbonium ions which probably *do not* involve alkyl-bridging. The carbonium ions from **1** and **2** have similar ultraviolet spectra, which would not be expected from a non-classical ion where charge delocalization into two *p*-anisyl groups at once should give a different spectrum than in the case where only one *p*-anisyl group is present. The di-anisyl cation is less stable than the mono-anisyl, the opposite being expected for a non-classical structure for these ions. The n.m.r. spectrum of solutions of the di-anisyl cation should be symmetrical for the non-classical structure. It would also be symmetrical for rapidly equilibrating classical structures, but cooling should, and in fact does, change the n.m.r. spectrum, thus indicating rapidly equilibrating ions. The non-classical ion should have positive charge delocalized into both anisyl rings, thus making sulfonation and bromination slow. In fact, the mono-anisyl cation substitutes slowly while the di-anisyl cation substitutes rapidly, indicating a classical structure for the di-anisyl ion, in which *one* anisyl group has no positive charge delocalized within it and thus is very reactive.

On the other hand, an analysis of the rates of solvolysis of 2-norbornyl tosylates led to the conclusion that alkyl-bridging must be important in the transition state for the *exo*-isomer

(91b). It was concluded that the intermediate carbonium ion must be alkyl-bridged, but this does not rigorously follow even if the transition state is alkyl-bridged.

Since camphene hydrochloride (**1**) undergoes ethanolysis 13,600 times faster at 25° than *tert*-butyl chloride (92), a non-

classical bicyclic ion might be involved. However, the ethanolysis of the non-bicyclic compound **2** is only 5.7 times slower than **1**, and it was thus concluded that the rapid rate for **1** is not necessarily evidence for a non-classical ion intermediate (92). Since the product from **2** is unrearranged alcohol, its fast rate cannot be explained by neighboring group participation of a methyl group. The fast rate could conceivably be explained by assuming that **2** also forms a non-classical ion (with a bridged methyl group) which, however, reacts with water at only one position to form unrearranged product. It could also be explained by increased steric (B-) strain in both **1** and **2** (92).

It appears, then, that the case for alkyl-bridging, while providing a simple interpretation of many experimental results, is not really unambiguously proved in any reaction, although this situation is subject to rapid change.

I believe that the delocalization energies in ions such as the bridged-alkyl or homoallylic would probably be very small, but differences of the order of only 2–3 kcal./mole could easily alter the course of reaction.

CONCLUSION

Many complexities still exist in the interpretation of solvolysis mechanisms. It will take all the ingenuity the chemist can bring to bear to understand even one such mechanism. But that goal is rapidly being approached. The major unsolved problems, in the opinion of the author, are (1) the question of whether or how much nucleophilic assistance is required in the transition state and (2) the question of how (or whether!) an intermediate such as [S---R---X] may be transformed into a symmetrically solvated carbonium ion [S---R---S]$^+$. The understanding of mechanisms more complex than the simple displacements will require much more information about the role of neighboring groups, non-classical ions, and perhaps many other mechanistic influences which are now no more than a gleam in their discoverers' eyes!

REFERENCES

Here again, much of the pertinent material is covered in Refs. (1), (2), and (3). In addition, some interesting discussion of steric effects and related topics is in Newman's book (40, 84). The paper by Doering and Zeiss (62) and related discussion in (3) are of special interest with regard to some of the major problems of solvolysis mechanisms. Hammett's book (73) is the most critical discussion up to 1940 of solvolysis mechanisms in general; much of the book is timely and interesting in spite of its age. Papers by Brown and by Maccoll (22) are also recommended. A recent monograph, C. A. Bunton, *Nucleophilic Substitution at a Saturated Carbon Atom* (Elsevier Publishing Co., Amsterdam, 1963), presents an interesting discussion of topics in this chapter.

5

Reaction Rates

Although it is difficult to interpret rate data in a unique way in terms of molecular properties unless the differences are very large, much of the literature on solvolysis reactions is concerned with rates, rate correlations, and the effects of temperature on rates. It is amazing that semiquantitative correlations of rates (*e.g.*, where the rates of one series of reactions parallel those of another, similar series) are as successful as they are.

LINEAR FREE ENERGY RELATIONSHIPS

A number of so-called linear free energy relationships are known, the two classical examples being the Brønsted catalysis law and the Hammett equation. The Brønsted law (93) for base-catalysis is

$$k = GK_b^\beta$$

where k is the rate of a base-catalyzed reaction with a certain base B, K_b is the basicity constant of B, and G and β are constants which depend only on the reaction and are supposed to be the same for all bases B. The equation works rather well, provided the series of bases does not differ too widely in structure. The exponent β is frequently thought of as measuring the product-like character of the transition state, since it is

141

almost always $0 < \beta < 1$. When β is close to 1, the transition state is product-like (the full basicity K_b affects the rate); when β is close to 0, the transition state is reactant-like (little of the basicity difference between different bases affects the rate).

It seems very reasonable to suppose that a similar relationship might hold for *nucleophilic substitution* reactions

$$X + RY \underset{k_{-1}}{\overset{k_1}{\rightleftarrows}} XR + Y$$

in the form

$$k_1 = GK^\beta \tag{5-1}$$

where $K = k_1/k_{-1}$ is the equilibrium constant for the reaction. A small amount of data is available on *carbon basicities* (94), *i.e.*, the basicities of various nucleophiles toward carbon, and is in Table 5-1. The orders are certainly different for

TABLE 5-1

Carbon Basicities: Equilibrium Constants for the Reactions of Various Anions with the Substrate in the Solvent Indicated

Anion, as $(C_2H_5)_4N^+$ Salt	$CH_3CH_2CH_2CH_2Br$ in $C_6H_5NO_2$, 80°	CH_3Br in H_2O, 25°	CH_3Br in Acetone, 25°
N_3^-	4×10^5	—	—
Cl^-	1.5×10^2	10	1.7×10^2
Br^-	1	1	1
SCN^-	1	—	—
I^-	2×10^{-2}	13	8×10^{-2}

the two non-hydroxylic solvents than for water. The rates for $CH_3CH_2CH_2CH_2OBs$ in acetone at 25° (51), Cl^- (18), Br^- (4), I^- (1.0), give a fair correlation with the carbon basicities for CH_3Br in acetone at 25°, with $\beta \approx 0.4$, and give a good correlation with the carbon basicities for $CH_3CH_2CH_2\-CH_2Br$ in $C_6H_5NO_2$ at 80°, with $\beta = 0.32$. The rates for $X^- + CH_3Br$ in H_2O at 25° are about Cl^- (1), Br^- (10), I^- (140). They do not parallel the carbon-basicities listed in

Table 5–1, but the ratio for I^-/Br^-, $140/10 = 14$, is essentially equal to the ratio of carbon basicities, 13. The rate for Cl^- is out of order of basicity, and this may well be a result of the strong solvation of the ions, especially Cl^- since it is the smallest, as mentioned in Chapter 4. Thus such correlations hold some promise, and it would be especially interesting to collect more data for H_2O. The values of β are about what would be expected for transition states approximately halfway between reactants and products, which is what the Hammond postulate (Chapter 4) predicts for these reactions. In fact, these plots according to Eq. (5–1) are slightly curved and correspond to smaller values of β for Cl^- than for Br^- than for I^-, in accord with the rule of Chapter 4. Cl^-, being more electron-supplying (more basic) than Br^- or I^-, is predicted to have a longer Cl---C bond at the transition state, *i.e.*, to have a more reactant-like transition state, *i.e.*, a smaller β.

In hydrolysis, the relative rates for methyl halides at 30° are $CH_3Cl:CH_3Br:CH_3I = 1.00:15.47:3.19$ (95), an "unnatural" order in that bromide is faster than chloride or iodide rather than intermediate. The rates of these hydrolyses might correlate with the reverse of the carbon-basicity equilibrium, *i.e.*, with $1/K$:

$$Br^- + CH_3X \underset{}{\overset{1/K}{\rightleftharpoons}} CH_3Br + X^-$$

Values of $1/K$ are $Cl^-:Br^-:I^- = 0.100:1.000:0.077$. The fact that CH_3Br hydrolyzes fastest is correctly predicted by $1/K$, but the relative values for Cl^- and I^- are reversed. Further study of solvolytic reactions in this way, particularly in solvents other than water, would be very interesting.

Before the Hammett equation is discussed, the theoretical basis for linear free energy relationships should be examined. A linear free energy relationship simply means that the free energy changes for one series of reactions are linearly related to the free energy changes for another series of reactions, *i.e.*,

$$\Delta F_i = x\,\Delta F_i' + b$$

where the ΔF_i are a series of free energy differences for similar reactions (*e.g.*, they might be $\Delta F^{\ddagger}$ for hydrolysis of the four methyl halides), and the $\Delta F'_i$ are a series of free energy differences for another series of similar reactions in which the same structural changes are made as in the first series (*e.g.*, they might be $\Delta F^{\ddagger}$ for methanolysis of the four methyl halides). $\Delta F_1^{\ddagger}$ and $\Delta F_1^{\ddagger\prime}$ might refer to methyl fluoride; $\Delta F_2^{\ddagger}$ and $\Delta F_2^{\ddagger\prime}$ might refer to methyl chloride; and so on. Such a linear relationship means that the changes in free energies, on changing from one substituent to another, are proportional for two (or possibly more than two) series of reactions. When *several* series of reactions (several series of ΔF_i) are correlated well with a *single* series of $\Delta F'_i$ (using different x and b for each series of ΔF_i, of course), the reactions are of especial interest because they probably have common mechanistic features.

If we consider equilibrium constants, then

$$\Delta F_i = -\mathbf{R}T \ln K_i$$

where K_i is the equilibrium constant for the reaction with substituent i. The linear relationship then takes the form

$$-\mathbf{R}T \ln K_i = -x\mathbf{R}T \ln K'_i + b$$

or

$$\ln K_i = x \ln K'_i - \frac{b}{\mathbf{R}T}$$

If we consider rate constants (*cf.* Chapter 3), with activity coefficients left out for convenience, then

$$\Delta F_i^{\ddagger} = -\mathbf{R}T \ln K_i^{\ddagger} = -\mathbf{R}T \ln k_i + \mathbf{R}T \ln \left(\frac{\mathbf{k}T}{\mathbf{h}}\right)$$

The linear relationship then takes the form

$$-\mathbf{R}T \ln k_i = -x\mathbf{R}T \ln k'_i + (\boldsymbol{x} - 1)\, \mathbf{R}T \ln \left(\frac{\mathbf{k}T}{\mathbf{h}}\right) + b \quad (5\text{--}2)$$

Remembering that (Chapter 3)

$$K^{\ddagger} = \frac{Q^{\ddagger}}{Q_{\mathrm{A}}^0 Q_{\mathrm{B}}^0}\, e^{-\Delta E_0^{\ddagger}/\mathbf{R}T}$$

for a bimolecular reaction $A + B \rightarrow M^{\ddagger}$, substitution into the linear relationship gives, for any substituent,

$$\ln\left(\frac{Q^{\ddagger}}{Q_A^0 Q_B^0}\right) - \frac{\Delta E_0^{\ddagger}}{\mathbf{R}T} = x \ln\left(\frac{Q^{\ddagger\prime}}{Q_A^{0\prime} Q_B^{0\prime}}\right) - x \frac{\Delta E_0^{\ddagger\prime}}{\mathbf{R}T} - \frac{b}{\mathbf{R}T}$$

or

$$\ln\left[\left(\frac{Q^{\ddagger}}{Q_A^0 Q_B^0}\right)\left(\frac{Q_A^{0\prime} Q_B^{0\prime}}{Q^{\ddagger\prime}}\right)^x\right] + \left(\frac{x \Delta E_0^{\ddagger\prime}}{\mathbf{R}T} - \frac{\Delta E_0^{\ddagger}}{\mathbf{R}T}\right) = -\frac{b}{\mathbf{R}T} \quad (5\text{--}3)$$

The right-hand side of Eq. (5–3) is a constant, dependent on the two reaction series being compared and on the temperature, but independent of the substituent i, *i.e.*, the same for all substituents in the series. The second term of the left-hand side corresponds to the differences in *potential energy* of activation for reactions with the same substituent in the two different series. The first term of the left-hand side corresponds to the changes in partition function ratios for the two activation processes.

If the partition function ratios *happened* to be constant, *i.e.*, independent of substituent (a special case),

$$\frac{Q^{\ddagger}}{Q_A^0 Q_B^0} = C; \ \frac{Q^{\ddagger\prime}}{Q_A^{0\prime} Q_B^{0\prime}} = C'$$

the first term on the left-hand side of Eq. (5–3) would be constant and could be included with the constant terms on the right-hand side. The correlation would then work if the potential energies of activation were proportional for the two series of reactions

$$\Delta E_0^{\ddagger} = x \Delta E_0^{\ddagger\prime} + \text{constant}$$

which could happen if the *change* in $\Delta E_0^{\ddagger}$ wrought by each substituent were proportional to the change in $\Delta E_0^{\ddagger\prime}$ wrought by the same substituent. This proportionality would seem to be entirely reasonable for reaction series that were not too dissimilar, especially in cases where the substituent change is made fairly far from the reaction site, *e.g.*, in a substituted benzene ring attached to the reaction site. Provided a substituent could be expected to affect the electron probability distribution and the steric surroundings of the reaction site similarly in both reaction series, such a proportionality would be predicted. That the partition function ratios should be approximately constant is reasonable in most cases because the same atoms and mostly the same bonds are present in the transition state as in the reactants. Only a few bonds of the reactants change drastically in going to the transition state, and the remainder which do not change should make nearly the same contribution to $Q^{\ddagger}$ as to Q_A^0 or Q_B^0.

In most reactions, however, the partition function ratios are not *exactly* constant. This can be detected experimentally by measuring the temperature dependence of the reaction rate. If the entropy of activation $\Delta S_0^{\ddagger}$ is the same for different substituents, this can occur (except in some exceedingly exceptional case) only if the partition function term (excluding zero-point energies; see below) is constant. It frequently turns out that the linear free energy relationship works even though the $\Delta S_0^{\ddagger}$'s are not constant. Amazingly, the values of $\Delta S_0^{\ddagger}$ prove to be *proportional* to the corresponding values of $\Delta H_0^{\ddagger}$, which is sufficient for the correlation. The important point is that even if we measure $\Delta H_0^{\ddagger}$ and $\Delta S_0^{\ddagger}$, we still cannot ascribe any fundamental significance to them. Usually *both* are composed of kinetic *and* potential energy contributions and are therefore not simply interpretable in terms of molecular properties. $\Delta H_0^{\ddagger}$ and $\Delta S_0^{\ddagger}$ both involve a term containing

$$\frac{\partial}{\partial T}\left[\ln\left(\frac{Q^{\ddagger}}{Q_A^0 Q_B^0}\right)\right]$$

which would be unlikely to be independent of substituents if the partition function ratio itself were not. It is only when $\Delta S_0^{\ddagger}$ is constant with different substituents that the effect of substituents on rates is the result of changes in potential energy alone.

The form of the partition function term for one of the reactions is (*cf.* Chapter 3)

$$\ln\left(\frac{Q^\ddagger}{Q_A^0 Q_B^0}\right) = \ln\left[\left(\frac{m^\ddagger}{m_A m_B}\right)^{3/2}\left(\frac{A^\ddagger B^\ddagger C^\ddagger}{A_A B_A C_A A_B B_B C_B}\right)^{1/2}\frac{\sigma_A \sigma_B}{\sigma^\ddagger}\right.$$

$$\left.\frac{\displaystyle\prod^{3N_A-6}(1-e^{-h\nu_A/kT})\prod^{3N_B-6}(1-e^{-h\nu_B/kT})}{\displaystyle\prod^{3N^\ddagger-7}(1-e^{-h\nu^\ddagger/kT})}\right]$$

$$+\sum\frac{h\nu_A}{2kT}+\sum\frac{h\nu_B}{2kT}-\sum\frac{h\nu^\ddagger}{2kT}+\text{constant} \quad (5\text{--}4)$$

There are factors that involve the masses of the molecules, the moments of inertia, the symmetry numbers, the vibrations, and the zero-point energies of vibration, and a constant involving temperature, k, h, and numerical factors, but *independent* of which substituent of the series we are considering. The constant could be absorbed into the right-hand side of Eq. (5–3), and need not be further considered. A further simplification arises if we include the zero-point energy terms along with the $\Delta E_0^\ddagger$ term. This means that the entire partition function term need not be independent of substituents but only the term in square brackets in Eq. (5–4). It can be seen that this term is very complicated. However, according to Eq. (5–3) the effect tends to cancel between k and k'. Even if the effect did not completely cancel, it would frequently be expected to be only of the order of 1.5 or less. This would still allow a very good correlation if a change in substituent changed the rate by a factor of 10 or more, as is frequently the case. If the substituents were small, then the term involving the masses would be fairly constant for different substituents. The term involving the moments of inertia depends strongly on the geometry of the reactant and of the transition state, so it could be relatively constant or variable with substituent changes. It usually would be nearly constant if the substituents were very small relative to the mass of the rest of the molecule. The term involving $[1 - \exp{(-h\nu/kT)}]$ functions cannot be simply evaluated, but if the substituent change introduces only a small change in the normal modes of vibration of the reactant and transition state, this term could be reasonably constant for different substituents. Small substituents attached to a large molecule would leave most normal modes of vibration unchanged. All the terms in Eq. (5–4) discussed so far are rather complex, so it would be surprising if these terms remained constant with substituent changes. In fact, they do not in most cases, since $\Delta S_0^{\ddagger}$ is usually different for different substituents. What is amazing is that $\Delta S_0^{\ddagger}$ seems to parallel $\Delta F_0^{\ddagger}$, because the free energy depends greatly on electrical and delocalization effects of the substituent whereas the entropy appears to depend more on the mass and its effect on the moments of inertia and normal vibrations.

One term has been neglected so far, the symmetry number ratios. It has been pointed out (96) that, since this term depends only on the symmetry properties of reactants and transition states, it can usually be evaluated and a correction made for it. A term such as $\sigma_A \sigma_B / \sigma^{\ddagger}$ is called $K_{\sigma}^{\ddagger}$, so that $K^{\ddagger} = K_{\sigma}^{\ddagger} K_{\text{CHEM}}^{\ddagger}$, $K_{\text{CHEM}}^{\ddagger}$ being the *purely chemical* contribution, *i.e.*, excluding symmetry. Thus $k_{\text{CHEM}} = k/K_{\sigma}^{\ddagger}$ where k is the observed rate constant and k_{CHEM} is the corrected rate constant. *Internal* rotations can also be included in these rotational symmetry numbers (*e.g.*, $\sigma_{\text{ACETONE}} = 18$), but frequently their effect will be found to cancel between reactant and transition state. The Brønsted relation can be generalized in this way (96):

$$\frac{k}{K_{\sigma}^{\ddagger}} = G \left(\frac{K_b}{K_{\sigma}} \right)^{\beta}$$

It would be valuable to study the theoretical foundations of linear free energy relationships more thoroughly, considering in as much detail as possible the contributions to free energy changes such as molecular weight, moments of inertia, temperature, and solvation. Symmetry or lack of symmetry could arise because of strong solvation bonds, and we do not know exactly how to deal with this problem yet (96).

Another problem concerning solvation arises, too. When we consider the partition function ratios which determine the rate of a reaction, we have to consider the effect of solvation on reactants and transition state, and *also the effect of the reactants and transition state on the solvent.* The partition functions for solvent molecules around the reactants may be quite different from the partition functions for the solvent molecules around the transition state. If so, these partition functions must also be included. Fortunately, this effect may be expected to be constant for various substituents, at least non-charged substituents which do not act very strongly on the solvent.

Hammett Equation. A further simplification of the mathematical form of a linear free energy relationship is obtained by defining a *standard substituent.* For substituents on phenyl rings, the unsubstituted ring is usually used as the standard; *i.e.*, the standard substituent is hydrogen. In Eq. (5–2), the standard substituent is given the subscript $i = 0$. Subtracting the equation for substituent i from the standard equation, we get

$$\mathbf{R}T \ln k_i - \mathbf{R}T \ln k_0 = x\mathbf{R}T \ln k_i' - x\mathbf{R}T \ln k_0'$$

or, upon dividing through by 2.303 $\mathbf{R}T$ and collecting the logarithmic terms,

$$\log \left(\frac{k_i}{k_0} \right) = x \log \left(\frac{k_i'}{k_0'} \right)$$

The Hammett equation is of this form (see (73)),

$$\log \left(\frac{k_i}{k_0} \right) = \rho\sigma$$

where ρ is a proportionality constant depending upon the reaction and conditions but independent of substituents and σ is a constant supposedly depending only on the substituent and independent of the reaction and conditions. Hammett's σ

was defined not by rate constants but by the ionization constants of substituted benzoic acids in water at 25°:

$$C_6H_5CO_2H \overset{K_0'}{\rightleftharpoons} C_6H_5CO_2^- + H_3O^+$$
$$Z_i{-}C_6H_4CO_2H \overset{K_i'}{\rightleftharpoons} Z_i{-}C_6H_4CO_2^- + H_3O^+$$

$$\sigma \equiv \log\left(\frac{K_i'}{K_0'}\right)$$

This $\rho\sigma$ relationship might be expected to hold best for equilibria which are quite similar to the standard one, the ionization of the benzoic acids. It might also be expected to hold for other processes, *e.g.*, rates, in which the electronic requirements were very similar to those for benzoic acid ionization. *In fact*, it holds for a fantastic variety of rates, equilibria, and even spectral properties such as infrared and nuclear magnetic resonance absorptions of substituted benzene derivatives! There seems to be something very "fundamental" about a relationship which works so well, but it is difficult to see what it might be in terms of partition function ratios for different reaction series. It may have something to do with the fact that the free energy for a reaction is a minimized quantity, in the sense that for structural changes λ in molecules, $\partial F/\partial\lambda = 0$ since molecules are at equilibrium (under ordinary thermal reaction conditions) with respect to bond lengths, nuclear positions, and electron distributions. That is, when molecular structure is changed, the molecule "fights back" in such a way that the free energy change is minimized. For such big changes in structure as changing from one substituent to another we cannot expect that free energy changes will be zero, but perhaps this minimization makes us less surprised that free energies and entropies seem to follow similar patterns in different reaction series. A comprehensive review of the Hammett equation is available (97), from which a few pertinent results might be quoted. For the *standard reaction* $\rho \equiv 1$, obviously. For other reactions, ρ could be greater or less than one and could be positive or negative, the value being a measure of the sensitivity of the reaction to substituents Z_i. Since electron-withdrawing substituents such as NO_2 or Br increase the ionization constants of the benzoic acid, σ is positive for these substituents; $\sigma \equiv 0$ for hydrogen (no substituent); and $\sigma < 0$ for electron-donating substituents such as CH_3. A positive ρ is usually interpreted as meaning that substituents like NO_2 *facilitate* reaction, or more precisely, stabilize the transition state relative to the reactant. There is one problem with interpreting the values of ρ in terms of the structure of the transition state: there can be several different effects caused by one substituent, inductive, delocalization, field, and steric effects (*cf.* Chapter 2). Steric effects are rather complex, and Hammett correlations usually work only for *m*- and *p*-substituents. *Ortho*-substituents are too close to the reaction site in most cases and produce steric effects which are not independent of the nature of the reaction site. There are a number of substituents that have an electron-withdrawing inductive effect and an electron-donating delocalization effect, nuclei which are more electronegative than carbon but which bear unshared pairs of electrons (*e.g.*, $-\overset{\cdot\cdot}{\underset{\cdot\cdot}{N}}H_2$, $-\overset{\cdot\cdot}{\underset{\cdot\cdot}{F}}:$, $-\overset{\cdot\cdot}{\underset{\cdot\cdot}{O}}-CH_3$). The effects of such substituents may not be independent of the nature of the reaction because different kinds of reactions might utilize more or less delocalization of the unshared pair. This may be stated qualitatively by saying that the substituent affects the electron distribution in the ring and the reaction center affects the electron distribution in the ring, but in addition the substituent affects the reaction center and the reaction center affects the substituent *through* the ring.

A new theoretical interpretation of linear free energy relationships and the factors affecting the applicability is presented in a recent book (19). It is of interest that the substituent effects on the ionization of benzoic acids, the defining equilibrium for σ constants, are largely determined by *entropy* changes rather than enthalpy changes (see (19), pages 374–

TABLE 5–2

ρ Values for Acid Dissociation Constants of Substituted Acids

K_A for Substituted Derivatives of:	ρ [a]
C_6H_5OH	$+2.11$
$C_6H_5CO_2H$	(1.000) [b]
$C_6H_5CH_2CO_2H$	0.49
$C_6H_5CH=CHCO_2H$	0.47
$C_6H_5CH_2CH_2CO_2H$	0.21

[a] Ref. (97).
[b] By definition.

375). We might have expected it to be a "simple" enthalpy effect. The explanation is not yet clear.

Some representative ρ-values for different kinds of acid dissociation constants are listed in Table 5–2. It may be seen that the greater the distance of the reaction site ($CO_2H \rightarrow CO_2^-$) from the substituents, the smaller is ρ, just as would be expected.

Other similar types of linear free energy relationships have been investigated ((1), (2), Chapter 13 of (40)). As previously mentioned (Chapter 2), the acid ionization constants of the bicyclic acids

have been measured in 50% ethanol-water at 25° (6). A set of substituent constants σ' has been defined from these measurements. In order to make the σ' values comparable to σ values, ρ' was *defined* as 1.464, which is the value of ρ obtained for substituted benzoic acids in the same solvent. Therefore

$$\log\left(\frac{K_i'}{K_0'}\right) \equiv 1.464\,\sigma'$$

where the K_i' are the dissociation constants of the bicyclic acids under the standard conditions. The effects were found to be fairly large.

Recently the effect of solvent on ρ' has been investigated, by measuring the equilibrium constants K in various solvents (98):

$$ZC(CH_2CH_2)_3CCO_2H + p\text{-}O_2NC_6H_4O^- \overset{K}{\rightleftarrows}$$
$$ZC(CH_2CH_2)_3CCO_2^- + p\text{-}O_2NC_6H_4OH$$

Typical values of ρ' are CH_3OH, 1.22; 75% CH_3OH, 1.53; 50% CH_3OH, 1.22; CH_3CH_2OH, 1.44; 50% CH_3CH_2OH, 1.01; CH_3COCH_3, 1.99; 90% CH_3COCH_3, 1.70. Dimethyl sulfoxide and its mixtures with water were measured, but the plots were quite scattered. The substituents used for the correlation were $Z = H$, HO, $C_2H_5O_2C$, HO_2C, Br, and NC. Charged substituents were investigated also, and from the line determined by the uncharged substituents, values for σ' were calculated for the charged substituents. For $(CH_3)_3N^+$, σ' varied from 1.56 in acetone to 0.54 in 50% CH_3OH. For O_2^-C, σ' varied from -0.26 in 50% dimethyl sulfoxide to -1.11 in CH_3OH. Thus linear free energy relationships are not obeyed by charged substituents.

Calculations of the effect of the charge in mono-ionized dibasic acids on the value of the second dissociation constant have been made. By using a model of an elliptical area of relatively low dielectric constant (corresponding to the molecule) surrounded by a medium of high dielectric constant (the solvent), the field effect was found to explain the experimental results well (99).

The same type of calculation was applied to the uncharged substituents in $ZC(CH_2CH_2)_3CCO_2H$ dissociations (6) and found to account for easily half of the observed changes with substituent in the common solvent. Calculations have now been made (98) for the case where $Z = (CH_3)_3N^+$, in different solvents. For fourteen solvents and solvent mixtures, the predicted changes in $\log K$ were in good agreement with experiment, with one or two exceptions. This calculation indicates that the field effect may be responsible for non-linear free energy relationships for charged substituents and that possibly the σ' values determined for each solvent would give linear correlations of other reactions and equilibria in the same solvent. But it may be that a general breakdown of linearity occurs here as a result of specific interactions, so that σ' would depend not only on solvent but on reaction type. These two possibilities can be tested experimentally (98).

Another set of constants that is especially valuable for solvolysis reactions is the σ^+ values (100) defined by the solvolysis rates of substituted cumyl chlorides in 90% aqueous acetone (v/v) at 25°:

$$\log\left(\frac{k_i'}{k_0'}\right) \equiv -4.54\,\sigma^+$$

The value -4.54 comes from the finding that, for m-substituents there is an excellent linear correlation of least-squares slope -4.54 between σ and $\log(k_i'/k_0')$, the k_i' being the solvolysis rates of only the m-substituted cumyl chlorides. Thus $\sigma_m^+ \approx \sigma_m$, but usually $\sigma_p^+ \neq \sigma_p$ because the solvolysis transition states have much greater delocalization requirements than the benzoate anions. It is thought that the solvolysis transition states resemble carbonium ions. That other solvolysis reactions are well correlated by σ^+ is not surprising, since their mechanisms must be similar, although differing in details of electron density, bond-breaking, bond formation, and carbon hybridization at the transition state. For $ArCHClC_6H_5$ solvolyses in ethanol at 25°, $\rho^+ = -4.63$; for Ar_2CHCl in ethanol at 25°, $\rho^+ = -4.05$; for Ar_3CCl in 40% ethanol–60% ether at 0°, $\rho^+ = -2.68$ (100). These ρ^+ values may be compared with that observed for formation of benzyl carbonium ions from benzyl radicals in the gas phase (101), $\rho^+ = -20$. The value of ρ^+ for ionizing benzyl halides in the gas phase would also be very nearly -20 because the energy of dissociation of the carbon-halogen bond is almost the same for all substituents. Hence the differences in energy between substituents for ionizing differently substituted benzyl halides into carbonium ion + halide ion are essentially equal to the differences in energy for ionizing the corresponding free radicals. The surprising magnitude of ρ^+ indicates that the transition states for solvolysis reactions, where $\rho^+ \sim -4$ to -5, are certainly not really carbonium-ion-like, but must be heavily solvated (the difference in ρ^+ values of 15–16 corresponds to a factor of 10^{15}–10^{16} in rates or equilibria!). The fact that an excellent linear correlation of the ionization potentials with σ^+ is obtained is even more surprising, because it indicates that the nature of the electron demand of the transition states parallels that of the carbonium ions. In the solvolysis reactions, then, solvation effects must be very important, yet must parallel the stabilities of the corresponding carbonium ions!

There is a correlation of similar type for *aliphatic* compounds, in which steric hindrance may be important for some substituents (Chapter 13 of (40)). The substituent constants are called σ^*:

$$\sigma^* \equiv \frac{1}{2.48} \left[\log \left(\frac{k_i'}{k_0'} \right)_{\mathrm{B}} - \log \left(\frac{k_i'}{k_0'} \right)_{\mathrm{A}} \right]$$

where B and A refer to otherwise identical *basic* and *acidic* ester hydrolyses, respectively, *i.e.*, involving the same ester, solvent, and temperature. The logic behind this definition is that acid hydrolysis is very insensitive to electrical effects. For m- and p-substituted *benzoates*, ρ is between 2.2 and 2.8 in alkaline saponifications, but ρ is between -0.2 and $+0.5$ in acid-catalyzed ester hydrolysis or esterification. The transition states for acid- and base-catalyzed ester hydrolysis are very similar sterically, but have quite different charge distributions:

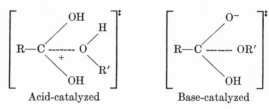

Acid-catalyzed   Base-catalyzed

The constant 2.48 is an average ($\rho_B - \rho_A$) for basic and acidic hydrolysis of m- and p-substituted benzoates, arbitrarily chosen to put σ^* on a similar scale to σ. The assumption is that for reactions in which steric effects are different for different substituents, as they are with aliphatic esters, the rate ratio for *acid* hydrolysis measures the steric effect only. The standard substituent for σ^* is methyl, *i.e.*, k_0' is the rate for an ester of *acetic* acid and k_i' are the rates for esters of various substituted acetic acids. Therefore

$$\log \left(\frac{k_i'}{k_0'}\right)_A = E_s$$

where E_s measures the steric effect of the substituent i relative to the steric effect of CH_3—. The equation for reactions which correlate with σ^* is then

$$\log \left(\frac{k_i}{k_0}\right) = \rho^* \sigma^* \tag{5-5}$$

Equation (5-5) has been applied to solvolysis reactions ((3), Sec. V, E). It is interesting that for ethanolysis of primary tosylates and benzenesulfonates at 100°, $\rho^* = -0.74$, while for solvolysis of substituted tertiary carbinyl halides in 80% ethanol-water (v/v) at 25°, $\rho^* = -3.29$, possibly indicating more requirement for electron-donation to the reactive center at the transition state in the case of the tertiary substrates than in the case of the primary substrates. The effect could be the result of the inherent bond-making and -breaking properties of the transition states, or of more steric hindrance

TABLE 5-3

Comparison of σ, σ^+, σ', and σ^* Constants

Substituent	$\sigma_p{}^a$	$\sigma_m{}^a$	$\sigma_m{}^{+b}$	$\sigma_p{}^{+b}$	$\sigma'{}^c$
(CH$_3$)$_2$N	-0.83	-0.211	—	-1.7	—
CH$_3$O	-0.268	+0.115	+0.047	-0.778	+0.23
CH$_3$	-0.170	-0.069	-0.066	-0.311	-0.05
None (H)	(0.0000)^d	(0.0000)^d	(0.0000)^d	(0.0000)^d	(0.0000)^d
F	+0.062	+0.337	+0.352	-0.073	+0.50
Cl	+0.227	+0.373	+0.399	+0.114	+0.47
Br	+0.232	+0.391	+0.405	+0.150	+0.454
I	+0.18	+0.352	+0.359	+0.135	+0.38
CH$_3$CO	+0.502	+0.376	—	—	+0.27
CF$_3$	+0.54	+0.42	+0.520	+0.612	+0.41
CN	+0.660	+0.56	+0.562	+0.659	+0.579
NO$_2$	+0.778	+0.710	+0.674	+0.790	+0.63
(CH$_3$)$_3$N$^+$	+0.88	+1.01	+0.359	+0.408	+0.86

Substituent	$\sigma^*{}^c$
—	—
CH$_3$OCH$_2$	+0.520
CH$_3$CH$_2$	-0.100
HCH$_2$	(0.0000)^d
FCH$_2$	+1.10
ClCH$_2$	+1.050
BrCH$_2$	+1.000
ICH$_2$	+0.85
CH$_3$COCH$_2$	+0.60
CF$_3$CH$_2$	+0.92
CNCH$_2$	+1.300
—	—
(CH$_3$)$_3$N$^+$CH$_2$	+1.90
NO$_2$(CH$_2$)$_2$	+0.50
Cl(CH$_2$)$_2$	+0.385
CF$_3$(CH$_2$)$_2$	+0.32
CH$_3$(CH$_2$)$_2$	-0.115
(CH$_3$)$_3$C	-0.300

[a] Ref. (1), page 87; (100).
[b] Ref. (100).
[c] Ref. (40), Chapter 13; see also Ref. (6).
[d] By definition.

to solvent participation in the tertiary transition states, the presence of solvent molecules in the primary transition states reducing the requirement for electron-donation by the substituents. Values of representative σ constants are listed for comparison in Table 5–3.

Normally the electronic effects on the values of σ constants have been considered to be simply inductive and delocalization effects. Five possible effects have been recently discussed (102): (1) the field effect, the electrostatic interaction of charges across space; (2) the σ-inductive effect, the inductive polarization of electrons in σ-bonds; (3) the π-inductive effect, the inductive polarization of electrons in π-bonds; (4) the delocalization ("mesomeric") effect, the polarization of electrons in π-bonds by delocalization to or from the substituent; and (5) mutual conjugation between the substituent and the reacting center, a delocalization effect through the π-electrons. Thirty-three substituted 1-naphthoic acids were studied. Effect (2) was found to be probably small, as might be expected since inductive effects usually are very small if more than one bond is between interacting centers. Effect (5) was eliminated from consideration by choosing systems where it did not occur. Effects (3) and (4) are difficult to separate, but should be in the same direction, so they were lumped together. Effect (1), which has usually not been considered, must be of considerable importance in view of the calculations on the dissociation constants of charged acids (99, 98).

Therefore, a model was used (102) which combined the field effect and the delocalization and/or polarization of the π-electrons by the substituent. The σ constant, σ_{ij}, where i and j are the numbers of the carbon atoms to which the substituent and the reactive group, respectively, are attached, is then given by

$$\sigma_{ij} = \frac{F}{r_{ij}} + Mq_{ij} \tag{5–6}$$

or

$$\sigma_{ij} = \frac{F'}{r_{ij}} - M'\pi_{ij} \tag{5–7}$$

The field effect is approximated as being inversely proportional to the distance between *ring carbons* i and j, r_{ij} (measured in units of the carbon-carbon bond length of benzene). In the second terms, q_{ij} is the formal charge at position j which would be produced by attaching the group —CH_2^- at position i, and π_{ij} is the "atom-atom polarizability" of atoms i and j (page 60). It can be shown that either of these terms should be approximately proportional to the π-inductive-delocalization effect.

In Eq. (5–6), q_{ij} is the *absolute value* of the quantity $(1 - q)$, where q is the charge on a carbon as defined in Chapter 3. For example, for benzyl$^-$ (*cf.* benzyl$^+$, Chapter 3) q_{14} is $\frac{1}{7}$ and q_{13} is 0. These values of q_{ij} are readily calculated for addition of —CH_2^- to even alternant hydrocarbons by the NBMO ("starring") method.

By using σ_{13} (σ_m) and σ_{14} (σ_p) for benzene, together with known values of $r_{13} = \sqrt{3}$, $r_{14} = 2$, $\pi_{13} = 0.009$, $\pi_{14} = -0.102$,

TABLE 5–4

Calculated and Observed σ Constants for Naphthalene-1-carboxylic Acids

Substituent	NO₂	Br	CH₃	CH₃O
F	1.23	0.68	−0.12	0.20
M	1.14	−0.77	−0.77	−2.58
F′	1.26	0.66	−0.14	0.13
M′	1.48	−1.00	−1.00	−3.36
σ_{31}[a] calc.	0.71(0.70)	0.39(0.40)	—	—
σ_{31}[b] exp.	0.61	0.34	—	—
σ_{41}[a] calc.	0.84(0.84)	0.19(0.19)	−0.21(−0.21)	−0.42(−0.40)
σ_{41}[b] exp.	0.86	0.30	−0.14	−0.36
σ_{51}[a] calc.	0.52(0.51)	0.22(0.23)	−0.07(−0.07)	−0.05(−0.03)
σ_{51}[b] exp.	0.54	0.30	0.01	−0.01
σ_{61}[a] calc.	0.41(0.41)	0.23(0.21)	−0.04(−0.05)	0.07(0.02)
σ_{61}[b] exp.	0.41	0.18	−0.05	−0.06
σ_{71}[a] calc.	0.53(0.52)	0.21(0.22)	−0.08(−0.08)	−0.07(−0.06)
σ_{71}[b] exp.	0.36	0.07	−0.07	−0.08

[a] From Eq. (5–6). Numbers in parentheses from Eq. (5–7).
[b] Experimental value (102).

$q_{13} = 0$, and $q_{14} = \frac{1}{7}$, F, M, F', and M' were calculated for each substituent. Then Eqs. (5–6) and (5–7) were used in reverse to calculate σ values for naphthalene-1-carboxylic acids, the calculated σ values being compared with those known from experimental measurements of the acid dissociation constants (102). Representative results for four substituents are in Table 5–4. The standard deviation for all values known experimentally is ± 0.08 σ-unit. The approach seems justified and emphasizes that the field effect is probably important.

Non-linear Hammett Plots. In some nucleophilic reactions of compounds such as substituted benzyl halides the Hammett plot (log (k_i/k_0) *vs.* σ) is smoothly curved rather than linear. In extreme cases both electron-withdrawing and electron-donating substituents increase the rate, a rate *minimum* occurring in the area of the unsubstituted compound. This behavior was interpreted (103) as reflecting changes in the relative importance of bond-making and bond-breaking in the SN2-type transition state, with different substituents. If bond-making were more complete than bond-breaking, the benzylic carbon atom should bear a net negative charge in the

transition state, which should be stabilized by electron-withdrawing substituents. If bond-breaking were more complete than bond-making, the carbon atom should bear a net positive charge in the transition state, which should be stabilized by electron-donating substituents. The curvature of the plot is then explained by a changing ρ, ρ being a measure of the change in negative charge on the central carbon atom.

For example, curved plots are obtained for the reactions of benzyl chlorides with $(CH_3)_3N$ in benzene at $100°$ and of benzyl bromides with pyridine in acetone at 20°. Another feature is that the curved plot sometimes separates into two branches, one of greater curvature and higher rates for p-substituents and one of less curvature and lower rates for m-substituents. Clearly the delocalization effects (more important for p-substituents) are significant in such reactions, a reasonable conclusion as discussed theoretically in Chapter 3.

Electron-withdrawing substituents are predicted to decrease the C---X and C---Y bond lengths at the transition state (47), which would tend to produce the effects observed. However, a number of other factors could also be important, such as solvation of nucleophile and of leaving group, repulsions between X and Y, the exact electron distributions in the C---X and C---Y bonds, and the effect of the transition state on the solvent. Therefore we cannot be certain of the interpretation. It is conceivable that a curved plot could be obtained even though the central carbon atom had a net negative charge in the transition states for *all* substituents. Rate minima could then be explained by saying that there is some substituent which produces a *least favorable* transition-state charge distribution, and any deviation from this least favorable situation will produce a rate increase.

Part of the problem is that rates are almost always composed of so many different influences that they cannot be simply interpreted in terms of transition-state structure. It would be valuable to investigate this non-linearity phenomenon more thoroughly from a theoretical as well as an experimental point of view (see also (19)).

Non-linearity has been noted in solvolysis of benzyl tosylates (104). In aqueous acetone and aqueous dioxane solvents, ρ increases with an increase in reaction rate, *i.e.*, with electron-donating substituents. Further study of such solvolyses would be valuable in conjunction with similar study of SN2 reactions.

Nucleophilicity. The factors determining nucleophilic reactivity have been discussed (105) and will be briefly mentioned, although most of the data are for ions rather than the neutral molecules which would be involved in nucleophilic solvolysis mechanisms. The most important factors are (1) basicity, (2) polarizability, and (3) the presence of unshared pair(s) of electrons on an atom adjacent to the attacking atom. Basicity is certainly expected to be important, because it is a measure of the affinity of the nucleophile for a proton. In fact good correlations of nucleophilicity with basicity are obtained for displacements by substituted phenols or anilines, *i.e.*, where the bond formation is with the same nucleus (oxygen in the case of phenols) throughout the series. Polarizability is important because a polarizable nucleophile can rearrange its electron distribution in such a way as both to enhance its ability to form a bond by polarization of electrons toward the atom being attacked and to reduce repulsions of non-bonded electrons in the transition state by polarizing unshared pairs *away from* the electrons in the bonds of the substrate being attacked. Effect (3) is more or less a delocalization effect which favors bond formation.

A linear free energy relationship (106),

$$\log \left(\frac{k_i}{k_0} \right) = sn \tag{5-8}$$

was suggested, where n is the "nucleophilicity" of the attacking nucleophile and s is the sensitivity of the substrate (in a particular solvent at a particular temperature) to the nucleophilicity. For methyl bromide in any solvent at any temperature $s = 1.00$, and for water as the nucleophile $n = 0.00$; *i.e.*, k_0 is the rate constant for reaction of the substrate with water. The pseudo-first-order rate constant for the reaction with water was divided by the water concentration (55.5 M for pure H_2O) to give the second-order rate constant k_0. Some values of n are listed in Table 5–5. Nucleophilicity should play a part in many solvolysis reactions, at least those involving nucleophilic assistance in the transition state.

TABLE 5–5

Nucleophilic Constants, n, According to Eq. (5–8)

Nucleophile	n^a	Nucleophile	n^a
ClO_3^-, ClO_4^-, BrO_3^-, IO_3^-	<0	Br^-	3.89
H_2O	0.00	N_3^-	4.00
$p\text{-}CH_3C_6H_4SO_3^-$	<1.0	$(NH_2)_2CS$	4.1
NO_3^-	1.03	HO^-	4.20
Picrate$^-$	1.9	$C_6H_5NH_2$	4.49
F^-	2.0	SCN^-	4.77
$SO_4^=$	2.5	I^-	5.04
$CH_3CO_2^-$	2.72	CN^-	5.1
Cl^-	3.04	SH^-	5.1
C_5H_5N	3.6	$SO_3^=$	5.1
HCO_3^-	3.8	$S_2O_3^=$	6.36
$HPO_4^=$	3.8	$HPSO_3^-$	6.6

[a] (106); (1), page 161.

More data on nucleophilicities of neutral molecules would be very interesting.

Leaving-Group Ability. Of more importance in discussing solvolysis reactions is the relative ability of various leaving groups to depart from carbon. The same factors that affect nucleophilicity are likely also to be important in leaving-group ability. An important simplification is in solvation effects. In Chapter 4 we discussed the probability that solvation bonds to a nucleophile must be broken before or during nucleophilic attack. This problem should be less important for a leaving group where we are reversing the process, because the leaving group could easily break its bond to carbon before replacing it by a solvation bond to solvent. Monatomic leaving groups like halide ions have three unshared pairs of electrons in the reactant. The product ion has four. Each pair could form a hydrogen bond with solvent. In the transition state, where the ion is partially formed, it is probable that very strong solvation bonds to the three unshared pairs have already formed. The solvation energy of a halide ion in water could easily be of the order of 50–100 kcal./mole. In many solvolytic reactions, "ion-pair" intermediates are thought to be formed, *e.g.*, [S---R---X]. The reason why there is an energy barrier to recombination of such ion pairs is not completely obvious, because the energy of the R---X bond should simply become less and less as it becomes longer and longer. In all probability, strong solvation bonds are what keep recombination from being almost instantaneous. If both R and X are strongly solvated, it is possible that they would have to overcome an energy barrier in order to recombine. B-strain in R could also be very important. The reason for calling such a structure an ion pair is simply its energy and electronic distribution. If [S---R---X] is an intermediate, it must correspond to a free energy minimum. If S and X are relatively electronegative, they may well make R electron-poor. A good representation of the structure might then be a "solvated carbonium ion," [S---R$^+$---X$^-$], *i.e.*, a relatively loosely bonded intermediate. In a true SN2 reaction, the intermediate (if there were one) would be much "tighter" and less ion-pair-like.

A recent study of leaving-group ability gives a quantitative measure for one reaction type (107):

$$CH_3O^- + CH_3X \xrightarrow[25°]{CH_3OH} CH_3OCH_3 + X^-$$

A linear free energy relationship was proposed,

$$\log\left(\frac{k_i}{k_0}\right) = \gamma L \tag{5–9}$$

where L is a constant characteristic of the leaving group X and = 0.00 for Br, γ is characteristic of the reaction system and = 1.00 for reactions of CH_3X with CH_3O^- in CH_3OH at 25°, k_i is the rate for R—X, and k_0 is the rate for R—Br. Values of L are listed in Table 5–6, along with approximate values for the pK_a of HX. It can be seen that L generally correlates with acidity of HX, but not too well, possibly because of polarizability effects and, with charged species, differences in

TABLE 5–6

Leaving-Group Constants (L) According to Eq. (5–9)[a]

X	L	pK_a of HX
$OClO_3$	3.34	$>H_2SO_4$
OSO_2OCH_3	1.57	$>HOSO_2C_6H_4CH_3\text{-}p$
$OSO_2C_6H_4CH_3\text{-}p$	0.63	$>HBr$
Br	0.00	-7.74
I	-0.04	-10.74
OH_2^+	-0.17	-1.74
Cl	-1.61	$-7.1, -4.74$
ONO_2	-1.90	-1.34
$OSOOCH_3$	-2.05	1.77
$S(CH_3)_2^+$	-3.01	—
$N(CH_3)_3^+$	-3.54	9.91
F	-3.60	3.14
SSO_2^-	-3.72	1.21
OSO_2^-	-4.58	1.70
$OCOCH_3$	-4.68	4.72
OCH_3	<-6.45	14.4

[a] Ref. (107).

specific solvation. The correlation of a number of other reaction series, for most of which only fragmentary data exist, is illustrated in Table 5–7. The correlations are generally good, but by no means perfect. The fact that solvolyses correlate about as well as SN2 reactions indicates that there is no

TABLE 5–7

Reaction Constants at 25°[a]

Reaction	γ	$\log k_0$
CH_3X with CH_3O^- in CH_3OH (second-order)	(1.000)	-3.55
CH_3X with CH_3OH in CH_3OH (first-order)	1.064	-7.47
CH_3X with HO^- in H_2O (second-order)	0.749	-3.84
CH_3X with H_2O in H_2O (first-order)	1.082	-6.48
$(CH_3)_3C$—X (halides) with CH_3OH in CH_3OH (first-order)	1.585	-4.46
CH_3CH_2X with $C_2H_5O^-$ in C_2H_5OH (second-order)	0.921	-4.63

[a] Ref. (107).

unexpected different order, and that leaving group ability is probably relatively independent of other mechanistic details.

However, for *tert*-butyl compounds, it was found that $(CH_3)_2S^+$ and O_2NO were far more reactive than predicted from Eq. (5–9), if γ was determined from the four halides alone, in both cases by a factor of *ca.* 100.

Solvent Effects.   The effect of solvent is especially complex in solvolysis reactions because of the possibility of solvation effects and, in addition, nucleophilic assistance effects.   Electrophilic assistance also may be relatively specific in some cases.   It is therefore interesting and surprising that a number of linear free energy relationships exist which correlate rates when solvents are changed.

We have already discussed the general idea that creation of charge should be accelerated in solvents that are better at solvating ions (Chapters 2 and 3).   The ability of a solvent to solvate ions depends on a number of factors such as the dielectric constant and the various specific interactions between solvent and ion.   It turns out to be an oversimplification to expect rates of solvolysis reactions to parallel dielectric constants.   Other effects must somehow be taken account of.

A very successful way to correlate solvolysis rates is to assign an *ionizing power* **Y** to each solvent.   Accordingly **Y** was defined (108) as the logarithm of the relative rate of solvolysis of *tert*-butyl chloride in solvent i and in the standard solvent, 80% ethanol-water (v/v), at $25°$:

$$\mathbf{Y} \equiv \log\left(\frac{k_i}{k_0}\right)_{(CH_3)_3CCl}$$

A linear free energy relationship between the rates for $(CH_3)_3CCl$ and for other compounds in a series of solvents then takes the form

$$\log\left(\frac{k_i}{k_0}\right) = m\mathbf{Y} \tag{5–10}$$

where m is a constant characteristic of the compound being solvolyzed and is a measure of the "sensitivity" of that compound to the "ionizing power" Y. In view of the complex factors making up Y, it is interesting to note that primary halides are correlated by Eq. (5–10). We have previously concluded that primary substrates probably involve considerably more nucleophilic assistance than tertiary. Yet $CH_3CH_2CH_2CH_2Br$ solvolysis rates are correlated just as well as those of $(CH_3)_3CBr$, at least in aqueous solvent mixtures. For the former, $m = 0.392$ at 59.4° and 0.331 at 75.1°; for the latter, $m = 0.917$ at 25°. The primary substrate is less sensitive to Y than the tertiary, as might be expected if Y really measures ionizing power.

Another feature of this type of correlation is that the plots for primary substrates drop off for non-aqueous solvents with high ionizing powers; considerable curvature eventually occurs. This effect is measured by measuring the rate of solvolysis in formic acid and in a C_2H_5OH-H_2O mixture of the same Y as formic acid. The formic acid is not very nucleophilic while the ethanol-water mixture is very nucleophilic, so the ratio $r = k_{ROH}/k_{HCO_2H}$ measures the effects related to nucleophilicity in various compounds, m values being calculated from data for aqueous ethanol mixtures only. For CH_3Br at 50°, $m = 0.258$ and $r = 200$; for CH_3CH_2Br at 55°, $m = 0.343$ and $r = 80$; for $(CH_3)_2CHBr$ at 50°, $m = 0.544$ and $r = 20$; for $(CH_3)_3CBr$ at 25°, $m = 0.940$ and $r = 1$; for the bicyclic compound $HC(CH_2CH_2)_3CBr$ (60) at 100°, $m = 0.88$ and $r = 0.5$. As mentioned previously (Chapter 4) the structure of the last of these compounds appears to prevent backside nucleophilic attack.

As with all empirical correlations, Eq. (5–10) is inadequate when pushed too far with very accurate data. For example, $(C_6H_5)_2CHCl$ gives somewhat different straight lines for C_2H_5OH-H_2O mixtures than for CH_3CO_2H-H_2O mixtures, m at 25° being 0.740 and 1.561, respectively. This separation into different lines for different binary solvent mixtures is characteristic of many compounds (109). More work might help us to understand the reasons for these differences in terms of the structure of the substrate and the properties of the solvent.

A more complicated relationship has been proposed in an attempt to take account of the nucleophilicity as well as ionizing power of the solvents (110):

$$\log\left(\frac{k_i}{k_0}\right) = c_1 d_1 + c_2 d_2 \qquad (5\text{--}11)$$

where k_i is the first-order rate constant for solvolysis of any compound in any solvent, k_0 is the corresponding rate constant in 80% ethanol–20% water (v/v) at the same temperature, c_1 and c_2 are constants depending only on the compound undergoing solvolysis, and d_1 and d_2 are constants depending only on the solvent. In order to fix the definitions of the four constants, it was arbitrarily assumed that

$$c_1 = 3.00c_2 \text{ for } CH_3Br$$
$$c_1 = c_2 = 1.00 \text{ for } (CH_3)_3CCl$$
$$3.00c_1 = c_2 \text{ for } (C_6H_5)_3CF$$
$$d_1 = d_2 = 0.00 \text{ for } 80\% \text{ } C_2H_5OH\text{--}20\% \text{ } H_2O \text{ (v/v)}$$

The order of c_1 and c_2 chosen is such that c_1 should measure sensitivity to the nucleophilic properties of the solvent (decreasing from CH_3Br to $(C_6H_5)_3CF$) and c_2 should measure sensitivity to the electrophilic properties of the solvent (increasing from CH_3Br to $(C_6H_5)_3CF$). The quantitative relationships chosen are open to objection, especially the definition that $(CH_3)_3CCl$ is *equally sensitive* to nucleophilic and electrophilic properties of the solvent. However, Eq. (5–11) gives an excellent correlation of the rates of 25 compounds ranging from *p*-nitrobenzoyl chloride to triphenylmethyl fluoride, using 18 different solvents ranging from methanol to formic acid (not all compounds have been studied in all solvents, of course).

Some representative values of d_1 and d_2, related to the nucleophilic and electrophilic properties of the solvent, respec-

TABLE 5–8

Constants from Eqs. (5–11) and (5–10)

Solvent	d_1[a]	d_2[a]	$d_1 - d_2$[a]	$\mathbf{Y}$[b]
HCO_2H	-4.40	$+6.53$	-10.9	$+2.054$
CH_3CO_2H	-4.82	$+3.12$	-7.9	-1.639
H_2O	-0.44	$+4.01$	-4.5	$+3.493$
$50\%\ CH_3COCH_3$	-0.25	$+0.97$	-1.2	$+1.398$
$90\%\ CH_3COCH_3$	-0.53	-1.52	$+1.0$	-1.856
$80\%\ C_2H_5OH$	(0.00)[c]	(0.00)[c]	(0.00)[c]	(0.000)[c]
C_2H_5OH	-0.53	-1.03	$+0.5$	-2.033
CH_3OH	-0.05	-0.73	$+0.7$	-1.090

Compound	c_1[a]	c_2[a]	$\dfrac{c_1}{c_2}$[a]	m[d]
CH_3Br	0.80	0.27	(3.0)[c]	0.26
$C_6H_5CH_2Cl$	0.74	0.44	1.7	0.43
$(CH_3)_2CHBr$	0.90	0.58	1.5	0.54
$C_6H_5CHClCH_3$	1.47	1.75	0.84	0.966
$(C_6H_5)_2CHCl$	1.24	1.25	0.99	0.740
$(C_6H_5)_2CHF$	0.32	1.17	0.27	0.98
$(CH_3)_3CCl$	(1.00)[c]	(1.00)[c]	(1.00)[c]	(1.000)[c]
$(C_6H_5)_3CF$	0.37	1.12	(0.33)[c]	0.890
$HC(CH_2CH_2)_3CBr$[e]	0.96	0.99	0.97	0.88

[a] Ref. (110).   [c] By definition.   [e] Ref. (60).
[b] Ref. (109).   [d] In C_2H_5OH-H_2O mixtures.

tively, along with $\mathbf{Y}$ values from Eq. (5–10), are in Table 5–8. Typical values of c_1 and c_2 are also in Table 5–8. The difference $d_1 - d_2$ is characteristic of the nucleophilic vs. electrophilic properties of the solvent, higher values corresponding to more nucleophilic solvents. The ratio c_1/c_2 tends to indicate the relative sensitivity of the substrate to nucleophilic vs. electrophilic properties of the solvent, higher values corresponding to relatively more sensitivity to nucleophilic character. Again the position of the bicyclic compound $HC(CH_2CH_2)_3CBr$ is odd; it appears to be as sensitive to nucleophilic assistance as $(CH_3)_3CCl$. Some other values are odd as well, for example $c_1 = 0.80$ for CH_3Br, indicating less nucleophilic sensitivity than $(CH_3)_3CCl$. The ratio c_1/c_2 increases only because of an even larger decrease in c_2. More theoretical as well as experimental work along these lines would be desirable in order to find out whether the parameters for CH_3Br and $HC(CH_2CH_2)_3CBr$ really are indicative of transition state properties. Other authors have suggested that the choice of definitions for c_1 and c_2 causes these apparently anomalous results. If, for example, we choose

$$c_2 = 0 \text{ for } CH_3Br$$
$$c_1 = c_2 = 1.00 \text{ for } (CH_3)_3CCl$$
$$c_1 = 0 \text{ for } (C_6H_5)_3CF$$

we obtain $c_1 = 1.06$ for CH_3Br and $c_2 = 1.50$ for $(C_6H_5)_3CF$.

The applicability of these solvent correlations to a substrate of a different charge type, $(CH_3)_3C–S^+(CH_3)_2$, is interesting (111). The reaction is a solvolysis, $i.e.$, does not involve the anion of the salt. The products are probably CH_3SCH_3 and compounds such as alcohol, ether, or olefin derived from the $tert$-butyl group. Therefore the solvolyses are similar to those of $(CH_3)_3C–Cl$, except that the leaving group is a neutral molecule instead of an anion. The rates of solvolysis were measured at $50.4°$ in 15 solvents: acetic acid, water, ethanol-water mixtures, methanol-water mixtures, and acetone-water mixtures. Correlation with $\mathbf{Y}$ gave a value of -0.107 for m. The correlation was not very good, partly because of large deviations for water and for acetic acid. As with other compounds, a rather good correlation is obtained for a single series of solvents, $e.g.$, various ethanol-water or acetone-water mixtures. Correlation with d_1 and d_2 gave $c_1 = -0.031$, $c_2 = -0.094$. As expected for reactions which involve dispersal of charge on going to the transition state, the sulfonium ion solvolyzes most rapidly in the least polar solvent. The sensitivities are rather small for both correlations. The authors (111) felt that the rates were determined by cation-solvating properties of solvents, which would explain why the correlations are not better. Alternatively, the results could be explained by the same factors that affect alkyl halide solvolyses.

Neighboring-Group Effects. We have previously mentioned neighboring-group effects (Chapter 4), but here we should discuss the effect which a neighboring group can have on reaction rates. Estimates have been made (112) of the amount of neighboring-group participation for different substituents on the β-carbon atom of an alkyl halide. The transition states presumably involve partial bonding of the neighboring group to the α-carbon atom:

The rate constant for solvolysis should be

$$k = k_c + k_\Delta$$

where k is the observed rate constant for reaction of the substrate, k_c is its rate constant for solvolysis in the absence of neighboring group participation, and k_Δ is its rate constant for neighboring-group participation. Neither k_c nor k_Δ can be determined experimentally, but k_c was calculated from the rate constants for X = H and Cl, both thought to produce no neighboring-group participation. The calculation was made by assuming that the major effect in the absence of participation would be the electrostatic interaction between the C-X dipole and the C-Y dipole in the transition state, and estimating the effective dielectric constant from the assumption that $k = k_c$ for both X = H and Cl. This approximation is crude, but the k_Δ effects are frequently so large that the error is negligible. Obviously the effect should depend on the nature

TABLE 5–9

Neighboring-Group Effects for β-Substituents

β-Neighboring-Group	$\dfrac{k_\Delta}{k_c}$	$\dfrac{k}{k_H}$ [a]
C_α = tertiary, C_β = primary		
I	7.2×10^2	0.486
Br	1.1	1.6×10^{-4}
Cl	(0.0) [b]	0.78×10^{-4}
OH or OCH_3	—	7.3×10^{-3}
C_α = secondary, C_β = secondary		
I	1.7×10^6	1120
Br	3.9×10^2	7.2×10^{-2}
Cl	(0.0) [b]	0.94×10^{-4}
OH or OCH_3	4.3	5.3×10^{-2}
C_α = tertiary, C_β = tertiary		
Br	4.7×10^2	3.5×10^{-2}
Cl	(0.0) [b]	0.85×10^{-4}
C_α = tertiary, C_β = secondary		
Br	44	3.4×10^{-3}

[a] Observed ratio for [(X = substituent listed in first column)/(X = H)] in same solvent at 25°.

[b] Assumed.

of R, R', R'', and R'''; it was investigated for certain cases where C_α and/or C_β were primary, secondary, and tertiary. Some results are presented in Table 5–9. From the experimental results further predictions for other types of compounds were made (112).

The results show that neighboring groups can have important effects on solvolysis *rates*, and that these effects can be correlated and explained in a simple manner. The problem of how to determine k_c more accurately is difficult, but may be solvable by using a σ^* correlation for compounds known *not* to involve participation, then estimating k_c (from ρ^*) for groups which *do* involve participation (3, 113).

The rates of ionization p-methoxyneophyl p-toluenesulfonate,

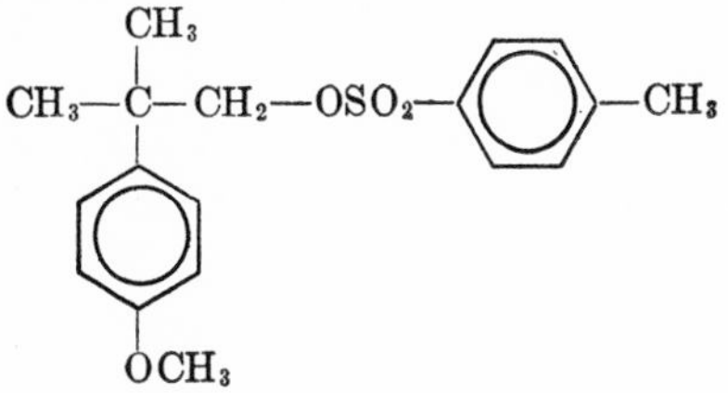

in various solvents have been reported (114).   The compound is known to involve neighboring group participation by the p-methoxyphenyl group, through an intermediate or possibly a transition state with phenyl-bridging:

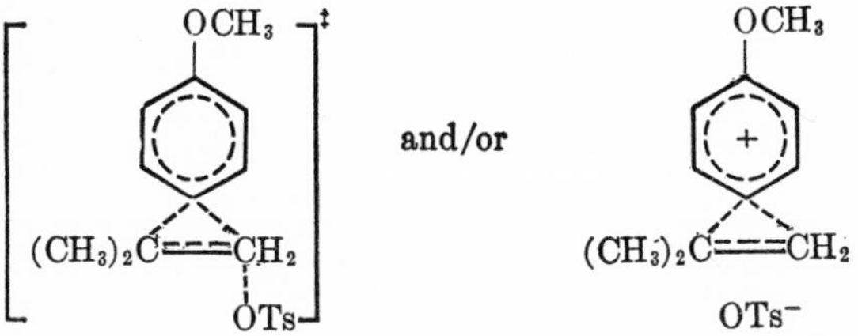

Therefore the rates of production of p-toluenesulfonic acid probably measure the rates of ionization (k_Δ) *uncomplicated by internal return*.   The results give satisfactory mY correlations over a wide range of solvents, but divide into branches for different binary solvent mixtures.   Values of m range from 0.421 for 60–100% C_2H_5OH-H_2O at 25° to 0.585 for 0–100% CH_3CO_2H-HCO_2H at 25°.   The relative rates are listed in Table 5–10.   They provide an interesting comparison of "ionizing power" over a wide range of solvents.   The lack of correlation with dielectric constant is particularly evident.

Data for the solvolysis of $[(CH_3)_2CH]_3CX$ where $X = p$-nitrobenzoate, and of derivatives in which isopropyl groups are successively replaced by cyclopropyl groups, are interesting

TABLE 5-10

Relative Rates of Solvolysis[a] of
p-Methoxyneophyl p-Toluenesulfonate

Solvent	D,[b] ca. 25°	Relative Rate, 75°[c]
H_2O	78.54	39.
HCO_2H	58.	153.
80% $C_2H_5OH–H_2O$	34.	1.85
CH_3CO_2H	6.2	(1.00)[d]
CH_3OH	32.63	0.947
C_2H_5OH	24.30	0.370
$(CH_3)_2SO$	45.	0.108
CH_3NO_2	36.7	7.3×10^{-2}
n-$C_7H_{15}CO_2H$	2.4	4.30×10^{-2}
CH_3CN	36.7	3.56×10^{-2}
$HCON(CH_3)_2$	36.71	2.94×10^{-2}
$CH_3CO_2COCH_3$	20.7	2.02×10^{-2}
C_5H_5N	12.3	1.27×10^{-2}
CH_3COCH_3	20.7	5.07×10^{-3}
$CH_3CO_2C_2H_5$	6.02	6.69×10^{-4}
$(CH_2)_4O$	7.39	5.0×10^{-4}
$(C_2H_5)_2O$	4.23	$ca.$ $3. \times 10^{-5}$

[a] Products presumably arise from substitution and/or elimination, depending on solvent, but rate-determining step is thought to be ionization.

[b] D = dielectric constant.

[c] Some of the numbers computed by extrapolation.

[d] By definition.

(115). In aqueous dioxane, a single cyclopropyl group increased the rate 246-fold; two cyclopropyl groups *further* increased the rate 95.6 fold; and three cyclopropyl groups *further* increased the rate 1080-fold (the last value was obtained from benzoates rather than p-nitrobenzoates because the tri-(cyclopropyl)carbinyl p-nitrobenzoate was unstable). These figures show that, in the latter two cases, two and three cyclopropyl groups participate *at the same time* in aiding solvolysis. If only one participated at a time, the rates should be approximately additive; *i.e.*, the rate with two should be twice the rate with one, and with three, thrice the rate with one. If all participate together the rates should be approximately multiplicative, *i.e.*, the rate with two should be the square of the rate with one, and with three, the cube of the rate with one. The latter is much more nearly the case than the former.

THERMODYNAMICS OF ACTIVATION

We have mentioned in Chapter 3 how the "pseudothermodynamic" quantities $\Delta H_0^{\ddagger}$ and $\Delta S_0^{\ddagger}$ can be derived and calculated by the transition state theory from measured rate constants at several temperatures. We will now discuss such quantities in more detail, and then some experimental results.

Potential Energy Surfaces. The potential energy curve for a reaction may be plotted, *e.g.*, with potential energy as the ordinate and the *reaction coordinate* as the abscissa (*cf.* Fig. 1). Such a curve is only a section of a complete potential energy surface. To really understand the mechanism of a reaction we should know how the potential energy changes as we displace the nuclei. The position of each nucleus could be specified by its three coordinates in space. Actually it is more instructive to specify the positions of the nuclei by means of the bond lengths and bond angles of the molecule. For a molecule in a very dilute solution and in the absence of a strong electrical or magnetic or centrifugal field, the molecular energy should be nearly independent of the rotational orientation and the translational direction. There are, for a non-linear molecule, three rotational degrees of freedom and three translational degrees of freedom, so to specify completely the nuclear positions we need only $3N - 6$ bond lengths and angles ($3N - 5$ for a linear molecule). Therefore, a graphical representation of the potential energy for all nuclear positions would require $3N - 6 + 1 = 3N - 5$ dimensions for a non-linear molecule (one dimension for energy, $3N - 6$ for bond lengths and angles), and $3N - 4$ dimensions for a linear molecule. For a simple diatomic molecule we would need two dimensions. A plot of this familiar type is shown in Fig. 9a, only the bond length being necessary to specify the relative positions of the nuclei.

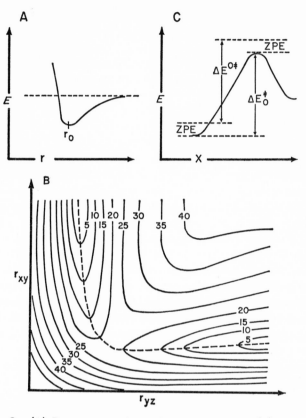

Fig. 9. (A) Energy curve for a diatomic molecule; (B) potential energy contour surface for reaction $X + YZ \rightarrow XY + Z$; (C) two kinds of energy of activation. ZPE stands for zero-point energy.

A plot for more than two nuclei does not fit into three-dimensional space. If we restrict ourselves to a linear triatomic molecule, making it very stiff so that the bonds cannot bend but can stretch, we would need three dimensions. This arises because there are two independent bending motions for a linear triatomic molecule, and $9 - 4 - 2 = 3$. By restricting our interest to linear configurations we can plot the potential energy for a reaction (*e.g.*, a SN2 displacement) like

$$X + YZ \rightarrow [X\text{---}Y\text{---}Z]^{\ddagger} \rightarrow XY + Z$$

on a three-dimensional contour diagram. The linear configuration should be most stable for such a reaction (in the absence of strong steric effects, *cf.* Table 3–2), particularly if it is a nucleophilic displacement, since electronic repulsions should be minimized. This fact provides a ready explanation for the Walden inversion (backside displacement) observed in nucleophilic substitution. Or, depending on one's point of view, the Walden inversion provides a ready explanation for the principle of linearity. The usual plot has the two bond lengths as ordinate and abscissa and contour lines of constant energy. This is illustrated in Fig. 9b.

The valence-bond or resonance theory of chemical bonding, which is very similar to, but more complex than, the MO theory, can be used to calculate the potential energy surface for a reaction. Although the results are crude because of the drastic approximations necessary to simplify the mathematics, it would be well worthwhile to make such calculations for reactions in which the nature of the activated complex is known from kinetic, stereochemical, or other studies. It is impossible to derive the results here (see (13)), but they are worth discussing. For a linear triatomic system,

$$E = A + B + C - \{\tfrac{1}{2}[(\alpha - \beta)^2 + (\beta - \gamma)^2 + (\alpha - \gamma)^2]\}^{1/2}$$

where A, B, and C are called coulombic terms and α, β, and γ are called resonance terms. The coulombic terms are related to the attraction of nuclei for the electrons and are therefore somewhat *analogous to* (but quite different from) the coulomb integral α of the MO theory (Chapter 3). The resonance terms are related to orbital overlap and are therefore somewhat analogous to the overlap integral β of the MO theory. The quantities A, B, C, α, β, and γ are very difficult to calculate and so must be evaluated empirically in order to get anywhere with calculating E. However, it is a feature of this valence-bond method that $A + \alpha$ is very nearly the energy of the diatomic molecule XY, $B + \beta$ the energy of YZ, and $C + \gamma$ the energy of XZ (13). The energies of the diatomic molecules can be determined from spectroscopic measurements, and expressed mathematically as a function of the distance between the two nuclei by a Morse function:

$$A + \alpha = D^e_{XY}[e^{-2a_{XY}(r_{XY}-r_{XY}{}^0)} - 2e^{-a_{XY}(r_{XY}-r_{XY}{}^0)}]$$
$$B + \beta = D^e_{YZ}[e^{-2a_{YZ}(r_{YZ}-r_{YZ}{}^0)} - 2e^{-a_{YZ}(r_{YZ}-r_{YZ}{}^0)}]$$
$$C + \gamma = D^e_{XZ}[e^{-2a_{XZ}(r_{XY}+r_{YZ}-r_{XZ}{}^0)} - 2e^{-a_{XZ}(r_{XY}+r_{YZ}-r_{XZ}{}^0)}]$$

since $r_{XY} + r_{YZ} = r_{XZ}$ for a linear XYZ system. In these equations D^e is the dissociation energy of the diatomic molecule D plus the zero-point energy $\mathbf{h}\nu/2$, and a is a constant (13):

$$a = 0.1227\omega_0(\mu/D^e)^{1/2}$$

where ω_0 is the equilibrium vibrational frequency and μ is the reduced mass of the molecule, ω_0 and D^e being expressed in wave numbers (cm.$^{-1}$). The bond lengths are r, the *actual* internuclear distance, and r^0, the *equilibrium* internuclear distance. The energy is zero when the nuclei are infinitely separated. The only thing we do not know theoretically is how the quantities $A + \alpha$, $B + \beta$, $C + \gamma$ should be divided between coulombic and resonance terms. The usual assumption is that the coulombic term comprises about 14 per cent of the total: $A = 0.14$ $(A + \alpha)$, $B = 0.14$ $(B + \beta)$, $C = 0.14$ $(C + \gamma)$. Using the above equations, E can be calculated for any chosen values of r_{XY} and r_{YZ} and thus the potential energy surface plotted. Simplified methods have been developed (13), but a complete plot still requires a lot of computation time unless an electronic computer is available.

There are two implicit assumptions in this method which we have not yet mentioned. First, we assumed the reaction is electronically adiabatic, meaning that we calculate E for each set of values of r_{XY} and r_{YZ} assuming the system remains in its *lowest* electronic energy level. This probably is true for most reactions at ordinary temperatures. What we are really assuming is that there is an *equilibrium* between all possible configurations of XYZ, not merely between reactants and transition state. Second, we assumed that the electronic and nuclear motions can be treated independently. This approximation, known as the Born-Oppenheimer approximation, is probably valid to a small fraction of a per cent. Because the electrons move much faster than the nuclei (since they are so much lighter), we can assume that the electrons adjust themselves to their most favorable distribution for each possible internuclear distance. If the nuclei move a slight distance, the electrons "follow along" immediately. This means that we can first solve the Schrödinger equation for the *electronic probabilities* as a function of the internuclear distance, then use the potential energy of this electronic distribution to solve another Schrödinger equation for the nuclei. The possibility of separation of electronic energy levels from vibrational energy levels in the calculation of partition functions (Chapter 3) is a result of the Born-Oppenheimer approximation.

Normally the reaction coordinate is considered to be the pathway of least resistance from reactants to products (dashed line in Fig. 9b). The transition state is the highest energy configuration on this pathway of least resistance. Such a surface has been vividly described by Moelwyn-Hughes (116; *cf.* Fig. 9b):

If we imagine ourselves to take the place of the representative point of the reacting system, we can gain a clearer view of what happens. Starting at [reactants], we climb a gentle ascent southwards in a valley flanked by mountains, those on our right being the steeper. Round about the [transition state] there is a virtually horizontal walk, beyond which we descend into a second valley eastwards. The height of the pass is the energy of activation.

We could then make a plot of energy *vs.* reaction coordinate by using the distance *along the dashed line* as the abscissa.

Kinds of Activation Energy. A rate constant can be expressed as (*cf.* Chapter 3):

$$k = \frac{\mathbf{k}T}{\mathbf{h}} e^{-\Delta H_0^{\ddagger}/\mathbf{R}T} e^{\Delta S_0^{\ddagger}/\mathbf{R}}$$

If we assume that $\Delta H_0^{\ddagger}$ and $\Delta S_0^{\ddagger}$ are independent of temperature, we can calculate them by measuring the rate constant at several temperatures. Up to this point we have used the same symbol F for both Gibbs and Helmholtz free energy. Almost all experimental measurements in solution are made at constant pressure, so that the experimental free energy differences (*e.g.*, $\Delta F_0^{\ddagger}$) which we calculate are really Gibbs free energies. But the calculation based on partition function ratios gives us Helmholtz free energies. We dismissed this discrepancy between theory and experiment by stating (page 30) that in solution the two quantities are essentially the same. They are related by the equation (in the case of activation free energies):

$$(\Delta F_0^{\ddagger})_{\text{GIBBS}} = (\Delta F_0^{\ddagger})_{\text{HELMHOLTZ}} + p\,\Delta V_0^{\ddagger}$$

p being the pressure and $\Delta V_0^{\ddagger}$ the difference in volume between transition state and reactants. For a typical bimolecular reaction in solution, $\Delta V_0^{\ddagger}$ turns out to be of the order of -20 cm.^{3}/mole, which corresponds to *ca.* -0.5 cal./mole at 1 atm. pressure. Thus in fact the differences will generally be less than one small calorie per mole, whereas typical values of $\Delta F_0^{\ddagger}$ are of the order of 20,000 cal./mole and cannot be measured with an accuracy better than *ca.* ± 50 cal./mole at present. Ignoring the difference between the two kinds of free energy therefore seems justified in solution.

The enthalpy of a pure element (in its most stable state at 25°C and 1 atm.) is *defined* as zero. The absolute enthalpy of any compound is then equal to its enthalpy of formation. Accordingly, ΔE^0 is given by the difference in enthalpies of formation at 0°K. between products and reactants (*cf.* page 30).

$\Delta H_0^{\ddagger}$, $\Delta S_0^{\ddagger}$, and $\Delta F_0^{\ddagger}$ are *average*, not molecular, quantities. The subscript zeroes indicate differences with each substance *in its standard state.* This distinction is slightly confusing. We say that the reactants and transition states are in equilibrium, and we know that at equilibrium the free energy difference is zero. In an actual reaction mixture, the free energy difference between reactants and transition states *is* really zero. There are far fewer transition states present at any given time than there are reactant molecules because the free energy of each transition state that is present is much higher than the free energy of the reactant molecule(s) which are brought together to form a transition state. The thermodynamic quantities like $\Delta F_0^{\ddagger}$ measure the free energy difference that there would be per mole if all the substances were present, *not* in equilibrium concentrations, but in standard state concentrations. These standard state concentrations can be chosen in any way we like, the usual choice for solutions being a hypothetical perfect 1-Molar solution, and the free energy difference may be somewhat different depending on the choice. Usually reactions are run at high dilution so that the solutions will behave like perfect solutions, and then the results are corrected to the standard state of unit concentration by the appropriate multiplicative factor.

Since, for the example of a reaction $A + B \rightarrow M^{\ddagger}$,

$$ k = \frac{\mathbf{k}T}{\mathbf{h}} \frac{Q^{\ddagger}}{Q_{A}^{0} Q_{B}^{0}} e^{-\Delta E_0^{\ddagger}/\mathbf{R}T} = \frac{\mathbf{k}T}{\mathbf{h}} e^{-\Delta H_0^{\ddagger}/\mathbf{R}T} e^{\Delta S_0^{\ddagger}/\mathbf{R}} $$

it is easy to show that

$$ \frac{d}{dT}\left[\ln\left(\frac{k}{T}\right) \right] = \frac{\Delta H_0^{\ddagger}}{\mathbf{R}T^2} = \frac{\Delta E_0^{\ddagger}}{\mathbf{R}T^2} + \frac{d}{dT}\left[\ln\left(\frac{Q^{\ddagger}}{Q_{A}^{0} Q_{B}^{0}}\right) \right] $$

or

$$ \Delta E_0^{\ddagger} = \Delta H_0^{\ddagger} - \mathbf{R}T^2 \frac{d}{dT}\left[\ln\left(\frac{Q^{\ddagger}}{Q_{A}^{0} Q_{B}^{0}}\right) \right] $$

The theoretical quantity $\Delta E_0^{\ddagger}$, which is the activation potential energy (from the potential energy surface), is therefore not easily calculated from $\Delta H_0^{\ddagger}$, the experimental activation enthalpy. If we really knew the potential energy surface completely, we could calculate the mass, moments of inertia, and vibrational frequencies of the transition state. From these the partition functions could be calculated. Knowing the partition functions and $\Delta E_0^{\ddagger}$ from the potential energy surface, $\Delta H_0^{\ddagger}$ could be calculated and compared with experiment. The important point is that $\Delta H_0^{\ddagger}$ is a composite quantity, *i.e.*, an average including both potential and kinetic energies. $\Delta E_0^{\ddagger}$ is *not* the activation energy at 0°K., $\Delta E^{0\ddagger}$, because the molecules still have their zero-point energies even at 0°K. If we include these zero-point energies,

$$\Delta E^{0\ddagger} = \Delta E_0^{\ddagger} + N_0 \sum \frac{h\nu^{\ddagger}}{2} - N_0 \sum \frac{h\nu_r}{2}$$

where Avogadro's number N_0 is used to put everything on a per-mole scale. The difference is shown in Fig. 9c, which is a plot of energy *vs.* reaction coordinate x. $\Delta E^{0\ddagger}$ and $\Delta E_0^{\ddagger}$ are *molecular*, rather than *average*, properties.*

The Arrhenius activation energy E_A is (*cf.* Chapter 3)

$$E_A = R T^2 \frac{d \ln k}{dT}$$

and is therefore, by simple differentiation

$$E_A = RT + \Delta H_0^{\ddagger}$$

There is some difference of opinion about which experimental activation parameters are "more significant." Obviously the potential energy difference $\Delta E_0^{\ddagger}$ is *most* significant because it is a molecular property rather than an average property. But all the experimental parameters, *e.g.*, $\Delta F_0^{\ddagger}$,

---

* Because free energy is an *average* property, it is obvious that we have not been justified in drawing free energy diagrams (*e.g.*, Figs. 1 and 7). Whereas potential energy is defined for all molecular configurations, free energy can be defined only at extrema of the potential energy surface. We can discuss free energies of reactants, transition states, intermediates, or products, but we should not connect their free energy values by a curve.

$\Delta H_0^{\ddagger}$, $\Delta S_0^{\ddagger}$, and E_A are average properties. The advantage of $\Delta F_0^{\ddagger}$ is that it is a *minimized* quantity. The advantage of $\Delta H_0^{\ddagger}$ is that it contains no entropy contribution. The unresolved question seems to be, "Is the free energy or the enthalpy a better measure of the quantity we want but cannot get experimentally, $\Delta E_0^{\ddagger}$?"

All the derivations and differentiations above are based on the assumption that $\Delta H_0^{\ddagger}$ is temperature-independent. In fact, it is not, as pointed out in Chapter 3 (*cf.* Eq. (3–1)). We could, as a better approximation, include a *heat-capacity* term:

$$\Delta H_0^{\ddagger} = \Delta H_0^{0\ddagger} + \Delta C_p^{\ddagger} T$$
$$\Delta S_0^{\ddagger} = \Delta S_0^{0\ddagger} + \Delta C_p^{\ddagger} \ln T$$

where $\Delta C_p^{\ddagger}$ is the heat capacity (at constant pressure) of the transition state minus the sum of the heat capacities of the reactants. Then

$$\log k = \log\left(\frac{k}{h}\right) + \log T - \frac{\Delta H_0^{0\ddagger}}{2.3026\ \mathbf{R}T} - \frac{\Delta C_p^{\ddagger}}{2.3026\ \mathbf{R}}$$
$$+ \frac{\Delta S_0^{0\ddagger}}{2.3026\ \mathbf{R}} + \frac{\Delta C_p^{\ddagger}}{\mathbf{R}} \log T$$

If the experimental data can be fitted to an equation of the form

$$\log k = \frac{A}{T} + B \log T + C$$

the thermodynamic quantities can be calculated (117):

$$A = -\frac{\Delta H_0^{0\ddagger}}{2.3026\ \mathbf{R}}$$
$$B = \frac{\Delta C_p^{\ddagger}}{\mathbf{R}} + 1$$
$$C = \log\left(\frac{k}{h}\right) + \frac{\Delta S_0^{0\ddagger} - \Delta C_p^{\ddagger}}{2.3026\ \mathbf{R}}$$

Some question exists as to whether $\Delta C_p^{\ddagger}$ might itself be temperature-dependent, but the most accurate data do not require it to be.

Experimental Results. At present rates have been measured accurately enough to evaluate $\Delta C_p^{\ddagger}$ for only a few reactions. The greatest accuracy has been attained by conductivity measurement.

The hydrolyses of the four methyl halides provide the most complete data (118). Because the thermodynamic quantities for the methyl halides in the vapor state, and for their solution in water, and for their hydrolysis reactions, are known, the thermodynamic quantities for the *hydrolysis transition states* can be calculated. The results are presented in Table 5–11. Although the entropy and heat capacity of the transition states increase regularly in the series F, Cl, Br, I, the enthalpy of the transition state for I is "out of order," causing CH_3I to hydrolyze more slowly than CH_3Br. Since both $\Delta H_0^{\ddagger}$ and $\Delta F_0^{\ddagger}$ are "anomalous" for CH_3I, it is probably safe to assume that $\Delta E_0^{\ddagger}$, the *molecular* property, is also anomalous and that there is some small mechanistic change in the CH_3I transition state as compared with the transition states for the other three methyl halides. One guess is that the solvation bonds to the incipient halide ion are different. It is probable that F^-, Cl^-, and Br^- are coordinated with four water molecules in aqueous solution. In the transition state, only three sites (three-fourths of the total) are available for hydration, because the fourth site is still partially bonded to carbon. It is probable that I^-, on the other hand, is coordinated with six water molecules in aqueous solution. In the transition state, it may not be possible for five of the six sites to be hydrated because of steric hindrance to solvation by the CH_3 group. If only four of the six sites (two-thirds of the total) are utilized, the solvation may not be proportionally as strong as with the other halides, and this could increase the energy required to reach the transition state for CH_3I $(27.36(\frac{2}{3}/\frac{3}{4}) = 24.32$, right "in order").

TABLE 5-11

Thermodynamic Description of Hydrolysis Transition States of the Four Methyl Halides

	Substrate			
	CH_3F	CH_3Cl	CH_3Br	CH_3I
At 298.16°K.				
$(H^0 - H_0{}^0)$, kcal. mole^{-1} [a]	2.42	2.49	2.54	2.59
$-\delta_s H$, kcal. mole^{-1} [b]	4.41	5.67	6.28	6.38
$\Delta H_0{}^\ddagger$, kcal. mole^{-1}	27.32	26.56	25.30	27.36
$(H_0{}^\ddagger - H_0{}^0)$, kcal. mole^{-1} [c]	25.33	23.38	21.56	23.59
$S_g{}^0$, cal. mole^{-1} deg. $^{-1}$ [d]	46.95	49.62	52.39	54.50
$\delta_s S^g$, cal. mole^{-1} deg.$^{-1}$ [e]	-14.11	-17.13	-18.30	-18.32
$\Delta S_0{}^\ddagger$, cal. mole^{-1} deg.$^{-1}$	-8.70	-4.31	-2.91	0.61
$S_\ddagger{}^0$, cal. mole^{-1} deg.$^{-1}$ [f]	24.14	28.18	31.18	36.79
$S_{ion}{}^0$, cal. mole^{-1} deg.$^{-1}$ [g]	-2.3	13.17	19.30	26.14
$C_p{}^0$, cal. mole^{-1} deg.$^{-1}$ [h]	8.94	9.73	10.14	10.55
$\delta_s C_p$, cal. mole^{-1} deg.$^{-1}$ [i]	35.26	43.02	44.22	85.35
$\Delta C_p{}^\ddagger$, cal. mole^{-1} deg.$^{-1}$	-69.0	-52.0	-46.5	-56.5
$C_{p\ddagger}{}^0$, cal. mole^{-1} deg.$^{-1}$ [j]	-14.81	0.77	7.91	39.41
At 373.16°K.				
$\Delta H_0{}^\ddagger$, kcal. mole^{-1}	22.141	22.664	21.819	23.125
$\Delta S_0{}^\ddagger$, cal. mole^{-1} deg.$^{-1}$	-24.19	-16.46	-13.37	-12.07

[a] Enthalpy of vapor.
[b] $-$ (Enthalpy of solution in H_2O).
[c] Enthalpy of transition state.
[d] Entropy of vapor.
[e] Entropy of solution in H_2O.
[f] Entropy of transition state.
[g] Entropy of halide *ion* in H_2O.
[h] Heat capacity of vapor.
[i] Heat capacity of solution in H_2O.
[j] Heat capacity of transition state.

It is interesting that $\Delta H_0^\ddagger$ and $\Delta S_0^\ddagger$ are highly temperature-dependent for these hydrolyses. Possible explanations have been offered (12, 119), assuming that several water molecules may be involved in the transition state. The basic idea is related to the generalized Boltzmann distribution (Eq. (3-2)). If we cast Eq. (3-1) into a form involving $\Delta C_p^\ddagger$, we find that $C/R = (\Delta C_p^\ddagger/R) + 1$. It followed from Eq. (3-2) that $C/R = -(s - 1)$, where $2s$ is the number of squared terms in the energy of activation, if $E \gg RT$. Therefore $s = -\Delta C_p^\ddagger/R$

and is 35 for CH_3F, 26 for CH_3Cl, 23 for CH_3Br, and 28 for CH_3I hydrolyses (based on the most recent values of $\Delta C_p^{\ddagger}$ (118)). It was assumed that $s - 1$ is the number of harmonic oscillators, *i.e.*, vibrational degrees of freedom, contributing to the activation process. For methyl bromide, not all the internal vibrations could participate in activation, but if about 6 do participate, and if about 4 vibrational degrees of freedom (including the hindered rotations) participate for each water molecule involved, then $s - 1 = 6 + 4n$ where n is the number of water molecules. For CH_3F, $n \approx 7$; for CH_3Cl, $n \approx 5$; for CH_3Br, $n \approx 4$; and for CH_3I, $n \approx 5$. If this sort of reasoning is correct, then CH_3I does indeed require one more, rather than two more, water molecules than CH_3Br. It should be emphasized that such calculations are only approximate explanations of the very negative values of $\Delta C_p^{\ddagger}$ observed in hydrolysis reactions and do not prove anything about the actual numbers of water molecules involved. It seems reasonable, however, that several water molecules might contribute to hydrolysis transition states.

Similar data are available for the hydrolysis of *tert*-butyl chloride (120): at 298.16°K., $\Delta H_0^{\ddagger} = 21.245$ kcal. mole^{-1}, $\Delta S_0^{\ddagger} = 5.68$ cal. mole^{-1} deg.$^{-1}$, and $\Delta C_p^{\ddagger} = -184$ cal. mole^{-1} deg.$^{-1}$. At 298.16°K., *tert*-butyl chloride hydrolyzes 1.24×10^6 times faster than methyl chloride, on account of both a lower enthalpy of activation and a higher entropy of activation. It is noteworthy that $\Delta C_p^{\ddagger}$ is over three times as negative for *tert*-butyl chloride as for methyl chloride, indicating that many more water molecules are involved in the activation of the tertiary substrate even if a much larger number of degrees of freedom of the substrate contributes. The rate of reaction of *tert*-butyl chloride is so great that even if its SN2 reaction with hydroxide ion were as fast as the SN2 reaction of methyl chloride with hydroxide ion, the SN2 reaction would be negligibly slow compared to the hydrolysis. This may be a result of solvation of the hydroxide ion (120). If a strongly bound water molecule must be removed from HO$^-$ before it can effect SN2 displacement, a lower limit to the activation energy is automatically set, regardless of the ease of breaking the C—Cl bond.

The methanolyses of *tert*-butyl chloride, bromide, and iodide have been studied in detail (121), with the result that $\Delta C_p^{\ddagger} = -45.52$ cal. mole^{-1} deg.$^{-1}$ for $(CH_3)_3CCl$, -40.45 for $(CH_3)_3CBr$, and -37.72 for $(CH_3)_3CI$; $\Delta H_0^{\ddagger}$ at 298.16°K. = 24.978 kcal. mole^{-1} for $(CH_3)_3CCl$, 24.087 for $(CH_3)_3CBr$, and 22.055 for $(CH_3)_3CI$. The important points are that in these cases the rate is greatest and the enthalpy is least for the iodide, as opposed to the results for the methyl halides in water, and that $\Delta C_p^{\ddagger}$ is much less for the methanolysis than for the hydrolysis of the chloride. Although we cannot be sure because we are comparing completely different solvents, it looks as if the methanolysis may be more SN2-like than SN1-like, the values of $\Delta C_p^{\ddagger}$ for methanolysis of the tertiary halides being close to those for hydrolysis of *methyl* halides rather than $(CH_3)_3CCl$. Such comparisons of $\Delta C_p^{\ddagger}$ may be useful mechanistic criteria when more data become available. Values for methanolysis of the methyl halides would be very interesting.

Some data for hydrolysis of other substrates also are available. Results for benzyl chloride and allyl chloride ($CH_2=CH—CH_2Cl$), bromide, and iodide are in Table 5–12. Some

TABLE 5–12

Thermodynamic Quantities for Hydrolysis of Allylic and Benzylic Halides[a]

Substrate	$\Delta H_0^{\ddagger}$, kcal. mole^{-1}		$\Delta S_0^{\ddagger}$, cal. mole^{-1} deg.$^{-1}$		$\Delta C_p^{\ddagger}$, cal. mole^{-1} deg.$^{-1}$
	298.16°K.	373.16°K.	298.16°K.	373.16°K.	
$CH_2=CH—CH_2Cl$	23.26	19.51	-7.73	-18.96	-50.1
$CH_2=CH—CH_2Br$	22.63	18.20	-4.46	-17.71	-59.1
$CH_2=CH—CH_2I$	24.08	20.58	-1.58	-12.05	-46.7
$C_6H_5—CH_2Cl$	21.40	18.37	-9.09	-18.15	-40.4

[a] Ref. (117).

interesting inversions of order occur between 25° and 100°, but the reasons for such behavior are not well enough understood for any interpretation. In the allyl halide hydrolyses, as in the methyl halide hydrolyses, the iodide falls in an "anomalous" order with respect to $\Delta H_0^{\ddagger}$. See also Ref. (22), page 179.

The hydrolyses of all the chloromethanes have been investigated (122). Reaction of CCl_4 with water is very unusual in that it appears to be second-order with respect to CCl_4. Possibly (122) this unexpected mechanism arises because there is no C—H bond in the substrate, so that no vibrational frequency of the substrate lies near enough to one of the three vibrational frequencies of H_2O to "couple" with it, the activation energy being of necessity supplied by a second substrate molecule. To explain these observations in terms of transition state theory will require a detailed study of the products and other mechanistic features.

We have been assuming that all rates were measured in "hypothetical perfect" solutions, *i.e.*, effectively at infinite dilution, and have therefore assumed that all activity coefficients were unity. The rates and activation parameters for $(CH_3)_3CCl$ hydrolysis have been measured (123) with unit (1 atm.) *pressure* of $(CH_3)_3CCl$ above an aqueous solution as the standard state, with the result that $\Delta H_p^{\ddagger}$ at 8° = 14.3 kcal. mole^{-1} and $\Delta S_p^{\ddagger}$ = 24.9 cal. mole^{-1} deg.$^{-1}$. These activation parameters include the change on solution of the vapor plus the change on activation. The usefulness of these results is that the same method can be applied to other solvent systems and the parameters directly interpreted in terms of transition state properties because the initial state in each case is the hypothetical perfect gas at 1 atm. pressure. The technique has been applied to aqueous solutions of electrolytes (123) up to 1 M. *Specific* salt effects on the transition states are found, thought to be caused by changes in "internal pressure" of the solvent resulting from the presence of the salt. But the specific effect of the salt on the transition state is practically equal to the specific effect of the salt on the substrate in solution. Thus, if one compares salt effects on *rate constants determined from concentrations in solution,* the specific effects cancel between initial and transition state and the salt effects in this case can be predicted from an electrostatic model, depending on ionic strength but not on the nature of the ions. The changes in rates of solvolysis of three chlorides in 40–85% aqueous acetone have been found to be caused largely by changes in the free energy of the *reactant* rather than the transition state (124).

For a number of series of compounds values for $\Delta H_0^{\ddagger}$ and $\Delta S_0^{\ddagger}$ are available. One of the most extensive is the solvolysis of substituted cumyl chlorides in 90% acetone-water (v/v). From the representative results in Table 5–13 (125), it can

TABLE 5–13

Enthalpy and Entropy of Activation for Solvolysis of Substituted Cumyl Chlorides ($C_6H_5C(CH_3)_2Cl$) in 90% Acetone-Water (v/v)

Substituent	$\Delta H_0^{\ddagger}$, kcal. mole^{-1}	$\Delta S_0^{\ddagger}$, cal. mole^{-1} deg.$^{-1}$
None	18.8	-12.5
$m\text{-}CO_2CH_3$	21.7	-11.2
$p\text{-}CO_2CH_3$	22.1	-11.1
$m\text{-}CF_3$	21.4	-15.5
$p\text{-}CF_3$	21.7	-16.3
$m\text{-}CN$	20.8	-18.3
$p\text{-}CN$	23.4	-11.5
$o\text{-}CH_3$	19.0	-10.4
$m\text{-}CH_3$	18.6	-11.8
$p\text{-}CH_3$	17.3	-12.0
$o\text{-}F$	20.3	-14.4
$m\text{-}F$	19.9	-17.0
$p\text{-}F$	18.8	-11.7
$m\text{-}NO_2$[a]	21.0	-10.0
$p\text{-}NO_2$[a]	21.9	-9.3
$p\text{-}OCH_3$[b]	12.9	-21.1

[a] In 60% acetone-water (by *weight*).
[b] In 94.8% acetone-water (by *weight*).

TABLE 5–14

Enthalpy and Entropy of Activation for Solvolysis p-$CH_3OC_6H_4C(CH_3)_2CH_2OTs$ at 50°

Solvent	$\Delta H_0^{\ddagger}$, kcal. mole^{-1}	$\Delta S_0^{\ddagger}$, cal. mole^{-1} deg.$^{-1}$
C_2H_5OH-H_2O (v/v)		
100%–0%	23.56	−5.8
80%–20%	21.75	−7.8
CH_3OH-H_2O (v/v)		
100%–0%	23.12	−5.2
80%–20%	21.31	−7.8
CH_3CO_2H	23.09	−5.2
CH_3CO_2H + 8.00 M H_2O		
+ 0.068 M $Li^+CH_3CO_2^-$	20.7	−9.

be seen that the differences are really very small and that the enthalpy and entropy usually tend both to increase or both to decrease, as expected (page 45).

The activation parameters will of course vary with solvent also. Those for solvolysis of p-$CH_3OC_6H_4C(CH_3)_2CH_2OTs$ (114) in a number of solvents are in Table 5–14. The entropies of activation are relatively more positive than for the cumyl chlorides, probably because neighboring-group participation eliminates the need for orienting as many solvent molecules.

It has been pointed out that the success of the linear free energy relationships involving solvent "ionizing power" with a wide variety of solvents is probably the result of the cancellation of specific *solvent* effects between reactant and transition state (123), so that mainly electrostatic interactions determine relative rates in different solvents. Mixed solvents can add complications; therefore, various *pure* solvents are probably more valuable to study than mixtures (123).

An example of the complexity of the problem for solvent mixtures is the solvolysis of *tert*-butyl chloride in various binary solvent mixtures (126). Although the free energy of activation tends to change smoothly as a function of solvent composition, the enthalpy and entropy of activation tend to go through one or more maxima or minima. The behavior is most complex in $C_2H_5OH-H_2O$ mixtures, where, for example, the entropy of activation goes through two maxima and two minima as the mole fraction of H_2O is varied from zero to one! The maximum change in $\Delta S_0^{\ddagger}$ is from -8.7 cal. deg.$^{-1}$ mole^{-1} to $+12.8$; in $\Delta H_0^{\ddagger}$, from 26.13 kcal. mole^{-1} to 20.20 (see (19), p. 397). The thermodynamic quantities for solvolysis of $(CH_3)_3CCl$ in pure solvents are in Table 5–15. The entropy of activation in H_2O is "anomalous," and possibly is related to the tetrahedrally hydrogen-bonded structure of liquid water. A similar "anomalous" $\Delta S_0^{\ddagger}$ is found for hydrolysis of other compounds, even methyl bromide (126), indicating that the peculiarity may be caused by some property of the liquid rather than any specific mechanistic details.

Volume of Activation. The effect of high pressure on the rates of reactions can be very useful. In principle, if activity coefficients are neglected,

$$\left(\frac{\partial \ln k}{\partial p}\right)_T = -\frac{\Delta V^{\ddagger}}{RT}$$

and $\Delta V^{\ddagger}$, the difference in volume between transition state and reactant(s) can be calculated. There are complications, however, in that the activity coefficients of ions can be highly

TABLE 5–15

Enthalpy and Entropy of Activation for Solvolysis
of $(CH_3)_3CCl$ in Pure Solvents at 25°

Solvent	$\Delta H_0^{\ddagger}$, kcal. mole^{-1}	$\Delta S_0^{\ddagger}$, cal. mole^{-1} deg.$^{-1}$
HOH	23.22	$+12.2$
HCO_2H	21.0	-1.7
$HCONH_2$	22.36	-3.8
CH_3OH	24.88	-3.1
CH_3CO_2H	25.80	-2.5
C_2H_5OH	26.13	-3.2

pressure-dependent (127, 128), especially in solvents of low dielectric constant. This is not a complication for non-ionic solutes, and even highly ionic transition states present no problem because their concentration must be very small so that their activity coefficients are essentially unity. The problem for non-ionic solutes is that transition states and reactants have a finite *compressibility*, making $\Delta V^{\ddagger}$ itself pressure-dependent. Extrapolation of $\Delta V^{\ddagger}$ to one atmosphere pressure is difficult, because pressure has only a small effect on rates and measurements must be made at several thousand atmospheres.

The standard states must be in molality or mole fraction units because the molarity *unit* is affected by pressure, because of the compressibility of the solution.

We might mention the methanolyses of ethyl chloride, bromide, and iodide at 65° (129). Pressure speeds up the methanolyses ($\Delta V^{\ddagger}$ is negative), speeding up that of C_2H_5Cl most and of C_2H_5I least. The reasons for these results are not completely clear, but a negative $\Delta V^{\ddagger}$ would be expected for a SN2 reaction where two molecules are brought together in the transition state. Since several solvent molecules may be involved, it is difficult to interpret the results uniquely, but the transition state for methanolysis of C_2H_5Cl seems to be more "compressed" (more negative $\Delta V^{\ddagger}$). It may be possible to make approximate empirical corrections for the compressibilities of reactant(s) and transition state (127). Probably differences in $\Delta V^{\ddagger}$ in related reactions are significant as long as they are determined in the same way.

REFERENCES

The book by Leffler and Grunwald (19) is a thorough discussion of linear free energy relationships and entropy-enthalpy relationships, and is the most complete work available on these subjects. There are many other discussions of linear free energy relationships (1, 2, 14, 93, 97), one of the most concise and informative discussions being in Hammett's book (73), although it lacks data gathered since 1940. The Kirkwood-Westheimer treatment of solvent effects in ionizations (99) is classical. The recent discussion of field effects of substituents (102) by Dewar and Grisdale is very interesting. Swain and Langsdorf's paper on curved Hammett plots (103) gives a good discussion of the subject. Edwards and Pearson's review on nucleophilicity (105) is well worth reading since it discusses in detail many possible factors determining nucleophilicity. The Swain (110, 111) and Winstein (108, 109, 114) discussions of solvent effects help provide a basis for understanding the factors which may influence such effects. The paper by Heppolette and Robertson (118), wherein the thermodynamics of the transition states for hydrolysis of the methyl halides is discussed, is a good example of the interesting information which can be obtained when a large amount of data is available about a single reaction. The *Advances in Physical Organic Chemistry* volumes have several articles of interest (100, 128). A number of interesting chapters in P. deMayo (ed), *Molecular Rearrangements*, (Interscience, New York, 1964), relate to the topics in this chapter and in Chapter 4.

6

Isotope Effects

An excellent discussion of the theoretical and experimental aspects of isotope effects is given by Melander's book in this Series (130). We will briefly discuss the theory and then experimental results for solvolysis reactions, especially some recent work.

THEORY

The transition-state theory is especially suited to discussion of isotope effects because the partition function ratios simplify considerably. The starting point is the excellent approximation that the potential energy surface (and therefore the bond lengths, bond angles, and force constants) is the same for isotopically substituted molecules. The potential energy surface is determined by the electron probability function (wave function) for the molecule. The wave function is determined by the electrostatic interactions between nuclei and electrons, which are the same because the nuclear charges are by definition the same for isotopic molecules. The only difference arises because the reduced mass of nucleus plus electron enters the kinetic energy expression for the electron. In Eq. (3–9) the reduced mass μ should replace m if we wish to be completely accurate. However, since a nucleus is several thousand times heavier than an electron, $\mu = m_e m_n/(m_e + m_n)$, where m_e is the mass of the electron and m_n is the mass of the nucleus, is essentially equal to m_e no matter what the mass of the nucleus. Thus the wave functions, and therefore the potential energies, of isotopic molecules are almost identical.

The other simplification is the possibility of approximating molecular vibrations as sums of normal vibrations (page 33), which we should discuss in a little more detail. The vibrations of a polyatomic molecule are very complex but may be expressed in a form which is easy to understand.* It is possible to find "coordinates" X such that

$$X = \sum_j h_j q_j$$

where the q's measure the displacement of the nuclei of the molecule from their equilibrium positions and the h's are constants determined by the equation

$$\frac{d^2X}{dt^2} + \lambda X = 0$$

which is easily seen to be the equation satisfied by a simple harmonic oscillator, t being time and λ a constant. The molecule can vibrate only by changing X, i.e., by changing all the q_j which contribute to X at the same time. A linear molecule has 5 values of $\lambda = 0$ and $3N - 5$ values of $\lambda \neq 0$, corresponding to 5 translational and rotational, and $3N - 5$ vibrational

* This simplification arises only if the vibrational displacements of the nuclei are considered to be "small," so that the vibrational potential energy V of the molecule can be expressed as

$$2V = \sum_{i,j}^{3N} k_{ij}q_iq_j$$

where the k_{ij} are force constants and the q_i are displacements of the nuclei from their equilibrium position. This is equivalent to the condition that the displacements of the nuclei be small enough that the restoring force is directly proportional to the displacement from equilibrium.

degrees of freedom, N being the number of nuclei in the molecule. A non-linear molecule always has 6 values of $\lambda = 0$ and $3N - 6$ values of $\lambda \neq 0$. Each $\lambda \neq 0$ determines a different X and these $3N - 5$ or $3N - 6$ X's are called the *normal coordinates* of the molecule. Thus the vibrations of a molecule can be treated as a series of $3N - 5$ or $3N - 6$ *independent* simple harmonic oscillators provided the rather complex coordinates X are used to describe these simple harmonic oscillators. The advantage is that, since the oscillators are independent, each has its own characteristic frequency, energy levels, etc., so that vibrational partition functions can be well approximated by a *product* of $3N - 5$ or $3N - 6$ simple harmonic oscillator partition functions. From the equations for simple harmonic oscillators, it turns out that $\lambda_i = 4\pi^2\nu_i^2$ where ν_i is the vibrational frequency. Since $\nu_i = (1/2\pi)\sqrt{k/\mu}$, $\lambda_i = k/\mu$ where k is the force constant for the particular normal vibration and μ is the reduced mass for that normal vibration.

There is one more simplifying feature of the normal vibrations of many molecules: frequently many of the X involve only a few q_j to any appreciable extent, *i.e.*, a few h_j are large (close to 1) and the rest of the h_j are very small. This is especially true for hydrogen nuclei, which do not "couple" very strongly with other nuclei of a molecule because the other nuclei are so much heavier. That is why we can usually legitimately speak of C—H stretching and bending vibrations separately from the vibrations of the rest of the molecule. The hydrogen nuclei vibrate so rapidly that the molecule acts as if all the other nuclei stand still while the hydrogen nucleus moves. In considering two isotopic molecules, therefore, many of the normal vibrations have essentially equal frequencies in both molecules.

The partition function ratio Q_A'/Q_A, where the prime refers to the *heavier* isotope, is then simply the product of the ratios for translation, rotation, and vibration (we neglect nuclear spins throughout this book because at temperatures as high as room temperature they are unimportant; also the electronic partition functions are equal for isotopic molecules because of equal electronic probability functions):

$$\frac{Q'_A}{Q_A} = \frac{Q'_t}{Q_t} \frac{Q'_r}{Q_r} \frac{Q'_v}{Q_v}$$

$$= \left(\frac{m'_A}{m_A}\right)^{3/2} \left(\frac{A'B'C'}{ABC}\right)^{1/2} \frac{\sigma}{\sigma'} \prod_i \frac{e^{-h\nu_i'/2kT}}{e^{-h\nu_i/2kT}} \frac{1 - e^{-h\nu_i/kT}}{1 - e^{-h\nu_i'/kT}}$$

for non-linear molecules. Most of the multiplicative constants cancel out. Since the same type of relationship holds for transition states, we can write an expression for the kinetic isotope effect in the reaction $A + B \rightarrow M^{\ddagger}$ (*cf.* page 40):

$$\frac{k}{k'} = \frac{K^{\ddagger}}{K^{\ddagger'}} = \frac{Q_A^{0'}}{Q_A^0} \frac{Q_B^{0'}}{Q_B^0} \frac{Q^{\ddagger}}{Q^{\ddagger'}}$$

Since the term $e^{-\Delta E_0^{\ddagger}/RT}$ is *the same* for k and k', it cancels. Also the activity coefficients can be assumed to be the same for isotopically substituted species as long as the standard states are properly chosen (*e.g.*, $\alpha^{\ddagger} = \alpha^{\ddagger'}$, $\alpha_A = \alpha'_A$, etc.). The standard states should be based exclusively on molecules or moles rather than volume or weight, e.g., a hypothetical perfect solution of concentration 1 mole per mole of solvent, 1 mole per 55.5 moles of solvent (in the case of water), or 1 molecule per molecule of solvent. We have assumed also that the transmission coefficients are equal for isotopic species and that no significant tunneling through the potential barrier occurs. Actually isotope effects are where tunneling should show up most obviously, because so many other effects cancel yet the probability of tunneling should be different for different isotopes because it depends strongly on the mass of the particle which tunnels. No completely unambiguous case of nuclear tunneling in a solvolysis reaction seems to be known at present, although it probably occurs in certain special reactions involving proton transfer (21).

If isotopic substitution is made only in reactant A, then $Q_B^0 \equiv Q_B^{0\prime}$, and

$$\frac{k}{k'} = \frac{Q_A^{0\prime}}{Q_A^0} \Big/ \frac{Q^{\ddagger\prime}}{Q^\ddagger} = \left(\frac{m_A'm^\ddagger}{m_Am^{\ddagger\prime}}\right)^{3/2} \left(\frac{A'B'C'A^\ddagger B^\ddagger C^\ddagger}{ABC A^{\ddagger\prime}B^{\ddagger\prime}C^{\ddagger\prime}}\right)^{1/2} \frac{\sigma_A\sigma^{\ddagger\prime}}{\sigma_A'\sigma^\ddagger}$$

$$\prod_A^{3N_A-6} \frac{e^{-h\nu_i'/2kT}}{e^{-h\nu_i/2kT}} \frac{1 - e^{-h\nu_i/kT}}{1 - e^{-h\nu_i'/kT}} \prod_{M^\ddagger}^{3N^\ddagger-7} \frac{e^{-h\nu_i/2kT}}{e^{-h\nu_i'/2kT}} \frac{1 - e^{-h\nu_i'/kT}}{1 - e^{-h\nu_i/kT}}$$

The product of vibrational partition functions for the transition state must be taken over $3N^\ddagger - 7$ different normal vibrations because the normal vibration corresponding to the reaction coordinate is missing from $Q^\ddagger$ (*cf.* Eq. (3–6)). If we knew all the bond lengths, bond angles, and normal vibrational frequencies of A, A', $M^\ddagger$, and $M^{\ddagger\prime}$, we could calculate the moments of inertia and then calculate k/k' exactly. Exact calculations of isotope effects can be made for *equilibria*, where we can in principle determine the structures and spectra of all reactants *and* products, but at present we cannot determine the structures or vibrational frequencies of transition states. Nevertheless, kinetic isotope effects k/k' can be measured and compared with theoretical isotope effects based on *models* for the transition state. Usually we know quite a lot about transition states from kinetic, stereochemical, and other measurements. From such knowledge a very reasonable model can be constructed. Thus by using isotopic substitution it might be possible to refine the transition state model considerably, and possibly in some cases even calculate some of the vibrational frequencies of the transition state.

It is usually time-consuming to calculate moments of inertia, and also difficult to guess at proper bond lengths and angles. Fortunately, this is not necessary because there is a rule for calculating the translational and rotational contributions to the isotope effect from the vibrational frequencies. The *product rule* may be arrived at as follows (131). The frequency of a simple harmonic vibration is given by Eq. (3–3):

$$\nu_i = \frac{1}{2\pi} \left(\frac{k}{\mu}\right)^{1/2} \tag{3–3}$$

where k is the force constant for the vibration and μ is the reduced mass. Therefore, if we take the ratios of frequencies of isotopic molecules and multiply them together,

$$\prod_i \frac{\nu_i'}{\nu_i} = \prod_i \left(\frac{\mu_i}{\mu_i'}\right)^{1/2}$$

Now the only cause for $\mu_i \neq \mu_i'$ is the presence of the isotopic nuclei. If there were a normal vibration where *only* a single isotopic nucleus moved, its reduced mass would be simply the mass of that nucleus, m_i or m_i', *i.e.*,

$$\left(\frac{\mu_i}{\mu_i'}\right)^{1/2} = \left(\frac{m_i}{m_i'}\right)^{1/2}$$

We cannot prove it here, but it is reasonable to assume that if the isotopic nucleus were to move in *several* normal vibrations, its effect would be *partially* felt in the reduced masses of each normal vibration. If we took a product over all nuclear motions,

$$\prod_i \frac{\nu_i'}{\nu_i} = \prod_i \left(\frac{\mu_i}{\mu_i'}\right)^{1/2} = \prod_i \left(\frac{m_i}{m_i'}\right)^{1/2}$$

where the products are taken over *all* 3N *degrees of freedom* of the molecule. If there were only *one* nucleus that changed in going from the unprimed to the primed molecule, the right-hand side of the above equation would be simply $(m_i/m_i')^{3/2}$ since each nucleus contributes three degrees of freedom of motion to the molecule. The translations and rotations have zero frequencies, of course, so that some of the terms on the left-hand side of the above equation are indeterminate (0/0). But if we consider the molecule to be in a very weak force field such that the translations and rotations are converted into vibrations, we can evaluate these ratios. In fact, for translations

$$\frac{\nu_i'}{\nu_i} = \left(\frac{m}{m'}\right)^{1/2}$$

where the m's are the masses of the *molecules*. Likewise, for rotations

$$\frac{\nu_i'}{\nu_i} = \left(\frac{I}{I'}\right)^{1/2}$$

where the I's are the corresponding principal moments of inertia. These relationships must also be true in the limit of a *vanishing* force field. For a non-linear molecule there are 3 translations, 3 rotations, and $3N - 6$ vibrations, so

$$\left(\frac{m}{m'}\right)^{3/2} \left(\frac{ABC}{A'B'C'}\right)^{1/2} \prod_i^{3N-6} \frac{\nu_i'}{\nu_i} = \prod_i^{3N} \left(\frac{m_i}{m_i'}\right)^{1/2}$$

The right-hand side is simply equal to $(m_i/m_i')^{3n/2}$ if only one *kind* of isotope is changed, where n is the number of isotopic nuclei that are changed. Then

$$\left(\frac{m_i'}{m_i}\right)^{3n/2} \prod_i^{3N-6} \frac{\nu_i'}{\nu_i} = \left(\frac{m'}{m}\right)^{3/2} \left(\frac{A'B'C'}{ABC}\right)^{1/2} = \frac{Q_t' Q_r'}{Q_t Q_r} \frac{\sigma'}{\sigma}$$

The translational and rotational parts of the partition function can be expressed in terms of simply the masses of the isotopically substituted nuclei and the vibrational frequencies. For a transition state the same relationship holds. It is important to note that the product of *frequency ratios* is taken over $3N^\ddagger - 6$ frequencies, not $3N^\ddagger - 7$ as used in the vibrational partition function. The imaginary frequency ratio must be evaluated, *as well as* those of the $3N^\ddagger - 7$ *real* frequencies.*

* The product rule is rigorous only for the so-called *zero-order* frequencies of vibration. The zero-order frequency is given by $\nu^0 = (1/2\pi)$ $\sqrt{k^0/\mu}$, where k^0 is a force constant evaluated *at the minimum of the potential energy surface*. The observed infrared transitions are the energy required for transition from the zero-point energy level to the next

To evaluate the vibrational frequencies of the transition state it is necessary to make educated guesses. One way of doing this is to use *bond vibrations* instead of true normal vibrations. The large number of infrared and Raman spectra now available for all kinds of molecules makes it possible to estimate stretching and bending frequencies for most kinds of bonds, and to guess how these frequencies might change when the hybridization and electron distribution are changed. Usually only a few stretching and bending frequencies need be included in the partition function ratios because all cancel for which $\nu = \nu'$. If the bond is actually being made or broken in the transition state, it will be unlike that of a "normal" molecule. Nevertheless, estimates of its vibrational frequencies can be made by means of empirical relationships such as Badger's rule (132), with which the stretching force constant can be calculated from the bond length. Frequencies are commonly expressed in wave numbers (cm.$^{-1}$) rather than sec.$^{-1}$; in this case $h\nu/kT = hc\omega/kT$, where c is the velocity of light and ω is the frequency in cm.$^{-1}$.

Normal vibrations are an approximation, as mentioned. They correspond to a parabolic potential, rather than the non-symmetrical curve such as Fig. 9a. It is possible to correct for the anharmonicity (see Dole, 18) if the extent is known. The anharmonicity of stretching vibrations can be empirically estimated (132).

In many cases the isotope effect is determined largely by the zero-point energy terms (and the symmetry numbers). This is especially true for deuterium and tritium isotope effects, where the vibrations are of high frequency. If $h\nu \gg kT$, the terms $1 - e^{-h\nu/kT} = 1$. In cases for which a bond has a smaller force constant in the transition state than in the reactant, the zero-point energy difference between A and A'

---

higher energy level and therefore involve anharmonicity effects. The use of the *observed* transitions leads to slight errors in the ν'/ν ratios; however, in the *vibrational* partition function, use of the observed transitions will help to take account of anharmonicity.

is greater than that between $M^\ddagger$ and $M^{\ddagger\prime}$. Since the zero-point energy of a heavier isotope is always less than that of the corresponding light molecule (greater μ in Eq. (3–3) for the heavier isotope), this case leads to $k/k' > 1$. In the diagram

$$M^\ddagger \text{———}$$
$$\text{———} M^{\ddagger\prime}$$
$$\text{———} A$$
$$\text{———} A'$$

the energy difference between A' and $M^{\ddagger\prime}$ is greater than that between A and $M^\ddagger$. From Eq. (3–3) it can be seen that a decrease in the force constant will tend to make $h\nu/2$ closer to $h\nu'/2$ unless μ changes greatly. The change in μ could be very important for *heavy* isotopic nuclei, but usually for hydrogen vibrations $\mu \sim 1$ and for deuterium vibrations $\mu \sim 2$ because the masses of hydrogen and deuterium are so small compared with the masses of other atoms in a molecule.

The relative importance of zero-point energy can be assessed by measuring the isotope effect at different temperatures. If it is not very temperature-dependent, it must arise in the temperature-independent factors (TIF) of the partition functions, mainly the translational and rotational contributions. If it is very temperature-dependent, it must arise in the vibrational contributions because they involve T. An empirical way of evaluating experimental results assumes the isotope effect can be approximated as

$$\log\left(\frac{k}{k'}\right) = A + \frac{B}{T}$$

so that a plot of the log of the isotope effect *vs.* $1/T$ should approximate a straight line, from which the TIF and the temperature-dependent factor (TDF) can be evaluated.

ISOTOPE EFFECTS IN SUBSTRATES

A number of investigations of isotope effects in solvolysis reactions utilize isotopic substitution of the substrate.

The hydrolysis of $(CH_3)_3C^{14}Cl$ in 60% dioxane–40% water at 24.8° gives $k_{12}/k_{14} = 1.03$ (133) which is a rather small effect for carbon-14. In SN2 reactions of methyl iodide under various conditions k_{12}/k_{14} is 1.09–1.14. These facts are disturbing, because we might expect the isotope effect to be large when we are completely breaking a bond in the transition state, and smaller if a bond is being formed simultaneously with a bond being broken. We would expect a large effect in a SN1 case because the stretching of the C—Cl bond is the *reaction coordinate*, and therefore makes *no* zero-point energy contribution to the transition state, but *does* to the reactant ($3N^{\ddagger} - 7$ normal vibrations contribute to the transition state zero-point energy; the reaction coordinate vibration does not contribute). The SN2 situation is more complex, because the C—I stretching vibration of the reactant is "converted" to *two* vibrations in the transition state, a periodic and an aperiodic vibration (page 37). The aperiodic vibration is the reaction coordinate, so it makes no zero-point energy contribution. The periodic vibration does make a zero-point energy contribution, and the difference in zero-point energies between $M^{\ddagger}$ and $M^{\ddagger\prime}$ contributed by the periodic vibration will depend on whether the central carbon atom *moves* in the periodic vibration. If the entering and leaving groups were identical, *e.g.*, $I^{-} + C^{14}H_3I \rightarrow [I\text{---}CH_3\text{---}I^{-}]^{\ddagger}$, then only the two I atoms would move in the periodic stretching vibration, and the C atom would be motionless. In this case the frequency of the periodic vibration would be the same no matter whether the C atom were C^{12} or C^{14}, and there would be no transition state zero-point energy difference caused by the periodic vibration. Therefore a large isotope effect should arise, because the zero-point energy difference between the C^{12}-I and C^{14}-I stretching frequencies of the reactants would not be canceled by a corresponding zero-point energy difference between the transition states. On the other hand, if the entering and leaving groups were different $(N + CH_3I)$, the N---C stretching force constant of the transition state might be quite different from the C---I stretching force constant. Then the C atom would move considerably in the periodic vibration and little in the aperiodic vibration. The periodic stretching vibration would give rise to a zero-point energy difference between the transition states, partially offsetting the zero-point energy difference between the reactants, and leading to a low isotope effect. Of course, if the stretching force constant were *much* smaller for the N---C than for the C---I bond of the transition state, the mechanism would approach SN1 instead of SN2. Eventually the aperiodic vibration would begin to involve motion of the C atom again, as the reaction coordinate became more like a simple C---I stretching vibration, and the periodic vibration would become simply the movement of N toward and away from the rest of the transition state nuclei. Thus it appears from this qualitative argument as if the isotope effect should be large, if the transition state were sufficiently SN1-like or symmetrical, and should pass through a minimum when the N---C bond had a small but finite force constant. It is tempting to conclude that the relatively small isotope effect for the hydrolysis of $(CH_3)_3C^{14}Cl$ may be a result of a transition state which is quite unsymmetrical but nevertheless involves nucleophilic assistance. The large effects for the SN2 reactions of $C^{14}H_3I$ could be caused by relatively "symmetrical" transition states (N---C and C---I stretching force constants nearly equal). This line of argument neglects bending vibrations, which could, of course, change in going from reactants to transition state. However, it might be expected that a "symmetrical" transition state would tend to have stronger bending vibrations than an asymmetrical one, and this tendency should make the isotope effect smaller than expected on the basis of the stretching vibrations alone.

A C^{13} isotope effect has been measured (134) for the ethanolysis of 1-phenyl-1-bromoethane $(C_6H_5CHBrCH_3)$ at the 1-carbon atom. Obviously a C^{13} isotope effect will be smaller than the C^{14} isotope effect for the same reaction because the former differs by only one mass unit from C^{12}, the latter, by two. The observed isotope effect is $k_{12}/k_{13} = 1.0065$, very small even for a C^{13} isotope effect. The isotope effect is smaller yet for the SN2 reaction of the same substrate with ethoxide ion (*ca.* 2 *M*) in ethanol, $k_{12}/k_{13} = 1.0032$. These results are perhaps reasonable if the ethanolysis transition state involves nucleophilic assistance and if both are reactant-like. Another possibility is that the transition states are both "carbonium-ion-like," but the effects are small because of large delocalization of electrons from the ring towards the carbonium ion center, causing an increase in zero-point energy of the vibrations involving the 1-carbon atom which nearly offsets the loss of zero-point energy caused by the C---Br stretching vibration's being the reaction coordinate (134). It is significant that the isotope effect for the benzyl carbon atom of benzyl bromide reacting with *ca.* 1 *M* methoxide ion in methanol (134) is 1.0531, an order-of-magnitude greater an effect than that for the compound containing an α-methyl group. This large effect is explainable if the transition state is nearly "symmetrical." The authors state that further experiments are underway (134). The results should be very interesting. It is likely that such measurements will provide precise information about transition state differences which do not show up in ordinary rate measurements.

The theory of such carbon isotope effects is not completely clear yet. For example, it has been found impossible to correlate TIF's for the reactions of CN^- with $C^{13}H_3Cl$, $C^{13}H_3Br$, and $C^{13}H_3I$ in water with any reasonable, simple model for the transition state (135).

Chlorine isotope effects have been measured for the leaving group in the hydrolysis of *p*-substituted benzyl chlorides in 80% aqueous dioxane (by weight) at 30°: For *p*-CH$_3$O, *p*-CH$_3$, H, *p*-Cl, and *p*-NO$_2$ substituents, $k_{35}/k_{37} = 1.0078$, 1.0075, 1.0078, 1.0078, and 1.0076 respectively (136). The differences are just within experimental error, indicating that these isotope effects are closely similar despite a rate factor of *ca.* 20,000 between CH_3O and NO_2 substituents. A Hammett plot of the rate constants is non-linear, but does not have a minimum. The isotope effects for reactions of these same substituted benzyl chlorides with two good nucleophiles, CN^- and $S_2O_3^=$, were also determined (136). These were somewhat more variable with substituents than the hydrolysis isotope effects. The authors found that some of the reactions with nucleophilic ions were kinetically first-order (SN1), although they did not carry these reactions very far toward completion. We cannot be sure they are really first-order. Nevertheless, those which gave straight-line first-order kinetic plots (and curved second-order kinetic plots) had isotope effects quite close to 1.0078, and those which gave straight-line second-order kinetic plots had isotope effects close to 1.0058. The few reactions which appear to have intermediate kinetics also had intermediate isotope effects. The authors conclude that the chlorine isotope effect will be near 1.0078 for SN1-type mechanisms and near 1.0058 for SN2-type mechanisms. The hydrolyses then appear to be all SN1-type with transition states involving essentially the same amount of C---Cl bond-weakening. These conclusions are quite surprising, especially for the p-NO_2 substituent, and if borne out by further experiment, may revise some of our ideas about solvolysis. It is difficult to believe that the hydrolyses are all SN1, so the possibility that strong solvation bonds may be influencing the chlorine isotope effects should be considered.

The SN1 solvolysis of $(CH_3)_3C$—$S^+(CH_3)_2$ has *sulfur* isotope effects (k_{32}/k_{34}) of 1.018 in H_2O at 60° and 1.010 in C_2H_5OH at 40° (137). These are rather large effects for sulfur, and imply considerable bond-breaking in the transition states. The large change upon changing solvents is also interesting, since the nucleophilicity of H_2O and C_2H_5OH should be similar. The effect may be the result of steric effects on solvation of reactant or transition state, or on nucleophilic assistance.

So far we have considered only *primary* isotope effects, *i.e.*, those from bond-making and/or -breaking with the isotopically substituted atom. Isotope effects which are not primary are termed *secondary*. Some very interesting secondary isotope effects have been obtained for solvolysis reactions, all of them involving hydrogen isotopes, where the effects would be larger than for heavier nuclei. A large amount of data is recorded in Table 6–1 for hydrolysis reactions of simple substrates (138). It is important to note that some of these isotope effects are for molecules containing more than one deuterium atom. To put them on an equal basis, the observed isotope effect should be raised to the $1/n$ power, where n is the number of deuterium atoms in the deuterium-substituted substrate (see below). In addition, the isotope effects have been measured at different temperatures for different substrates. Although they are not very temperature-dependent in most cases, the differences between substrates are sometimes very small. That the α-deuterium effects are *inverse* (<1) in the case of CD_3X can be explained by assuming that the approaching nucleophile, H_2O, inhibits the bending motions of the C—D (and C—H) bonds of the transition state. Inhibition would *increase* the frequency of vibration, giving a greater zero-point energy difference between the undeuterated and deuterated transition states than between the undeuterated and deuterated reactants, *i.e.*, making the deuterated substrate react faster. From the effects observed with ethyl, *n*-propyl, and isopropyl compounds, there appears to be a delicate balance of effects, sometimes leading to isotope effects <1, sometimes, >1. The other effect here may be on the *stretching* frequencies of the α-deuterium atoms. If the carbon atom happened to have a slight net charge, more than it had in the reactant, then the C—D (and C—H) bond could be weakened by the inductive effect and should then have a smaller force constant and frequency in the transition state than in the reactant. Also, to the extent that the transition state were *carbonium-ion-like*, the bending as well as stretching vibrations of the C—D bonds would be weakened. These latter two effects could explain isotope effects >1.

The β-deuterium isotope effects are all >1. Because of the small amounts of olefin formed, we know that the isotope

TABLE 6-1

Secondary Deuterium Isotope Effects for Hydrolysis of R-X Compounds

R	X	$\dfrac{k_H}{k_D}$	T, °C
CD_3	Cl	0.92	89.794
	OTs	0.96	70.05
	Br	0.90	79.94
	I	0.87	70.05
	ONO_2	0.92	100.005
	OSO_2CH_3	0.96	60.067
CH_3CD_2	OTs	1.038	54.285
	OSO_2CH_3	1.037	60.003
	Br	0.983	80.001
	I	0.966	80.000
$CH_3CH_2CD_2$	$OSO_2C_6H_5$	1.034	54.192
	OSO_2CH_3	1.036	60.004
	Br	0.980	80.009
	I	1.006	90.003
$(CH_3)_2CD$	OTs	1.134	30.001
	OSO_2CH_3	1.143	29.999
	Br	1.069	59.998
	I	1.050	59.996
CD_3CH_2[a]	OTs	1.018	59.935
	OSO_2CH_3	1.027	60.000
	Br	1.033	80.001
	I	1.037	80.000
$(CD_3)_2CH$[b]	OTs	1.551	30.001
	OSO_2CH_3	1.545	30.001
	Br	1.336	59.932
	I	1.313	60.003
$(CD_3)_3C$[c]	Cl	2.568	2.070
$CD_3CH_2CH_2$	$OSO_2C_6H_5$	0.947	54.133
	OSO_2CH_3	0.943	60.004
	Br	0.921	79.994
	I	0.926	90.003

[a] Olefin formation <0.3% for all leaving groups.
[b] Olefin formation <3% for all leaving groups.
[c] Olefin formation 2.9%.

effects are really for the solvolysis and are not affected appreciably by an E2-type elimination, which would involve breaking a C—D (C—H) bond, a primary deuterium isotope effect (primary deuterium isotope effects are frequently 5 to 7). The most important fact is that the effect per CD_3 group is about 1.03 for ethyl, 1.20 for isopropyl, and 1.37 for *tert*-butyl. It seems entirely possible that the principal cause of these effects is the inductive effect of any positive charge induced on the α-carbon atom in the transition state. Alternatively the effect might be caused by steric effects, the transition state being looser than the reactant, especially in the cases where the transition state has carbonium ion character. In any case, the effects for different alkyl groups seem best explained if the transition states for isopropyl and *tert*-butyl have more carbonium ion character than that for methyl.

It is amazing that there is any appreciable γ-deuterium effect at all. It seems as if this effect must be the result of steric causes, not the inductive effect.

In SN1 solvolysis, the β-deuterium isotope effect is much greater for 2-methyl-2-butyl chloride-β-d_8 in 80% aqueous ethanol at 25° ($k_H/k_D = 2.50$) than for the corresponding dimethylsulfonium ion in water at 59.75° ($k_H/k_D = 1.25$) (139). This is surprising, because we would predict that the C---S bond would be *more broken* in the transition state than the carbon-halogen bond. Further information about this difference, especially its solvent-dependence, would be most instructive.

The effect of β-hydrogen atoms in stabilizing positive charge has long been known as *hyperconjugation*. Much effort has been put into explaining the details of the effect. In the case of carbonium ion formation, either all β-hydrogen atoms could simultaneously stabilize the developing positive charge on the α-carbon atom, or they could do so one at a time by forming a "hydrogen bridge":

It is known that the more β-hydrogens the molecule possesses, the larger the effect. But this could result from a concerted effect or from the fact that the probability of forming a hydrogen bridge would be greater if more hydrogens were available. It appears to be possible to distinguish these two possibilities by means of β-deuterium isotope effects:

The solvolyses of **1**, **2**, and **3** in 60% aqueous ethanol (v/v) at 25° have isotope effects k_H/k_D of 1.3304, 1.7095, and 2.3271, respectively (140). We can calculate the isotope effects for **2** and **3** by assuming one mechanism for hyperconjugation and using the isotope effect for **1**. To prove the result is rather long and complicated, but the idea is quite simple: if the concerted mechanism applies, the effects should be *multiplicative* because one occurs "on top of" the other; if the stepwise (hydrogen-bridging) mechanism applies, the effects should be *additive* because only one hydrogen can presumably bridge at a time in the transition state. If k_0 is the rate of solvolysis of the undeuterated compound, k_1 the rate for **1**, k_2 the rate for **2**, and k_3 the rate for **3**, then for the concerted mechanism,

$$\frac{k_2}{k_0} = \left(\frac{k_1}{k_0}\right)^2 = (0.7516)^2 = 0.5649$$

$$\frac{k_0}{k_2} = \frac{1}{0.5649} = 1.770$$

$$\frac{k_3}{k_0} = \left(\frac{k_1}{k_0}\right)^3 = (0.7516)^3 = 0.4246$$

$$\frac{k_0}{k_3} = \frac{1}{0.4246} = 2.355$$

while for the stepwise mechanism

$$\frac{k_2}{k_0} = 1 + 2\left(\frac{k_1}{k_0} - 1\right) = 1 - 0.4968 = 0.5032$$

$$\frac{k_0}{k_2} = \frac{1}{0.5032} = 1.987$$

$$\frac{k_3}{k_0} = 1 + 3\left(\frac{k_1}{k_0} - 1\right) = 1 - 0.7452 = 0.2548$$

$$\frac{k_0}{k_3} = \frac{1}{0.2548} = 3.925$$

The experimental k_0/k_2 and k_0/k_3, 1.7095 and 2.3271, are obviously in much better agreement with the predictions of the concerted mechanism. This criterion should be applicable to many other kinds of reactions for deciding between concerted and stepwise mechanisms.

The acetolysis rates of cyclopentyl tosylates, undeuterated and with α- and β-deuterium atoms, have been reported (141). For cyclopentyl-1-d tosylate, k_H/k_D at $50° = 1.15$; for *trans*-cyclopentyl-2-d tosylate, k_H/k_D at $50° = 1.16$; for *cis*-cyclopentyl-2-d tosylate, k_H/k_D at $50° = 1.22$. Using the hydrogen atom of an aldehyde group as a model for an α-hydrogen atom of a carbonium ion, the maximum α-deuterium isotope effect was calculated as 1.38, mainly on account of a lowering of one bending vibration on going from sp^3 to sp^2 hybridization. Thus carbonium ion character seems not highly developed at the transition state. The β-deuterium effects are similar for *cis*- and *trans*-deuterium. This was taken as evidence that the "hyperconjugation" effect is not stereospecific (141), assuming that the *cis*- and *trans*-deuterium atoms would be in quite different positions with respect to the bond being broken. However, if the reactant approaches the envelope conformation (42) with the bulky tosylate group equatorial, as might be expected, these deuterium atoms would both be staggered about the same distance on either side of the tosylate group. To the extent that this approximate equivalence of cis- and trans-β-positions is maintained in the transition state, the respective isotope effects should be similar. There is good indication that in other solvolysis reactions the "hyperconjugation" effects are stereospecific (142). Stereospecificity is expected if the effects are caused by overlap of the incipient carbon p-orbital (vacant in the carbonium ion) of the transition state with the orbitals of the β C—D (and C—H) bonds, but probably not if the effects are σ-inductive.

The temperature dependence of the β-deuterium isotope effects for hydrolysis of $(CD_3)_2CH$—X compounds has been studied (143). They have been found to be almost temperature-independent. A possible explanation is (143) that they are the result of effects on the internal rotation of the methyl groups around the C—C bond. The lack of temperature dependence could be caused by *cancellation* of zero-point energy effects in the rotations and the vibrations of the C—D (C—H) bonds.

SOLVENT ISOTOPE EFFECTS

Isotopic substitution of the *solvent*, leaving the substrate unchanged, has also been studied. Almost all the work has so far been done in H_2O and D_2O, *i.e.*, in hydrolysis reactions. The main conclusion of this work is that the isotope effects are very much the same for many different substrates, in particular for primary, secondary, and tertiary alkyl halides. If the mechanism involves nucleophilic assistance in the primary substrates, but no nucleophilic assistance in the tertiary substrates, the similarity of isotope effects is unexpected. It is conceivable that more than one effect (*e.g.*, nucleophilic assistance *and* solvation effects) exists, and that the changes in these effects mutually compensate in going from primary to tertiary substrates. Some of the data are presented in Table 6–2 (144). There is one distinguishing feature: primary substrates appear to have isotope effects which are largely temperature-independent, while *tert*-butyl chloride appears to have an isotope effect which is very temperature-dependent.

TABLE 6-2

Solvent Isotope Effects for Hydrolysis of RX Substrates in
H$_2$O and in D$_2$O

R	X	$\dfrac{k_{H_2O}}{k_{D_2O}}$	$T°C$
CH$_3$	Cl	1.28	89.96
	Br	1.22	89.95
	Br	1.23	80.00
	Br	1.24	70.50
	I	1.23	79.99
	OSO$_2$C$_6$H$_5$	1.10	39.85
	OSO$_2$C$_6$H$_5$	1.11	49.97
	OSO$_2$C$_6$H$_5$	1.10	60.62
	OSO$_2$C$_6$H$_5$	1.10	70.26
CH$_3$CH$_2$	Cl	1.24	100.00
	Br	1.23	98.66
	I	1.24	98.64
CH$_3$CH$_2$CH$_2$	Cl	1.22	100.00
	Br	1.23	79.99
	I	1.22	100.00
(CH$_3$)$_2$CH	Cl	1.32	98.64
	Br	1.28	50.00
	I	1.31	80.01
	OSO$_2$C$_6$H$_5$	1.09	7.51
	OSO$_2$C$_6$H$_5$	1.09	15.00
	OSO$_2$C$_6$H$_5$	1.08	30.10
(CH$_3$)$_3$C	Cl	1.43	4.00
	Cl	1.35	14.03
	F	1.22	90.24
	S$^+$(CH$_3$)$_2$	1.05	70.02

However, this feature may be an artifact resulting from the different temperature ranges used. The *structure of water* is believed to change markedly between 0° and 25°, then to remain constant between 25° and 70° or so (145). The other significant trend is that the benzenesulfonates and the sulfonium salt have very low isotope effects. The reasons are probably different for the two kinds of leaving group, however. We should expect that the benzenesulfonates would have less charge development in the transition state than the halides, and also the reactant should be more polar than the halides because of the highly polar S—O bonds. Both of these effects should tend to make the isotope effect smaller (see below). The sulfonium salt, on the other hand, probably has a large isotope effect from strong nucleophilic assistance (see below), partially offset by a reverse effect from the fact that we are destroying rather than creating charge on going from reactant to transition state. The isotope effects for hydrolysis of a number of halides with neighboring groups (HO (DO), CH_3O, Br, I) in H_2O and in D_2O have been measured (146). Some are similar to the corresponding halides, while others are higher or lower. The effects are small and have been explained in terms of different solvation requirements depending on whether neighboring-group assistance is involved or not. It appears that the possible difference in nucleophilicity between HO and DO as neighboring groups may be important in pertinent cases, but the explanation was rejected by the authors (146).

It is important, in cases of small solvent isotope effects, to be concerned with solvation effects, and these could be different for reactants and transition states. The solvation isotope effects for reactants are experimentally accessible by measuring the solubility of reactant vapor in H_2O and in D_2O. The ratios of solubilities are the isotope effects for solvation of the reactants. Solubilities of the four methyl halides have been measured in H_2O and in D_2O at 29.4° and 40.3° (147). Each of the four methyl halides has nearly the same solubility in light water as in heavy water; therefore, a methyl halide molecule probably fits into a hole in the water and does not simply intrude between water molecules. D_2O and H_2O have tetrahedrally hydrogen-bonded structures. Each water molecule is bound to four others, two by utilizing the two protons of the water molecule to bond to unshared pairs of other water molecules and two by utilizing the two unshared pairs of electrons of the water molecule to bond to protons of other water molecules. The electronic probability distributions (and therefore potential energies) are of course almost identical for H_2O and D_2O because they are isotopic. But the zero-point energy of the *librations* (hindered rotations) of a D_2O molecule is less than that of a H_2O molecule because the heavier nuclei make the principal moments of inertia larger. These librations are observed at *ca.* 667 cm.$^{-1}$ for H_2O and *ca.* 483 cm.$^{-1}$ for D_2O. Their frequencies are as high as internal vibrations of some molecules; the *three* independent librations contribute a large zero-point energy and a sizable zero-point energy *difference* between H_2O and D_2O. Therefore, D_2O, having less rotational kinetic energy than H_2O at the same temperature, has a *firmer* hydrogen-bonded *structure* than H_2O. Any solute which tends to disrupt the structure of the water, *i.e.*, decrease the librational frequency, *i.e.*, decrease the force constant for libration (*cf.* Eq. (3–3)), will tend to make the *difference* in zero-point energies between H_2O and D_2O smaller and thus make the isotope effect larger. This can be seen from Eq. (3–3):

$$\nu = \frac{1}{2\pi}\left(\frac{k}{\mu}\right)^{1/2} \qquad (3\text{–}3)$$

$$\nu_H - \nu_D = \frac{k^{1/2}}{2\pi}\left(\frac{1}{\mu_H} - \frac{1}{\mu_D}\right)^{1/2}$$

Decreasing the force constant k will decrease the difference $\nu_H - \nu_D$ (μ_H and μ_D remain nearly constant), and thus the zero-point energy difference $h\nu_H/2 - h\nu_D/2$,* which costs more energy for D than for H.

If a methyl halide molecule broke down the structure of the water immediately surrounding it, the solubility should be much less in D_2O than in H_2O because D_2O has more

---

* If we consider the other contributions to the partition function, the result is still the same, because the internal vibrational frequencies, bond lengths, and bond angles are unaffected when the rotational force constant is changed slightly.

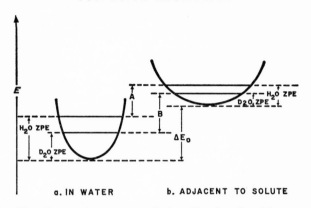

Fig. 10. Zero-point energy relationships for dissolving a solute which breaks down the structure of water (decreases the librational frequency); (a) potential curve for libration of a water molecule in pure liquid water; (b) potential curve for libration of a water molecule adjacent to a structure-breaking solute. ZPE stands for zero-point energy.

structure to start with, and therefore more to lose.   Figure 10 expresses the reason for this conclusion more accurately in terms of the zero-point energies of initial and final states. Both H_2O and D_2O gain energy (become less stable) in the presence of the solute molecule, but D_2O gains more (distance B is greater than distance A); the solute is therefore more soluble in H_2O.   If the water molecules surrounding a methyl halide molecule in solution were more restricted in motion than water molecules in pure liquid water at the same temperature, the methyl halide would be more soluble in D_2O than in H_2O.   The fact that the solubilities of the methyl halides are almost the same in H_2O and D_2O indicates that they leave the structure of water nearly unchanged.   For the equilibrium

$$CH_3X \ (g) \overset{K}{\rightleftarrows} CH_3X \ (solution)$$

the isotope effects K_{H_2O}/K_{D_2O} at 29.4° are 0.98 (CH_3F), 1.04 (CH_3Cl), 1.07 (CH_3Br), 1.10 (CH_3I); at 40.3°, 0.95, 1.03, 1.065, 1.08.   Methyl iodide is most soluble in water at 29.4°; methyl fluoride is least soluble.   Methyl iodide is probably surrounded by a shell of 28 water molecules (119).   Its isotope effect (the farthest from 1.0 of the four) could be accounted for by an average shift in librational frequency from 667 to 663 cm.$^{-1}$ in H_2O (483 to 480 cm.$^{-1}$ in D_2O) for 28 surrounding water molecules.   The initial-state isotope effect multiplied by the kinetic isotope effect gives the *isotope effect for the transition state*.   The data are listed in Table 6–3.   It was

TABLE 6–3

Transition-State Isotope Effects

Com- pound	Isotope Effects at 40°			Isotope Effects at 70°		
	Initial State	Kinetic	Transition State	Initial State	Kinetic	Transition State
CH_3Cl	1.03	1.36	1.40	1.02–1.03	1.322	1.35–1.36
CH_3Br	1.065	1.28	1.36	1.06–1.065	1.245	1.32–1.33
CH_3I	1.08	1.33	1.44	1.02–1.08	1.285	1.31–1.39

necessary to extrapolate the kinetic isotope effects to a lower temperature (40°) or the initial-state isotope effects to a higher temperature (70°) for comparison; both are listed in Table 6–3.   The transition-state isotope effect is the equilibrium constant of the reaction

$$\left[\begin{array}{c} D \\ \diagdown \\ \diagup \\ D \end{array} O\text{---}CH_3\text{---}X \right]^{\ddagger} \text{ in } D_2O + H_2O \text{ in } H_2O \rightleftarrows$$

$$\left[\begin{array}{c} H \\ \diagdown \\ \diagup \\ H \end{array} O\text{---}CH_3\text{---}X \right]^{\ddagger} \text{ in } H_2O + D_2O \text{ in } D_2O$$

where the standard states are hypothetical perfect 1 M solutions *in the solvents indicated*. It is therefore the product of the initial-state isotope effect, *i.e.*, the equilibrium constant for

$$CH_3X \text{ in } D_2O \rightleftarrows CH_3X \text{ in } H_2O$$

and the kinetic isotope effect, *i.e.*, the equilibrium constant for

$$\left[\begin{array}{c} D \\ \diagdown \\ \diagup \\ D \end{array} O\text{---}CH_3\text{---}X \right]^{\ddagger} \text{ in } D_2O + CH_3X \text{ in } H_2O + H_2O \text{ in } H_2O \rightleftarrows$$

$$\left[\begin{array}{c} H \\ \diagdown \\ \diagup \\ H \end{array} O\text{---}CH_3\text{---}X \right]^{\ddagger} \text{ in } H_2O + CH_3X \text{ in } D_2O + D_2O \text{ in } D_2O$$

It should be noted that this is a different standard-state convention from that used sometimes (145).* This conclusion that the kinetic isotope effects reflect the transition-state difference much more than an initial-state difference is quite contrary to the idea that they result from "freezing" of water molecules (*i.e.*, increase in water structure) around the initial state, CH_3X.

It has proved possible, using spectral measurements of librational frequencies, to evaluate theoretically the isotope effects for transfer of individual ions from H_2O to D_2O (145). For example, for fluoride ion, it has been found that the water molecules adjacent to the ion have a librational frequency of

---

* The problem of standard states can be quite confusing. Sometimes it is convenient to make the standard state a hypothetical perfect 1 M solution in H_2O or in D_2O (as above). In this case isotope effects are the result of differences in free energy of standard states; this is the more customary practice in chemical thermodynamics. However, since H_2O and D_2O are really so much alike, it is sometimes convenient to make the standard state a hypothetical perfect 1 M solution *in H_2O* (even for solutions that are really in D_2O). In this case isotope effects are the result of differences in free energy caused by *activity coefficients,* and activity coefficients are usually not unity in D_2O even under "infinitely dilute" conditions. The standard state can also be taken as the *perfect gas* at 1 M or 1 atm. (145).

698 cm.$^{-1}$ instead of the 667 cm.$^{-1}$ observed for water molecules adjacent to other water molecules. Therefore, the equilibrium constant K_F for the reaction

$$F^-(4D_2O) \text{ in } D_2O + 4H_2O \text{ in } H_2O \overset{K_F}{\rightleftarrows} F^-(4H_2O) \text{ in } H_2O + 4D_2O \text{ in } D_2O$$

can be approximated by assuming that the water molecules have identical partition function ratios Q_{D_2O}/Q_{H_2O} except for the librational frequency changes. These librations can be effectively treated as vibrations in the partition function ratio (145). Then

$$K_F = \left(\frac{Q_{D_2O}}{Q_{H_2O}}\right)^4 \left(\frac{Q_{H_2O}^F}{Q_{D_2O}^F}\right)^4$$

$$= \left[\frac{e^{-hc\omega_D/2kT}(1 - e^{-hc\omega_H/kT})}{(1 - e^{-hc\omega_D/kT})e^{-hc\omega_H/2kT}}\right]^{12} \left[\frac{e^{-hc\omega_H^F/2kT}(1 - e^{-hc\omega_D^F/kT})}{(1 - e^{-hc\omega_H^F/kT})e^{-hc\omega_D^F/2kT}}\right]^{12}$$

where the fourth powers appear because we have four separate water molecules of each type, Q is for water molecules surrounded by other water molecules, Q^F is for water molecules surrounding a fluoride ion, $\omega_H = 667$ cm.$^{-1}$, $\omega_D = 483$ cm.$^{-1}$, $\omega_H^F = 698$ cm.$^{-1}$, $\omega_D^F = 506$ cm.$^{-1}$, and the twelfth powers appear because each water molecule has three degrees of librational freedom (we assume that the observed librational frequencies are *averages* for the three separate degrees of librational freedom). The calculated value is $K_F = 0.83$; and analogously for the other halide ions, $K_{Cl} = 1.48$, $K_{Br} = 1.69$, and $K_I = 1.95$ (all at 25°C).

Since the transition-state isotope effect is smaller for methyl bromide than for methyl chloride in spite of a larger isotope effect for solution of bromide ion than for chloride ion, C—X bond-breaking at the transition state must be more complete for methyl chloride than for methyl bromide. This is in accord with the previously mentioned rule (Chapter 4 and Ref. (47)).

It is interesting to try to evaluate the possible secondary isotope effect which might arise from nucleophilic attack by

D_2O instead of H_2O.   The equilibrium constant

$$2D_3O^+ + 3H_2O \overset{K_2}{\rightleftharpoons} 2H_3O^+ + 3D_2O$$

has a value 8.20 at 25° (145); *i.e.*, D_3O^+ is a stronger acid than H_3O^+.*   It makes no difference whether the water molecules or hydronium ions are in H_2O, D_2O, or a mixture (145).   The librational frequency of water molecules around hydronium ions is found to be unchanged from the librational frequency of water molecules around other water molecules.   Thus the free energy of transfer of H_3O^+ in D_2O (if it existed) to H_2O is zero; *i.e.*, there is no *solvation* isotope effect as there was for halide ions.   If we assume that all LO^+ bonds (L = H or D) are exactly like those in L_3O^+, we can calculate the maximum possible isotope effect contributed by the difference in nucleophilicity between H_2O and D_2O.   It is

$$D_2O + \tfrac{2}{3}H_3O^+ \underset{\longleftarrow}{\overset{(K_2)^{-1/3}}{\longrightarrow}} H_2O + \tfrac{2}{3}D_3O^+$$

or

$$D_2O + H_2O^+\!\!-\!\!C\!\!\diagdown \quad \underset{\longleftarrow}{\overset{(K_2)^{-1/3}}{\longrightarrow}} \quad H_2O + D_2O^+\!\!-\!\!C\!\!\diagdown$$

the two equations having the same equilibrium constant because we assumed all LO^+ bonds are equivalent to the LO^+ bonds in L_3O^+. $(K_2)^{-1/3} = 0.50$ at 25°, which means that if a hydrolysis reaction had a transition state with a full positive charge on the oxygen atom, there should be an isotope effect of $k_D/k_H = 0.50$ ($k_H/k_D = 2.0$).   This effect is certainly much larger than the effects observed in hydrolysis of alkyl halides, presumably because only a *partial* positive charge is present on the oxygen atom of the transition state in those cases in which water is acting as a nucleophile.   If there is no nucleo-

---

* The ratios Q_D/Q_H are large for most molecules because of the much greater zero-point energies associated with H than with D bonds.   Representative values are (145): $Q_{D_2O}/Q_{H_2O} = 1437$; $Q_{D_3O^+}/Q_{H_3O^+} = 19023$; $Q_{HD_2O^+}/Q_{H_2DO^+} = 26.70$, all at 25°.

philic assistance by water in the transition state, the kinetic isotope effect is determined by solvation effects, *i.e.*, by the librational frequencies of the water molecules surrounding the transition state (148). The effect of converting one HO^+ bond to a HO bond (and simultaneously one DO bond to a DO^+ bond) is $(K_2)^{-1/6} = K_n = \sqrt{2}/2$. The problem is in separating the isotope effects caused by solvation from those caused by nucleophilic assistance.

Measurement of isotope effects in mixtures of H_2O and D_2O seems to offer some hope of unraveling the problem (149), although there are differences of opinion about the value of this approach (150). The author believes that such studies may be valuable. Equations for certain specialized cases have been derived (149). Another, more general, approximation for hydrolysis reactions is to assume that the isotopic free energy difference resulting from *solvation* is linearly related to the fraction of deuterium nuclei in the H_2O-D_2O mixture. The fraction is $\alpha = D/(D + H)$.

There are two cases for which equations can be derived: (a) the case in which the transition state is L_2O---S, with two water-like LO bonds (zero charge on oxygen) for reaction of L_2O with a substrate S; and (b) the case in which the transition state is $L_2O^+S^-$, with two hydronium-ion-like LO^+ bonds (+1 charge on oxygen). The equations allow one to calculate k_α/k_H, the rate in a H_2O-D_2O mixture of atom fraction deuterium α divided by the rate in pure H_2O, from the isotope effect k_D/k_H measured experimentally. Curves for k_α/k_H *vs.* α can then be drawn for the two extreme types of transition state: (a) reactant-like and (b) product-like. The *experimental* curve should fall between curves (a) and (b), depending on how reactant- or product-like the transition state is. Usually the difference between curves (a) and (b) is only a few per cent even at $\alpha = 0.5$ (where the difference is usually largest). In this case quantitative conclusions about the nature of the transition state may be unwarranted, but differences between experimental curves for different reactions should tell which reaction has a more product-like transition state.

For case (a), there are three possible transition states:

$$H_2O + S \underset{\longleftarrow}{\overset{K_H^\ddagger}{\longrightarrow}} [H_2O\text{---}S]^\ddagger$$

$$HDO + S \underset{\longleftarrow}{\overset{K_H^\ddagger}{\longrightarrow}} [HDO\text{---}S]^\ddagger$$

$$D_2O + S \underset{\longleftarrow}{\overset{K_H^\ddagger}{\longrightarrow}} [D_2O\text{---}S]^\ddagger$$

where the $K^\ddagger$'s are all equal because we are defining the standard states as the hypothetical perfect solutions of concentration 1 mole per 55.5 moles of H_2O (so that the solvation isotope effects come into the activity coefficients, not $K^\ddagger$). According to the definition, $K^\ddagger$ is an imaginary quantity (*cf.* page 38) because the reaction coordinate vibration has already been factored out of the partition function of the transition state. But we can use it to define an *effective concentration* of transition states $[M^\ddagger]^\ddagger$ which is also an imaginary number but can be used to calculate rates (this merely simplifies the algebra):

$$K^\ddagger = \frac{[M^\ddagger]^\ddagger}{[H_2O][S]} \frac{\gamma^\ddagger}{\gamma_{H_2O}\gamma_S}$$

$K^\ddagger$ is the same for every α, but the activity coefficients γ (γ is used as a symbol for activity coefficients to avoid confusion with α, the atom fraction of deuterium) are in general different for different α. Then

$$\frac{k_\alpha}{k_H} = \frac{[H_2O\text{---}S]_\alpha^\ddagger + [HDO\text{---}S]_\alpha^\ddagger + [D_2O\text{---}S]_\alpha^\ddagger}{[H_2O\text{---}S]_H^\ddagger}$$

$$= \frac{\left\{ \dfrac{K_H^\ddagger[H_2O]_\alpha[S]_\alpha(\gamma_{H_2O})_\alpha(\gamma_S)_\alpha}{(\gamma^\ddagger)_\alpha} + \dfrac{K_H^\ddagger[HDO]_\alpha[S]_\alpha(\gamma_{HDO})_\alpha(\gamma_S)_\alpha}{(\gamma^\ddagger)_\alpha} + \dfrac{K_H^\ddagger[D_2O]_\alpha[S]_\alpha(\gamma_{D_2O})_\alpha(\gamma_S)_\alpha}{(\gamma^\ddagger)_\alpha} \right\}}{\dfrac{K_H^\ddagger[H_2O]_H[S]_H(\gamma_{H_2O})_H(\gamma_S)_H}{(\gamma^\ddagger)_H}}$$

where the subscripts refer to the atom fraction deuterium, either α or H ($\alpha = 0$). We know that water molecules do not change the structure of water, so all the water activity coefficients are unity. Therefore

$$\frac{k_\alpha}{k_H} = \frac{K_H^{\ddagger}\{[H_2O]_\alpha + [HDO]_\alpha + [D_2O]_\alpha\}[S]_\alpha(\gamma_S)_\alpha(\gamma^{\ddagger})_H}{K_H^{\ddagger}[H_2O]_H[S]_H(\gamma_S)_H(\gamma^{\ddagger})_\alpha}$$

$$= \frac{(\gamma_S)_\alpha/(\gamma^{\ddagger})_\alpha}{(\gamma_S)_H/(\gamma^{\ddagger})_H} = y$$

since the sum of concentrations of H_2O, HDO, and D_2O must equal the concentration of H_2O when $\alpha = 0$ (55.5 moles per 55.5 moles of solvent), and we have assumed for simplicity that the concentrations [S] are equal in the two solvents (this is not strictly true, but it would have been possible to define the rate ratio so that it was concentration-independent in the first place, with the same end result). All that remains is the solvation part of the isotope effect (activity coefficients).*

It is the logarithm of y which is proportional to the isotopic free energy difference. Therefore, we assume

$$\log y = m\alpha + b$$

When $\alpha = 0$, $k_\alpha/k_H = 1$, so $b = 0$. When $\alpha = 1$, $k_\alpha/k_H = k_D/k_H$, so $m = \log (k_D/k_H)$. Finally,

$$\frac{k_\alpha}{k_H} = \left(\frac{k_D}{k_H}\right)^\alpha \tag{6-1}$$

For case (b), there are also three possible transition states:

$$H_2O + S \underset{\longleftarrow}{\overset{K_H^{\ddagger}}{\longrightarrow}} [H_2O^+S^-]^{\ddagger}$$

$$HDO + S \underset{\longleftarrow}{\overset{K_nK_H^{\ddagger}}{\longrightarrow}} [HDO^+S^-]^{\ddagger}$$

$$D_2O + S \underset{\longleftarrow}{\overset{K_n^2K_H^{\ddagger}}{\longrightarrow}} [D_2O^+S^-]^{\ddagger}$$

* We assume that the rates are all measured under "infinite-dilution" conditions so that the activity coefficient term need only take account of differences *between solvents* (H_2O *vs.* H_2O-D_2O mixtures), and not concentration effects as well.

Now

$$
\begin{aligned}
\frac{k_\alpha}{k_H} &= \frac{\left\{ \dfrac{K_H^\ddagger[H_2O]_\alpha[S]_\alpha(\gamma_{H_2O})_\alpha(\gamma_S)_\alpha}{(\gamma^\ddagger)_\alpha} + \dfrac{K_nK_H^\ddagger[HDO]_\alpha[S]_\alpha(\gamma_{HDO})_\alpha(\gamma_S)_\alpha}{(\gamma^\ddagger)_\alpha} \right.}{\dfrac{K_H^\ddagger[H_2O]_H[S]_H(\gamma_{H_2O})_H(\gamma_S)_H}{(\gamma^\ddagger)_H}} \\
&\qquad\qquad\left. + \dfrac{K_n^2K_H^\ddagger[D_2O]_\alpha[S]_\alpha(\gamma_{D_2O})_\alpha(\gamma_S)_\alpha}{(\gamma^\ddagger)_\alpha} \right\} \\[4pt]
&= \frac{\{(\gamma_S)_\alpha/(\gamma^\ddagger)_\alpha\}\{[H_2O]_\alpha + K_n[HDO]_\alpha + K_n^2[D_2O]_\alpha\}}{\{(\gamma_S)_H/(\gamma^\ddagger)_H\}[H_2O]_H}
\end{aligned}
$$

The equilibrium constant for the reaction

$$ H_2O + D_2O \rightleftarrows 2HDO $$

is very nearly 4 because of statistical factors.* Algebraic manipulation shows that

$$
\begin{aligned}
[H_2O]_\alpha/[H_2O]_H &= (1 - \alpha)^2 \\
[HDO]_\alpha/[H_2O]_H &= 2\alpha(1 - \alpha) \\
[D_2O]_\alpha/[H_2O]_H &= \alpha^2
\end{aligned}
$$

whence

$$
\begin{aligned}
\frac{k_\alpha}{k_H} &= y[(1 - \alpha)^2 + 2K_n\alpha(1 - \alpha) + K_n^2\alpha^2] \\
&= y[1 + \alpha(K_n - 1)]^2 \\
&= y[1 - 0.293\alpha]^2
\end{aligned}
$$

In this case, when $\alpha = 0$, $b = 0$; and when $\alpha = 1$,

$$
\begin{aligned}
\log\left(\frac{k_D}{k_H}\right) &= m + \log[(1 - 0.293)^2] = m + \log(0.5) \\
m &= \log\left(2\,\frac{k_D}{k_H}\right)
\end{aligned}
$$

* HDO is "twice as probable" as either H_2O or D_2O because it could "really" be HDO or DHO (which are of course identical except for rotation). It may be puzzling why a statistical correction does not come into the $K_H^\ddagger$ constants for reactions of H_2O or D_2O *vs.* HDO. The answer is that, although $[H_2O^+S^-]^\ddagger$ should be twice as probable as $[HDO^+S^-]^\ddagger$ on statistical grounds, there are *two possible* $[HDO^+S^-]^\ddagger$ transition states which are optical isomers. Therefore, as is frequently the case, the statistical corrections cancel out in considering relative rates.

Finally

$$\frac{k_\alpha}{k_H} = \left(2\,\frac{k_D}{k_H}\right)^\alpha (1 - 0.293\alpha)^2 \qquad (6\text{--}2)$$

Values of $(1 - 0.293\alpha)^2$ are 0.8589 for $\alpha = 0.25$, 0.7285 for $\alpha = 0.50$, and 0.6088 for $\alpha = 0.75$.

Application of these equations to typical isotope effects for alkyl halide solvolysis, $k_D/k_H = 0.77$, gives from Eq. (6–1) $k_{0.5}/k_H = 0.877$, and from Eq. (6–2) $k_{0.5}/k_H = 0.905$. There is a 3 per cent difference between the predictions for the two extreme types of transition states, and this should be detectable with modern conductivity apparatus. Precision of 0.03 per cent has been attained in solvolysis rate constants (151). For $(CH_3)_3CS^+(CH_3)_2$, with $k_D/k_H = 0.952$, Eq. (6–1) gives $k_{0.5}/k_H = 0.976$, and Eq. (6–2) gives $k_{0.5}/k_H = 1.006$. Again the difference is about 3 per cent, so that it might be possible to determine whether significant nucleophilic assistance is involved in this hydrolysis transition state. No data appear to be available for any simple hydrolysis reaction in H_2O—D_2O mixtures.

Similar experiments should be possible for other solvents.

The smallness of the predicted difference between extreme mechanisms is perhaps a little discouraging, but the idea works *in principle*, and is apparently the only way currently available which might allow mechanistic distinctions to be made.

Values for the acidity and basicity constants, and for ion solvation isotope effects have been calculated for H_2O^{18} *vs.* H_2O^{16} (152). The differences are very small, but conductivity measurements should be accurate enough to detect the solvent isotope effects. No experimental data are available.

The hydrolysis of $(CH_3)_3C$—Cl in a solvent 60% dioxane–40% H_2O or D_2O (v/v) has an isotope effect k_{H_2O}/k_{D_2O} of 1.05 at 20.1° whereas in the pure waters the isotope effect is 1.35 (153). This large change in isotope effect was interpreted as meaning that dioxane breaks down the solvent structure around the initial state, so that less structure-breaking is necessary in the activation process. However, the results could also be explained with other factors, *e.g.*, rate-determining nucleophilic attack by dioxane, forming an oxonium ion which should rapidly be hydrolyzed. Data for other substrates under these conditions should be very interesting.

"INDUCTIVE" AND "STERIC" ISOTOPE EFFECTS

In recent years speculation has arisen that the effects of anharmonicity (page 201) may be important in determining certain isotope effects. Because a C—H bond has a larger zero-point energy associated with it than a C—D bond, vibration in a non-parabolic (anharmonic) potential field makes the *average* C—H bond length slightly greater than the average length if D is substituted for H. It is reasoned that the C—H bond should be electron-attracting relative to the C—D bond because the proton (+1 charge) is on the average slightly further from the carbon nucleus than the deuteron (+1 charge). This effect is certainly real, but its magnitude must be very small.

If we neglect anharmonicity, the isotope effect is determined by changes in molecular masses, moments of inertia, and harmonic vibrational frequencies on proceeding from reactants to transition state. If a given experimental result is adequately explained by these factors, we can assume that anharmonicity is unimportant.

Naturally, it would be interesting to be able to distinguish anharmonicity effects from the other effects. The distinction could be described as between an inductive effect *of* deuterium (anharmonic) and an inductive effect *on* deuterium (harmonic). Harmonic isotope effects arise because changes in electronic distribution in the bonds cause changes in vibrational frequencies (and other properties) on proceeding from reactants to transition state, the electronic distribution being considered to be identical for C—H and C—D bonds. Anharmonic effects are the results of slight *differences in electronic distribution* between C—H and C—D bonds. Some authors have not distinguished these two effects clearly.

Solvolysis of ring-deuterated benzhydryl chlorides in 80% aqueous acetone at 25° gives rise to isotope effects k_D/k_H of 1.010 to 1.018 per deuterium atom, depending on the position of substitution (154). These inverse effects ($k_D > k_H$) are conveniently explained if deuterium is electron-supplying relative to protium, *i.e.*, by anharmonicity. They are also explained if some C—H vibrational frequency is increased on going from reactant to transition state (see page 207). It might be guessed that on going to the transition state, where a partial positive charge is induced in the rings, the C—H bond stretching frequency would be decreased (decreased force constant). However, in the infrared spectra of substituted benzyl chlorides, the most intense ring C—H stretching band decreases from 3076 cm.$^{-1}$ for p-NO_2 to 3042 for p-F to 3031 for unsubstituted to 3025 for p-CH_3 (155). These frequencies *increase with electron withdrawal* from the ring, and the changes are far more than necessary to account for the observed isotope effects in the benzhydryl system.

There is another possible effect of anharmonicity—a steric effect. The slightly longer average C—H bond length makes a C—H group slightly *larger*, on the average, than a C—D group. In the case of steric effects, too, we must keep clear the distinction between a steric effect *of* deuterium (anharmonic) and a steric effect *on* deuterium (harmonic). Steric interactions could very well increase vibrational frequencies of C—H bonds, especially bending vibrations, giving a harmonic isotope effect. The smaller size of the C—D group could also give an isotope effect in the *same direction*, as a result of anharmonicity. It is difficult to distinguish these effects. Steric isotope effects have not been directly implicated in solvolysis reactions yet. However, in the racemization of the biphenyls

in benzene at 42° the isotope effect is $k_D/k_H = 1.14$ (156). This was ascribed to the smaller average size of the CD_3 groups than of the CH_3 groups (156), but seems much more likely to be caused by increased crowding of the CD_3 and CH_3 groups in the transition state, giving increased bending frequencies and therefore $k_D > k_H$. An investigation of the racemization of 2,2'-dibromo-4,4'-dicarboxybiphenyl and its 6,6'-dideutero derivative gave $k_D/k_H = 1.19$ at $-19.8°$ in ethanol (157). Although calculations based on the smaller average size of deuterium gave reasonable agreement with experiment, the possibility of changes in force constants was not considered.

CONCLUSION

The measurement of isotope effects is probably the most subtle means available at present for learning about transition-state structure. The limiting factor is mainly the smallness of many isotope effects. Although improvements in experimental technique will undoubtedly help solve this problem, new problems may be created at the same time. Effects that many now consider to be negligible, *e.g.*, tunneling, transmission coefficient, anharmonicity, and differences between potential energies of isotopic molecules, may become important with more precise measurements of isotope effects. It is therefore a challenge to the investigator, not only to invent new problems, but also to design experiments in which the effects will be large enough to answer subtle questions about reaction mechanisms.

REFERENCES

The book by Melander (130) is an excellent introduction to all kinds of isotope effects and features chapters on experimental method and theory, plus extensive discussion of representative isotope effects, critically evaluated by means of approximate calculations with appropriate models. A chapter on kinetic isotope effects by Saunders in Ref. (23), Part I of Vol. VIII, Chapter IX, is excellent as well. The outstanding review by Bigeleisen and Wolfsberg (130) is a highly theoretical and rigorous discussion of isotope effects. The review by K. B. Wiberg, *Chem. Rev.*, **55,** 713 (1955), on the experimental aspects of isotope effects as applied to reaction mechanism, is highly recommended. An article by F. H. Westheimer, *Chem. Rev.*, **61,** 265 (1961), on the magnitude of primary isotope effects is recommended, as the discussion of primary deuterium isotope effects also applies to primary carbon isotope effects. Secondary deuterium isotope effects are discussed by Streitwieser and coworkers (141). The theory of isotope effects in H_2O and D_2O is presented by Swain and Bader (145). For a discussion of secondary isotope effects from a viewpoint which claims that anharmonicity effects are important, see the chapter by E. A. Halevi, *Progr. Phys. Org. Chem.*, **1,** 109 (1963). This discussion treats isotopic substituents as being equivalent to other kinds of substituents, but seems largely to ignore the unique characteristic of isotopic substitution, that the electronic probabilities are almost the same for compounds differing only by isotopic substitution. A recent article on isotopes by C. J. Collins, *Advan. Phys. Org. Chem.*, **2,** 1 (1964) is also of interest.

APPENDIX 1

Translational and Rotational Partition Functions

Quantum theory shows that a particle of mass m in a rectangular box of dimensions a, b, and c has stationary energy levels

$$E = \frac{h^2}{8m}\left(\frac{n_a^2}{a^2} + \frac{n_b^2}{b^2} + \frac{n_c^2}{c^2}\right)$$

where n_a, n_b, and n_c are quantum numbers which can have only integral values from 1 to ∞. Then

$$Q_t = \sum_{n_a=1}^{\infty} e^{-h^2 n_a^2/8ma^2kT} \sum_{n_b=1}^{\infty} e^{-h^2 n_b^2/8mb^2kT} \sum_{n_c=1}^{\infty} e^{-h^2 n_c^2/8mc^2kT}$$

We have mentioned that translational energy levels are $\ll kT$ for ordinary temperatures in ordinary-size containers. Therefore each of the exponentials in the above summations is $\ll 1$ or does not change much with n, so it is permissible to make the summations into integrals,

$$Q_t = \int_0^{\infty} e^{-h^2 n_a^2/8ma^2kT}\, dn_a \int_0^{\infty} e^{-h^2 n_b^2/8mb^2kT}\, dn_b$$

$$\int_0^{\infty} e^{-h^2 n_c^2/8mc^2kT}\, dn_c$$

Each integral is of a standard form,

$$\int_0^{\infty} e^{-ax^2}\, dx = \frac{1}{2}\sqrt{\frac{\pi}{a}}$$

from integral tables, so that

$$Q_t = \frac{(2\pi \mathbf{m k} T)^{1/2}}{\mathbf{h}} \, a \, \frac{(2\pi \mathbf{m k} T)^{1/2}}{\mathbf{h}} \, b \, \frac{(2\pi \mathbf{m k} T)^{1/2}}{\mathbf{h}} \, c$$
$$= \frac{(2\pi \mathbf{m k} T)^{3/2}}{\mathbf{h}^3} \, V$$

since $V = abc$ is the volume of the box. This is the expression used in Chapter 3 and is valid for any shape of box, and therefore for any flask, bulb, etc. In this formula V should be in cm.^{3} to be consistent with the usual units of $\mathbf{h}$ and $\mathbf{k}$.

Q_t is the translational partition function for a single, isolated molecule. If we consider a collection of non-localized, non-interacting molecules (a perfect gas), the molecules are indistinguishable, and the partition function for N molecules must be divided by N!, the number of ways N indistinguishable molecules can be permuted, giving

$$\frac{Q_t^N}{N!} \text{ not merely } Q_t^N$$

The free energy (assuming no rotational, vibrational, or electronic contributions) is, for N molecules,

$$F = -\mathbf{k}T \ln \frac{Q_t^N}{N!}$$

or, since $N_0 \mathbf{k} = \mathbf{R}$ and, for large values of N,

$$\ln N! = N \ln N - N$$
$$F = -\mathbf{R}T \left(\ln \frac{Q_t}{N_0} + 1 \right)$$

for one mole (N_0). Since, for a mole of perfect gas molecules, $pV = \mathbf{R}T$, the Gibbs free energy G is

$$G = F + pV = -\mathbf{R}T \ln \frac{Q_t}{N_0}$$

Since it is G which determines equilibria, the translational part of the partition function Q^0 for the standard state will be given simply by Q_t/N evaluated for the standard state. For a standard state of one molecule per cm.³,

$$Q_t^0 = \frac{(2\pi \mathbf{m} \mathbf{k} T)^{3/2}}{\mathbf{h}^3}$$

since $V = 1$ and $N = 1$. For a standard state of one mole per liter,

$$Q_t^0 = \frac{(2\pi \mathbf{m} \mathbf{k} T)^{3/2}}{\mathbf{h}^3} \cdot \frac{1000}{N_0}$$

since in this case $V = 1000$ cm.³ and $N = N_0$. Q_t must certainly be modified for molecules in solution, and this is a very complicated problem. As mentioned in Chapters 3 and 6, the modifications which must be made are *the same* for different isotopic molecules, and so cancel out in taking the ratio of isotopic partition functions Q'/Q.

The translational partition function having been modified to take account of the indistinguishability of non-localized molecules, all other partition function contributions are correctly given by the formulas of Chapter 3, so that

$$Q^0 = Q_t^0 Q_r Q_v Q_e$$

The rotational partition function can be derived by a similar integration. We will consider the case of a linear molecule; the non-linear case is analogous. Quantum theory shows that the rotational energy levels are

$$E_j = \frac{\mathbf{h}^2}{8\pi^2 I} J(J + 1)$$

where I is the moment of inertia and J is a quantum number which can be assigned integral values from 0 to ∞. For each J it turns out, however, that there are $2J + 1$ levels of the *same* energy E_j, and all of these must be counted in the partition function. Then

$$Q_r = \sum_{J=0}^{\infty} (2J + 1)e^{-\mathbf{h}^2 J(J+1)/8\pi^2 I \mathbf{k} T}$$

At ordinary temperatures this summation can be replaced by an integration, giving

$$Q_r = \int_0^\infty e^{-h^2 J(J+1)/8\pi^2 I k T}(2J + 1)\, dJ = \frac{8\pi^2 I k T}{h^2}$$

These partition functions Q_t and Q_r should be valid for all ordinary molecules near room temperature, but it is well to remember that they are slightly approximate.

APPENDIX 2

Alternate Derivation of Transition-State Rate Equation

A more satisfying way of arriving at the rate equation of the transition-state theory is to consider the motion of reactant complexes along the reaction coordinate as a *translational* motion (this derivation is from Ref. (158), pages 306–307). This is not strictly true, but we will consider a region in the reactant valley far removed from the potential energy barrier separating reactants from products. If we consider only a very short distance dx along the reaction coordinate, the motion may be considered to be almost like a free translation. As we shall see, this distance cancels out in the course of setting up the rate equation, so it can be taken to be very short.

Suppose that $C_n(p)$ is the number of complexes in length dx along the reaction coordinate which have linear momentum in the direction of the potential energy maximum between p and $p + dp$, and energy ϵ_n in all other $(3N - 1)$ degrees of freedom. N is the number of nuclei in a complex. Since the linear momentum is p, the velocity is p/m where m is the mass of a complex. The number of complexes which pass a given point of the reaction coordinate, traveling towards the barrier, is therefore $C_n(p)p/dx$ m per second. Since we are considering only systems moving *towards* the barrier, p has only positive values.

Note that we are considering the momentum to be a continuous variable, *i.e.*, not quantized. This is almost always justified for translational motion at any temperature anywhere near room temperature because the spacing of translational energy levels is so small that they practically form a continuum.

Of the systems passing a given point on the reaction coordinate, the fraction which reacts is

$$\sum_k \kappa_{nk}(p)\, \frac{C_n(p)p}{dx\, \mathrm{m}}$$

where $\kappa_{nk}(p)$ is the *transmission coefficient* for the transition from reactant energy level n to product energy level k.

The translation along the reaction coordinate can be treated by classical statistical mechanics. The *classical* probability of a state with momentum between p and $p + dp$ and simultaneously position between x and $x + dx$, and with energy ϵ_n in all other degrees of freedom, is

$$\frac{1}{\mathrm{h}}\, e^{-(\epsilon_n + p^2/2\mathrm{m})/kT}\, dx\, dp$$

(It can be very easily shown that the integral of this probability with $\epsilon_n = 0$ over all values of x and p leads to the same expression as that derived in Appendix 1 for a single degree of translational freedom.)

If we assume that the number of complexes is determined by a Boltzmann distribution, *i.e.*, an equilibrium distribution of the different excited states of the reactants, then

$$\frac{C_n(p)}{(\mathrm{A})(\mathrm{B})\, \cdots} = \frac{e^{-\epsilon_n/kT} e^{-p^2/2\mathrm{mk}T}}{Q_\mathrm{A} Q_\mathrm{B}\, \cdots}\, \frac{dx\, dp}{\mathrm{h}}$$

where (A), (B), . . . are the concentrations of reactants and Q_A, Q_B, . . . are the partition functions of the reactants.

The rate of reaction is obtained by integrating the fraction (with momentum p) which reacts over all possible values of p

(0 to ∞) and summing over n, *i.e.*, over all possible states ϵ_n, giving

$$\text{rate} = \frac{(A)(B)}{Q_A Q_B} \int_0^\infty \sum_n \sum_k \kappa_{nk}(p) e^{-\epsilon_n/kT_e - p^2/2mkT} \frac{p\,dp}{mh}$$

Now in order to simplify this expression, we need to know κ_{nk} as a function of p. This is a very difficult quantum mechanical problem. However, if we assume that $\kappa_{nk} = 0$ if $p^2/2m \leq \Delta\epsilon_0^\ddagger$ and is equal to some average value κ if $p^2/2m > \Delta\epsilon_0^\ddagger$, we can obtain an approximate answer:

$$\text{rate} = \frac{(A)(B)}{Q_A Q_B} \kappa \sum_n e^{-\epsilon_n/kT} \int_{\sqrt{2m(\Delta\epsilon_0^\ddagger)}}^\infty e^{-p^2/2mkT} \frac{p\,dp}{mh}$$

$$= \frac{(A)(B)}{Q_A Q_B} \kappa \sum_n e^{-\epsilon_n/kT} \frac{kT}{h} e^{-\Delta\epsilon_0^\ddagger/kT}$$

The sum $\displaystyle\sum_n e^{-\epsilon_n/kT}$ is over all possible energies ϵ_n which the complexes can have in $3N - 1$ degrees of freedom and is therefore almost like a partition function, so we will call it $Q^\ddagger$. Converted to a molar scale, $\Delta\epsilon_0^\ddagger/kT$ becomes $\Delta E_0^\ddagger/RT$. Also, since the rate constant equals the rate divided by the concentrations of reactants,

$$k = \kappa \frac{kT}{h} \frac{Q^\ddagger}{Q_A Q_B} e^{-\Delta E_0^\ddagger/RT}$$

$$= \kappa \frac{kT}{h} K^\ddagger$$

which, aside from the factor κ, is identical with the equation derived previously (page 39) using the same definition of $K^\ddagger$ except that here we have not bothered with activity coefficients.

In this derivation it is merely necessary to assume that excited states of the reactants (complexed together) are formed in accordance with the Boltzmann distribution. The function $Q^{\ddagger}$ then factors out as a consequence of the Boltzmann distribution, and it is not necessary to *assume* that some transition-state species actually has a partition function analogous to that of a normal molecule. The equilibrium condition (Boltzmann distribution) should be maintained provided that, from the excited levels near (but not quite at) the transition state, many more molecules lose energy and become reactants than gain more energy and so pass over to products. Since it is so unlikely that a molecule will gain enough thermal energy to reach the transition state, the chances of an energetic molecule's losing rather than gaining energy seem to be very great, especially in solution. Thus a difficulty inherent in the usual transition-state theory, that quantum mechanical stationary-state partition functions do not seem appropriate for a species as transient as a transition state, is overcome by this derivation. The more common derivation may be saved if we say that we can calculate the concentration and probability of decomposition of transition states *as if* they existed in a reasonably stationary state, and that the actual rate should be equal to the rate calculated by assuming that transition states exist as stationary states.

APPENDIX 3

Hybridized Orbitals

If we call the four valence shell atomic orbitals of carbon s, p_x, p_y, p_z where the p orbitals have their axes along the x, y, and z axes, respectively, the three kinds of hybridized orbitals can be written as linear combinations of these atomic orbitals.

The sp hybrid orbitals have axes in the $+x$ and $-x$ directions (180° angle):

$$\frac{1}{\sqrt{2}}\,(s + p_x)$$

$$\frac{1}{\sqrt{2}}\,(s - p_x)$$

The sp^2 hybrid orbitals have axes in the $+x$ direction and the two directions which make 120° angles with the $+x$ direction and lie in the xy plane:

$$\frac{1}{\sqrt{3}}\,(s + \sqrt{2}\,p_x)$$

$$\frac{1}{\sqrt{6}}\,(\sqrt{2}\,s - p_x + \sqrt{3}\,p_y)$$

$$\frac{1}{\sqrt{6}}\,(\sqrt{2}\,s - p_x - \sqrt{3}\,p_y)$$

The sp^3 hybrid orbitals have axes in the directions of the four corners of a regular tetrahedron with the nucleus in the center (109°, 28′ angles between each axis and each of the other 3):

$$\frac{1}{2}(s + p_x + p_y + p_z)$$

$$\frac{1}{2}(s + p_x - p_y - p_z)$$

$$\frac{1}{2}(s - p_x - p_y + p_z)$$

$$\frac{1}{2}(s - p_x + p_y - p_z)$$

A detailed discussion of these and other kinds of hybridized orbitals is in Chapter XII of Ref. (158).

References

1. J. HINE, *Physical Organic Chemistry*, McGraw-Hill Book Company, Inc., New York, 1962.
2. E. S. GOULD, *Mechanism and Structure in Organic Chemistry*, Holt, Rinehart and Winston, Inc., New York, 1959.
3. A. STREITWIESER, JR., *Solvolytic Displacement Reactions*, McGraw-Hill Book Company, Inc., New York, 1962; the book is a reprint, with an appendix on newer work, of *Chem. Rev.*, **56**, 571–752 (1956).
4. E. D. HUGHES, F. JULIUSBERGER, S. MASTERMAN, B. TOPLEY, and J. WEISS, *J. Chem. Soc.*, 1525 (1935).
5. L. C. BATEMAN, E. D. HUGHES, and C. K. INGOLD, *J. Chem. Soc.*, 1011 (1940).
6. J. D. ROBERTS and W. T. MORELAND, JR., *J. Am. Chem. Soc.*, **75**, 2167 (1953).
7. See E. L. ELIEL, *Stereochemistry of Carbon Compounds*, McGraw-Hill Book Company, Inc., New York, 1962.
8. E. D. HUGHES and C. K. INGOLD, *J. Chem. Soc.*, 244 (1935).
9. C. G. SWAIN, *J. Am. Chem. Soc.*, **70**, 1119 (1948).
10. F. C. WHITMORE, E. L. WITTLE, and A. H. POPKIN, *J. Am. Chem. Soc.*, **61**, 1586 (1939).
11. N. C. DENO, J. BOLLINGER, N. FRIEDMAN, K. HAFER, J. D. HODGE, and J. J. HOUSER, *J. Am. Chem. Soc.*, **85**, 2998 (1963); N. C. DENO, N. FRIEDMAN, J. D. HODGE, and J. J. HOUSER, *ibid.*, **85**, 2995 (1963); N. C. DENO, H. G. RICHEY, JR., N. FRIEDMAN, J. D. HODGE, J. J. HOUSER, and C. U. PITTMAN, JR., *ibid.*, **85**, 2991 (1963).
12. E. A. MOELWYN-HUGHES, *The Kinetics of Reactions in Solution*, 2nd ed., Oxford University Press, London, 1947.
13. S. GLASSTONE, K. J. LAIDLER, and H. EYRING, *The Theory of Rate Processes*, McGraw-Hill Book Company, Inc., New York, 1941.

14. Possibly the most mechanistically oriented is A. A. FROST and R. G. PEARSON, *Kinetics and Mechanism*, 2nd ed., John Wiley and Sons, Inc., New York, 1961.

15. P. D. BARTLETT, C. E. DILLS, and H. G. RICHEY, JR., *J. Am. Chem. Soc.*, **82**, 5414 (1960).

16. See Ref. (12), pp. 9, 12, 24, 68.

17. For a discussion of more complex cases, see Ref. 12, p. 22.

18. For the derivation of these results see, *e.g.*, M. DOLE, *Introduction to Statistical Thermodynamics*, Prentice-Hall, Inc., Englewood Cliffs, N. J., 1954; or K. S. PITZER, *Quantum Chemistry*, Prentice-Hall, Inc., Englewood Cliffs, N. J., 1953; or G. S. RUSHBROOKE, *Introduction to Statistical Mechanics*, Oxford University Press, London, 1949; all of which are excellent introductions to the subject on a level which does not involve highly specialized mathematics.

19. J. E. LEFFLER and E. GRUNWALD, *Rates and Equilibria of Organic Reactions*, John Wiley and Sons, Inc., New York, 1963.

20. R. P. BELL, *The Proton in Chemistry*, Cornell University Press, Ithaca, N. Y., 1959, Chap. XI.

21. H. S. JOHNSTON, *Adv. Chem. Phys.*, **3**, 131 (1960).

22. *The Transition State*, Special Publication No. 16, The Chemical Society, London, 1962.

23. M. M. KREEVOY, in S. L. FRIESS, E. S. LEWIS, and A. WEISSBERGER (eds.), *Investigation of Rates and Mechanisms of Reactions*, Part II, Interscience Publishers, New York, 1963, Chap. XXIII.

24. See Ref. (14), p. 131.

25. A. STREITWIESER, JR., *Molecular Orbital Theory for Organic Chemists*, John Wiley and Sons, Inc., New York, 1961, pp. 310–311.

26. J. W. LINNETT, *Wave Mechanics and Valency*, John Wiley and Sons, Inc., New York, 1960.

27. C. A. COULSON, *Valence*, 2nd ed., Oxford University Press, London, 1961.

28. R. DAUDEL, R. LeFEBVRE, and C. MOSER, *Quantum Chemistry Methods and Applications*, Interscience Publishers, Inc., New York, 1959.

29. J. D. ROBERTS, *Notes on Molecular Orbital Calculations*, W. A. Benjamin, Inc., New York, 1962.

30. M. J. S. DEWAR, *J. Am. Chem. Soc.*, **74**, 3341, 3345, 3350, 3353, 3355, 3357 (1952).

31. M. J. S. DEWAR and R. J. SAMPSON, *J. Chem. Soc.*, 2789 (1956), 2946 (1957).

32. G. W. WHELAND and D. E. MANN, *J. Chem. Phys.*, **17**, 264 (1949).

33. A. STREITWIESER, JR., *J. Am. Chem. Soc.*, **82**, 4123 (1960).

34. M. SIMONETTA and S. WINSTEIN, *J. Am. Chem. Soc.*, **76**, 18 (1954).

35. W. G. WOODS, R. A. CARBONI, and J. D. ROBERTS, *J. Am. Chem. Soc.*, **78**, 5653 (1956).

36. H. E. ZIMMERMAN and A. ZWEIG, *J. Am. Chem. Soc.*, **83**, 1196 (1961).
37. C. G. SWAIN and W. R. THORSON, *J. Org. Chem.*, **24**, 1989 (1959).
38. R. D. BROWN, *J. Chem. Soc.*, 2615 (1953).
39. Ref. (28), pp. 253 ff.
40. For a discussion of the theory behind steric effects, see F. H. WESTHEIMER in M. S. NEWMAN (ed.), *Steric Effects in Organic Chemistry*, John Wiley and Sons, Inc., New York, 1956, Chap. 12.
41. K. S. PITZER and W. E. DONATH, *J. Am. Chem. Soc.*, **81**, 3213 (1959).
42. F. V. BRUTCHER, JR., T. ROBERTS, S. J. BARR, and N. PEARSON, *J. Am. Chem. Soc.*, **81**, 4915 (1959).
43. F. V. BRUTCHER, JR., and W. BAUER, JR., *J. Am. Chem. Soc.*, **84**, 2233, 2236 (1962).
44. C. K. INGOLD, *Quart. Rev.*, **11**, 1 (1957).
45. P. B. D. DE LA MARE, L. FOWDEN, E. D. HUGHES, C. K. INGOLD, and J. D. H. MACKIE, *J. Chem. Soc.*, 3169 ff. (8 papers) (1955).
46. G. S. HAMMOND, *J. Am. Chem. Soc.*, **77**, 334 (1955).
47. C. G. SWAIN and E. R. THORNTON, *J. Am. Chem. Soc.*, **84**, 817 (1962).
48. (a) S. WINSTEIN, S. SMITH, and D. DARWISH, *Tetrahedron Letters*, **16**, 24 (1959); (b) S. WINSTEIN, E. C. FRIEDRICH, and S. SMITH, *J. Am. Chem. Soc.*, **86**, 305 (1964).
49. G. KOHNSTAM, A. QUEEN, and T. RIBAR, *Chem. and Ind. (London)*, 1287 (1962).
50. V. GOLD, *J. Chem. Soc.*, 4633 (1956).
51. S. WINSTEIN, L. G. SAVEDOFF, S. SMITH, I. D. R. STEVENS, and J. S. GALL, *Tetrahedron Letters*, **9**, 24 (1960).
52. H. C. BROWN, *Record Chem. Progr.*, **14**, 83 (1953); see also P. D. BARTLETT and M. S. SWAIN, *J. Am. Chem. Soc.*, **77**, 2801 (1955).
53. H. C. BROWN and H. L. BERNEIS, *J. Am. Chem. Soc.*, **75**, 10 (1953).
54. J. D. ROBERTS and V. C. CHAMBERS, *J. Am. Chem. Soc.*, **73**, 5034 (1951).
55. S. WINSTEIN, D. DARWISH, and N. J. HOLNESS, *J. Am. Chem. Soc.*, **78**, 2915 (1956).
56. C. A. VERNON, *J. Chem. Soc.*, 4462 (1954).
57. R. E. ROBERTSON, *Can. J. Chem.*, **31**, 589 (1953).
58. C. G. SWAIN and A. MACLACHLAN, *J. Am. Chem. Soc.*, **82**, 6095 (1960).
59. P. D. BARTLETT and L. H. KNOX, *J. Am. Chem. Soc.*, **61**, 3184 (1939); D. E. APPLEQUIST and J. D. ROBERTS, *Chem. Rev.*, **54**, 1065 (1954).
60. W. E. DOERING, quoted by STREITWIESER (3), pp. 64–65, 70.
61. J. L. FRANKLIN and F. H. FIELD, *J. Chem. Phys.*, **21**, 550 (1953).
62. W. E. DOERING and H. H. ZEISS, *J. Am. Chem. Soc.*, **75**, 4733 (1953).

63. A. STREITWIESER, JR., and T. D. WALSH, *Tetrahedron Letters*, **1**, 27 (1963).
64. H. C. BROWN and H. M. BELL, *J. Org. Chem.*, **27**, 1928 (1962).
65. H. WEINER and R. A. SNEEN, *J. Am. Chem. Soc.*, **84**, 3599 (1962); *Tetrahedron Letters*, **20**, 1309 (1963).
66. A. STREITWIESER, JR., and S. ANDREADES, *J. Am. Chem. Soc.*, **80**, 6553 (1958).
67. C. G. SWAIN, C. B. SCOTT, and K. H. LOHMANN, *J. Am. Chem. Soc.*, **75**, 136 (1953).
68. L. C. BATEMAN, M. G. CHURCH, E. D. HUGHES, C. K. INGOLD, and N. A. TAHER, *J. Chem. Soc.*, 979 (1940).
69. C. A. BUNTON and B. NAYAK, *J. Chem. Soc.*, 3854 (1959).
70. M. G. CHURCH, E. D. HUGHES, and C. K. INGOLD, *J. Chem. Soc.*, 966 (1940).
71. K. A. COOPER, E. D. HUGHES, C. K. INGOLD and B. J. MACNULTY, *J. Chem. Soc.*, 2038 (1948).
72. M. COCIVERA and S. WINSTEIN, *J. Am. Chem. Soc.*, **85**, 1702 (1963).
73. L. P. HAMMETT, *Physical Organic Chemistry*, McGraw-Hill Book Company, Inc., New York, 1940, pp. 167–169.
74. C. C. SWAIN and R. W. EDDY, *J. Am. Chem. Soc.*, **70**, 2989 (1948).
75. C. G. SWAIN and E. E. PEGUES, *J. Am. Chem. Soc.*, **80**, 812 (1958).
76. Ref. (12), pp. 203–204.
77. W. G. YOUNG, S. WINSTEIN, and H. L. GOERING, *J. Am. Chem. Soc.*, **73**, 1958 (1951).
78. H. L. GOERING, *Record Chem. Progr.*, **21**, 109 (1960).
79. See, for example, S. WINSTEIN, P. E. KLINEDINST, JR., and E. CLIPPINGER, *J. Am. Chem. Soc.*, **83**, 4986 (1961).
80. (a) C. G. SWAIN and G. TSUCHIHASHI, *J. Am. Chem. Soc.*, **84**, 2021 (1962); (b) D. DARWISH and E. A. PRESTON, *Tetrahedron Letters*, 113 (1964).
81. (a) H. L. GOERING and J. F. LEVY, *J. Am. Chem. Soc.*, **84**, 3853 (1962); (b) see also H. L. GOERING, R. G. BRIODY, and J. F. LEVY, *J. Am. Chem. Soc.*, **85**, 3059 (1963); H. L. GOERING and J. F. LEVY, *ibid.*, **86**, 120 (1964); B. L. MURR and C. SANTIAGO, *Abstracts of Papers*, 22 N, 147th Meeting, ACS, April, 1964.
82. See E. GRUNWALD and S. WINSTEIN, *J. Am. Chem. Soc.*, **70**, 841 (1948).
83. S. WINSTEIN, M. BROWN, K. C. SCHREIBER, and A. H. SCHLESINGER, *J. Am. Chem. Soc.*, **74**, 1140 (1952).
84. For an admirable discussion of this topic, see D. J. CRAM, Ref. (40), Chap. 5.
85. R. B. SANDIN and A. S. HAY, *J. Am. Chem. Soc.*, **74**, 274 (1952).
86. R. BAIRD and S. WINSTEIN, *J. Am. Chem. Soc.*, **85**, 567 (1963).
87. (a) H. C. BROWN and H. M. BELL, *J. Am. Chem. Soc.*, **85**, 2324 (1963); (b) S. WINSTEIN, A. H. LEWIN, and K. C. PANDE, *ibid.*, **85**, 2324 (1963).
88. D. BETHELL and V. GOLD, *Quart. Rev.*, **12**, 173 (1958).

89. J. D. Roberts, *Abstracts of Sixteenth National Organic Symposium,*
    A. C. S., 1959, p. 1.
90. J. D. Roberts, C. C. Lee, and W. H. Saunders, Jr., *J. Am.*
    Chem. Soc., **76,** 4501 (1954).
91. (a) P. R. Schleyer, D. C. Kleinfelter, and H. G. Richey, Jr.,
    J. Am. Chem. Soc., **85,** 479 (1963); (b) P. R. Schleyer, *ibid.,*
    86, 1854, 1856 (1964); C. S. Foote, *ibid.,* 1853.
92. H. C. Brown and F. J. Chloupek, *J. Am. Chem. Soc.,* **85,** 2322
    (1963).
93. J. N. Brønsted, *Chem. Rev.,* **5,** 231 (1928).
94. A. J. Parker, *Proc. Chem. Soc.,* 371 (1961).
95. E. A. Moelwyn-Hughes, *Proc. Roy. Soc.* (*London*), **A220,** 386 (1953).
96. S. W. Benson, *J. Am. Chem. Soc.,* **80,** 5151 (1958).
97. H. H. Jaffé, *Chem. Rev.,* **53,** 191 (1953).
98. C. D. Ritchie and E. S. Lewis, *J. Am. Chem. Soc.,* **84,** 591 (1962).
99. J. G. Kirkwood and F. H. Westheimer, *J. Chem. Phys.,* **6,** 506,
    513 (1938).
100. H. C. Brown and Y. Okamoto, *J. Am. Chem. Soc.,* **80,** 4979 (1958);
     Y. Okamoto and H. C. Brown, *J. Org. Chem.,* **22,** 485 (1957);
     L. M. Stock and H. C. Brown, *Advan. Phys. Org. Chem.,* **1,** 89
     (1963).
101. A. G. Harrison, P. Kebarle, and F. P. Lossing, *J. Am. Chem.*
     Soc., **83,** 777 (1961).
102. M. J. S. Dewar and P. J. Grisdale, *J. Am. Chem. Soc.,* **84,** 3539,
     3541, 3546, 3548 (1962).
103. C. G. Swain and W. P. Langsdorf, Jr., *J. Am. Chem. Soc.,* **73,**
     2813 (1951).
104. G. S. Hammond, C. E. Reeder, F. T. Fang, and J. K. Kochi,
     J. Am. Chem. Soc., **80,** 568 (1958).
105. J. O. Edwards and R. G. Pearson, *J. Am. Chem. Soc.,* **84,** 16
     (1962); R. G. Pearson, *ibid.,* **85,** 3533 (1963).
106. C. G. Swain and C. B. Scott, *J. Am. Chem. Soc.,* **75,** 141 (1953).
107. C. G. Swain and K. H. Lohmann, paper in process; K. H. Loh-
     mann, Ph.D. Thesis in Organic Chemistry, M.I.T., 1959.
108. E. Grunwald and S. Winstein, *J. Am. Chem. Soc.,* **70,** 846 (1948);
     S. Winstein, E. Grunwald, and H. W. Jones, *J. Am. Chem.*
     Soc., **73,** 2700 (1951).
109. A. H. Fainberg and S. Winstein, *J. Am. Chem. Soc.,* **79,** 1597,
     1602, 1608 (1957); **78,** 2770 (1956); S. Winstein, A. H. Fain-
     berg, and E. Grunwald, *ibid.,* **79,** 4146 (1957).
110. C. G. Swain, R. B. Mosely, and D. F. Bown, *J. Am. Chem. Soc.,*
     77, 3731 (1955).
111. C. G. Swain, L. E. Kaiser, and T. E. C. Knee, *J. Am. Chem.*
     Soc., **80,** 4092 (1958).
112. S. Winstein and E. Grunwald, *J. Am. Chem. Soc.,* **70,** 828 (1948).
113. A. Streitwieser, Jr., *J. Am. Chem. Soc.,* **78,** 4935 (1956).
114. S. G. Smith, A. H. Fainberg, and S. Winstein, *J. Am. Chem.*
     Soc., **83,** 618 (1961).

115. H. HART and P. A. LAW, *J. Am. Chem. Soc.*, **86**, 1957 (1964).
116. E. A. MOELWYN-HUGHES, *Physical Chemistry*, Pergamon Press, New York, 1957.
117. R. E. ROBERTSON and J. M. W. SCOTT, *J. Chem. Soc.*, 1596 (1961).
118. R. L. HEPPOLETTE and R. E. ROBERTSON, *Proc. Roy. Soc. (London)*, **A252**, 273 (1959).
119. D. N. GLEW and E. A. MOELWYN-HUGHES, *Discussions Faraday Soc.*, **15**, 150 (1953).
120. E. A. MOELWYN-HUGHES, *J. Chem. Soc.*, 1517 (1961).
121. J. BIORDI and E. A. MOELWYN-HUGHES, *J. Chem. Soc.*, 4291 (1962).
122. I. FELLS and E. A. MOELWYN-HUGHES, *J. Chem. Soc.*, 398 (1959).
123. G. A. CLARKE, T. R. WILLIAMS, and R. W. TAFT, *J. Am. Chem. Soc.*, **84**, 2292 (1962); G. A. CLARKE and R. W. TAFT, *J. Am. Chem. Soc.*, **84**, 2295 (1962).
124. W. FEATHERSTONE, E. JACKSON, and G. KOHNSTAM, *Proc. Chem. Soc.*, 175 (1963).
125. Y. OKAMOTO, T. INUKAI, and H. C. BROWN, *J. Am. Chem. Soc.*, **80**, 4969 (1958); H. C. BROWN, J. D. BRADY, M. GRAYSON, and W. H. BONNER, *J. Am. Chem. Soc.*, **79**, 1897 (1957); H. C. BROWN, Y. OKAMOTO and G. HAM, *J. Am. Chem. Soc.*, **79**, 1906 (1957); Y. OKAMOTO, and H. C. BROWN, *J. Am. Chem. Soc.*, **79**, 1909 (1957).
126. S. WINSTEIN and A. H. FAINBERG, *J. Am. Chem. Soc.*, **79**, 5937 (1957).
127. S. W. BENSON and J. A. BERSON, *J. Am. Chem. Soc.*, **84**, 152 (1962); *ibid.*, **86**, 259 (1964).
128. E. WHALLEY, *Advan. Phys. Org. Chem.*, **2**, 93 (1964).
129. S. D. HAMANN and D. R. TEPLITZKY, *Discussions Faraday Soc.*, **22**, 114 (1956).
130. L. MELANDER, *Isotope Effects on Reaction Rates*, The Ronald Press Company, New York, 1960; for a more complete treatment, see J. BIGELEISEN and M. WOLFSBERG, *Advan. Chem. Phys.*, **1**, 15 (1958).
131. See E. B. WILSON, JR., J. C. DECIUS, and P. C. CROSS, *Molecular Vibrations*, McGraw-Hill Book Company, Inc., New York, 1955, p. 182.
132. See D. R. HERSCHBACH and V. W. LAURIE, *J. Chem. Phys.*, **35**, 458 (1961); also D. R. HERSCHBACH, H. S. JOHNSTON, and D. RAPP, *J. Chem. Phys.*, **31**, 1652 (1959).
133. M. L. BENDER and G. J. BUIST, *J. Am. Chem. Soc.*, **80**, 4304 (1958); see also A. J. KRESGE, N. N. LICHTIN, and K. N. RAO, *J. Am. Chem. Soc.*, **85**, 1210 (1963).
134. J. B. STOTHERS and A. N. BOURNS, *Can. J. Chem.*, **40**, 2007 (1962).
135. K. R. LYNN and P. E. YANKWICH, *J. Am. Chem. Soc.*, **83**, 3220 (1961).
136. J. W. HILL and A. FRY, *J. Am. Chem. Soc.*, **84**, 2763 (1962).
137. W. H. SAUNDERS, JR., and S. AŠPERGER, *J. Am. Chem. Soc.*, **79**, 1612 (1957); W. H. SAUNDERS, JR., and S. E. ZIMMERMAN, unpublished results.

138. J. A. LLEWELLYN, R. E. ROBERTSON, and J. M. W. SCOTT, *Can. J. Chem.*, **38**, 222 (1960); K. T. LEFFEK, J. A. LLEWELLYN, and R. E. ROBERTSON, *Can. J. Chem.*, **38**, 1505, 2171 (1960); *Chem. and Ind. (London)*, 588 (1960).

139. S. AŠPERGER and N. ILAKOVAC, *Chem. and Ind. (London)*, 1191 (1960).

140. V. J. SHINER, JR., B. L. MURR, and G. HEINEMANN, *J. Am. Chem. Soc.*, **85**, 2413 (1963).

141. A. STREITWIESER, JR., R. H. JAGOW, R. C. FAHEY, and S. SUZUKI, *J. Am. Chem. Soc.*, **80**, 2326 (1958).

142. V. J. SHINER, JR., and J. S. HUMPHREY, JR., *J. Am. Chem. Soc.*, **85**, 2416 (1963).

143. K. T. LEFFEK, R. E. ROBERTSON, and S. E. SUGAMORI, *Can. J. Chem.*, **39**, 1989 (1961).

144. P. M. LAUGHTON and R. E. ROBERTSON, *Can. J. Chem.*, **34**, 1714 (1956); R. E. ROBERTSON and P. M. LAUGHTON, *Can. J. Chem.*, **35**, 1319 (1957); P. M. LAUGHTON and R. E. ROBERTSON, *Can. J. Chem.*, **37**, 1491 (1959).

145. See C. G. SWAIN and R. F. W. BADER, *Tetrahedron*, **10**, 182 (1960); C. G. SWAIN, R. F. W. BADER, and E. R. THORNTON, *ibid.*, **10**, 200 (1960); V. GOLD, *Proc. Chem. Soc.*, 141 (1963); A. J. KRESGE and A. L. ALLRED, *J. Am. Chem. Soc.*, **85**, 1541 (1963).

146. P. M. LAUGHTON and R. E. ROBERTSON, *Can. J. Chem.*, **39**, 2155 (1961).

147. C. G. SWAIN and E. R. THORNTON, *J. Am. Chem. Soc.*, **84**, 822 (1962).

148. C. G. SWAIN and E. R. THORNTON, *J. Am. Chem. Soc.*, **83**, 3884 (1961).

149. C. G. SWAIN and E. R. THORNTON, *J. Am. Chem. Soc.*, **83**, 3890 (1961).

150. V. GOLD, *Trans. Faraday Soc.*, **56**, 255 (1960); E. A. HALEVI, F. A. LONG, and M. A. PAUL, *J. Am. Chem. Soc.*, **83**, 305 (1961). P. SALOMAA, L. L. SCHALEGER, and F. A. LONG, *J. Am. Chem. Soc.*, **86**, 1 (1964).

151. B. L. MURR, JR., and V. J. SHINER, JR., *J. Am. Chem. Soc.*, **84**, 4672 (1962).

152. E. R. THORNTON, *J. Am. Chem. Soc.*, **84**, 2474 (1962).

153. W. G. CRAIG, L. HAKKA, P. M. LAUGHTON, and R. E. ROBERTSON, *Can. J. Chem.*, **41**, 2118 (1963).

154. A. STREITWIESER, JR., and H. S. KLEIN, *J. Am. Chem. Soc.*, **85**, 2759 (1963).

155. M. HOFFMAN, unpublished work.

156. K. MISLOW, R. GRAEVE, A. J. GORDON, and G. H. WAHL, JR., *J. Am. Chem. Soc.*, **85**, 1199 (1963); **86**, 1733 (1964).

157. L. MELANDER and R. E. CARTER, *J. Am. Chem. Soc.*, **86**, 295 (1964).

158. H. EYRING, J. WALTER, and G. E. KIMBALL, *Quantum Chemistry*, John Wiley and Sons, Inc., New York, 1944.

Author Index

Numbers in parentheses are reference numbers.

Subject Index